To Marty,
for 30 years and counting.

Travis

NAKED SNOW ANGELS

The Authorized Biography of

Travis A. Naughton

By

Travis A. Naughton

Author's note: An insignificant percentage of the events described in this book are real. Certain character and place names have been changed to keep friends, family, and the author out of prison. Liberal doses of hyperbole, blatant misstatements of facts, and complete fabrications can be expected throughout and should be overlooked by the reader.

© Travis A. Naughton 2011

Dedicated to my family, who is dedicated to me.

Contents

Introduction
The Two Travises
Tits and Asphalt
The Incontinent Letterman
Tromboners, Too
Tromboners Two
Remember When I Asked Your Mom to the Prom?
Hail to the Chief
I'm a Drinker, Not a Fighter
Secret Squirrel
Going Kerouac on Everyone's Ass*
I Want To Be Near The Beer
The Not-So-Cratic Method
The Lord of the Fruit Flies
Like a Rock
Dr. Cactus Fingers and the Prostate Exam
Finding Truman
Stay-at-Home Roller Coaster
Dogma Day Care
Reason for Leaving
Going Overboard
Are Those Goats?
Mr. Badwrench
Butterbean
Rosie Crane Rides the Crazy Train
Rude, Crude, and Socially Unacceptable
Big Fish
Great Scot
Paging Doctor Naughton
The Intercontinental Man of Letters
Timeline of Major Events

Introduction

After reading *A Farewell to Arms,* I was convinced that I could be the next Hemingway, but gave up that goal when I realized that although I could drink as much as Papa, I couldn't manage to grow a beard. When I read *On the Road*, I started writing a book that could best be described as Kerouac-ish, only not as well-written, interesting, or original. Next I fell in love with the wit of David Sedaris and began writing my own collection of humorous, awkward, and sometimes poignant essays. I compiled a couple dozen of these into a single volume, taking particular care to order them as randomly as possible in an attempt to make it appear as though they were a collection of previously published works from national magazines. Soon the world would think of me as the Hetero-Sedaris.

After reading my confounding mish-mash of random stories, I realized that I had in fact written a memoir, albeit a memoir with no semblance of a chronology whatsoever. I believe Mark Twain is the only writer who has ever told his life's story in this haphazard manner with any degree of success, although it took one hundred years for his editors to make sense of his no rhyme or reason form. I doubt history will have that amount of patience with me, regardless of the fact that both Samuel Clemens and I hail from the same hometown of Hannibal, Missouri where we spent our formative years of boyhood playing on the banks of the Mississippi. A *memoir*? The very thought of it made me thoroughly disgusted with myself. The notion of writing one's life story and thinking people would want to read it seems incredibly arrogant to me. Memoirs are for celebrities, former presidents, and porn stars — not stay-at-home dads who only leave the house to catch the school bus or buy more diapers. Nevertheless, I reluctantly rearranged the chapters of my book which resulted in a well-written, chronologically ordered, highly entertaining memoir of an ordinary guy that no one had ever heard of. Although the quality of the work was better than most celebrity tell-alls I'd read, I was no celebrity. And I was certain that if I tried to get my book published in that form, I never would be. I needed to come up with a format that was so completely original that readers would be drawn to my book despite my anonymity.

At thirty-eight years of age, I felt I was too young to have accumulated a full "life's story," so I instead endeavored to write what I imagine my life's story would be by the time I am seventy-six, working under the assumption that by that time, I will have become the most successful and famous writer of my generation. The following pages are the result of countless hours of interviews conducted by myself, Travis Naughton, a young, up and coming writer/biographer, of the world-renown author, lecturer, and humorist, Dr. Travis A. Naughton. I have incorporated various letters, journal entries, essays, short stories, and book excerpts penned by the internationally acclaimed writer into this volume wherever my thorough yet emotionally detached academic documentation of my subject fails to capture the genius wit of the wildly imaginative author. The resulting work is the first comprehensive accounting of the life of one of the 21st century's most creative minds. I am confident that the elder Naughton would approve of the finished product were he alive today to read it. Moreover, I am sure that you the reader will glean a fair measure of enjoyment from the *Authorized Biography*, too.

The Two Travises

When I first sat down with the legendary Travis A. Naughton at his sprawling four thousand square foot lodge-pole pine manor set upon two hundred and forty acres of pristine Colorado mountainside wilderness in July of 2048, I was, I must admit, more than slightly intimidated by being in such close proximity to the hero of my youth. The imposing view of Ansel Adams's Rocky Mountains through the windows of the home's study juxtaposed with the larger than life personality of the storied author nearly caused me to politely excuse myself from the impending interview session in favor of retreating to my humble, ramshackle house back in the familiar confines of Missouri, never daring to leave the self-imposed incarceration of my Fortress of Cowardice again. Luckily for me, the esteemed humanitarian sensed and allayed my discomfort before I had a chance to flee.

He was not as tall as I had imagined him to be. I was surprised to note that he and I were actually the same height, although seeing his image in print, on television, and online gave me the impression that he was much bigger in stature. He was a frighteningly handsome fellow, who at his advanced age still had a head full of thick, dark brown hair that matched the color of his warm and intelligent eyes. Although he was born seventy-six years ago on September 25, 1971, in Kirksville, Missouri, Travis Alexander Naughton still looked as young to me as a man half his age. He extended his hand as he entered the well-appointed room and said, "You must be Travis. I am so very glad to meet you. Won't you please make yourself at home?" My anxieties assuaged, I accepted his welcoming invitation and began the first in a series of interviews that would shape not only this book, but also the writer I would eventually become

Most of these interviews were tape recorded and later transcribed for this book. In order to more easily follow which Travis Naughton is speaking while reading through these transcripts, I have opted to use the designations "Travis the Younger" and "Travis the Elder," which have been shortened to Younger and Elder in most cases.

(Younger): First of all, Dr. Naughton, I would like to tell you what an honor it is to be in your company and in your beautiful home. Thank you for consenting to meet with me.

(Elder): The honor is strictly mine, young man. I have been made aware of some of your earlier works and am convinced that you have a very promising career as a writer ahead of you.

(Younger): Sir, you flatter me. I can only hope to one day be half the man you are today.

(Elder): Well, you are already there my young friend. Now, what do you say we get started?

(Younger): Of course. I understand that you grew up in Hannibal, Missouri, which is by coincidence the same boyhood hometown of another famous author, Mark Twain. Can you tell me some of your recollections of that "White Town Drowsing?"

(Elder): Hannibal in the 1980s still bore an unnatural resemblance to the town Twain last visited in 1902. His boyhood home and several other historic buildings in the downtown area were preserved by some forward thinkers who had the intention of turning the town into the Midwest's preeminent tourist trap at the expense of their favorite son. In that endeavor, they succeeded. People flocked to the town from all corners of the globe to see from where the inspiration for Tom Sawyer and Huckleberry Finn came. It always amused me as a kid living there to watch Japanese families snapping pictures of my boring little town in the heart of America as if they were taking in the spectacle of the Great Pyramids for the first time. Frankly, I never understood the attraction. But the town fully revolved around the legacy of Twain, and once a year, during "National Tom Sawyer Days" *[around the Fourth of July holiday],* I must admit it was actually pretty fun to be one of the "locals" in Hannibal. Fence painting and frog-jumping contests and a Tom & Becky look-alike pageant were all great fun for the youth of a town with very little else to offer in the form of entertainment.

(Younger): Aside from the Twain-related trappings, what did a boy from Hannibal do in those days to entertain himself?

(Elder): Unlike Tom & Huck, I never fashioned a raft and floated down the Mississippi, although I've enjoyed the river in a few motorboats over the years. My friends and I did have our share of adventures, though…

Naughton wrote an essay about his childhood experiences that was first published in 2008 in a "once reputable literary magazine back east" as he put it, that he claims still owes him "monies in excess of tens of dollars." The subject of the call to letters was "The End of Innocence." Naughton's submission bore a slight resemblance to the style of his idol Twain, with a decidedly updated feel. The reaction in the literary community was a virtual shot heard 'round the world and would place the writer squarely in line as the heir apparent to his long-dead Hannibalian predecessor. The title of this work, Tits and Asphalt, *both shocked and intrigued the editors of the prestigious magazine in which it appeared. After their initial hesitation to publish the work of such an unrefined and unknown literary voice, they decided to take a chance on this audacious young man from Twainland. Response from the journal's elite readership was surprisingly and resoundingly positive. Letters poured in to the editorial office demanding more pieces from this new American storyteller. Seemingly overnight, a star was born. His now famous essay is reprinted with the author's permission in the following chapter.*

Tits and Asphalt

In the years following our parents' divorce, my younger brother Blake and I were left home alone with alarming regularity. This isn't to say that my dad, whom we lived with most of the time, was in any way a negligent father. Back in those days, it was pretty common for school-aged kids to be alone at home for an hour or two while waiting for mom and dad to get home from work. It was perfectly normal for children to ride their bikes (without helmets) across town to buy ice cream cones without their folks' supervision or in many cases knowledge. But my brother and I enjoyed a freedom that most kids our age only dreamed about.

Our dad was a schoolteacher, and during summers when the other teachers were home with their families, Dad worked at a nearby state park as a park ranger. I was about eleven years old and my brother was around seven the first summer our dad left us to fend for ourselves. Our mother lived in another town at the time, so Blake and I were on our own for up to nine hours per day. Dad's girlfriend would stop by once in a while to make us lunch or just to make sure we were still alive, but by and large we were free to do whatever we pleased all day, every day. I am happy to report that the house never caught fire, we were never abducted, and the only emergency room trip was for a few measly stitches on Blake's chin after he crashed his bike while going over a ramp a la Evel Knievel.

Our next-door neighbor was a goofy lummox named Don, who was two years younger than me and two years older than Blake. He was a great source of entertainment during the years we lived beside one another. For example, Don had a dog that he allowed to hump his leg (or arm when he was sitting on the ground) all the way to the point of climax. That was fun to watch once or twice, but after that we really started to question the kid's sanity.

     Don loved fireworks almost as much as he loved food, and each year around the fourth of July we would have bottle rocket wars. He would set up a mini mortar cannon on his side of the cow pasture that ran behind our two houses while Blake and I would sit opposite him on our hill, and we would take shots at each other over the small gully between us. We rarely came close to hitting our targets, save for one time when I got lucky and fired off a shot that headed straight toward Don as he sat with his chubby legs spread apart on the facing slope, mortar held tight between his feet in a yoga-like pose that I think was called "Fat Boy Holding Plastic Pipe and Shouldn't Be Wearing Short-shorts." As I tracked the flight of the rocket, time seemed to slow down, affording me a perfect view of the unfolding scene. When Don realized the projectile was on a collision course with his partially-exposed testicles, his eyes widened, his feet hopelessly tried to find purchase on the eroding hillside, and his rolls of fat jiggled in waves of desperation while the explosive missile bore down on its target. The fear in his eyes was plain to see from a hundred yards away, even through the coke-bottle glasses that perpetually adorned his cherubic face. With all the agility of Jabba the Hutt, Don tried in vain to jump clear of the bottle rocket just as it impacted him squarely in his groin. As the report sounded, Don miraculously lifted off from the earth, defying gravity for a brief moment before landing with a thud, a cloud of dust, and a primal moan that left Blake and me in a fit of uncontrollable laughter. It was hard to tell who was crying harder, Don or us.

     Most of our days were spent riding our bikes throughout Hannibal. It was not unusual for us to ride for ten or more miles in a single day and on a few occasions, we rode well over twenty miles. (It is embarrassing to admit that I can only ride a fraction of that distance these days before debilitating ass-pain forces me to go home and slather myself in hemorrhoid cream. Oh, to be eleven again!) In the heat and humidity of a Missouri summer afternoon, we would inevitably be drenched with sweat whenever we arrived at our destination, which was often a pizza place across town. When we paid for our sodas or ice cream, the clerk would shoot us a death glare of disgust as we handed him the perspiration-infused cash.

Blake, Don, and I joined forces with a band of marauding neighborhood kids and formed a non-motorized motorcycle gang of sorts that we called "The Conrads." I don't know for sure where this name came from but can only venture a guess that one of our young members must have meant to say "comrades." At any rate, we weren't much of a "gang" in the traditional sense of the word. We didn't frequent biker bars or get into knife fights, but then again there weren't many traffic laws left unbroken whenever we rode. Amazingly, none of us were ever struck by a car, and our lack of head protection never came back to haunt us.

Sometimes, the thrill of the ride wasn't thrill enough to satisfy our lust for new adventures, so we would ratchet the danger level up a notch or two every once in a while to keep things interesting. Some of the older kids developed a network of off-road bike trails in the woods bordering our neighborhood. That was where Blake flew over his handlebars and split open his chin. Gosh, that was neat to watch. On another occasion, we fled from the police (and were apprehended) after hurling stones from a riverview blufftop down to the control booth on the railroad bridge that crossed the Mississippi. Apparently, the poor dope who occupied the dilapidated shack thought he was being ambushed by a well-armed militia and therefore called the cops. Scaring the locals, jumping over bike ramps, and watching kids cry and/or bleed was all great fun, but not nearly as thrilling as the time we discovered someone's secret stash of nudie magazines hidden in a makeshift clubhouse deep within the woods that contained our riding trails. A door to a whole new world was opened up to my curious mind that day. I would be entering junior high in the fall, and at that age nudity was something that piqued my interest a bit more than riding bikes with my brother did. A stop at the clubhouse became a regular part of our daily outings from then on. To us kids, the pictures in the magazines were fascinating, if not disgusting; but not nearly as gross as watching Don's dog hump his bare arm.

One day during that same summer, Don rode over to our

house towing a little red wagon behind his bike with a length of nylon rope. He suggested taking turns pulling each other around the neighborhood and naturally Blake and I couldn't think of any reason not to. I was the oldest, so I insisted on taking the first ride in the wagon. Don pulled me across the street to an apartment building that had a very steep driveway. He pedaled as fast as his blubbery, ankle-less legs could go until we reached the bottom of the hill where the driveway opened up to a parking lot. For reasons that he was never able to explain, Don turned sharply to his left just as we reached terminal velocity at the bottom of the hill. As Newton correctly observed, objects in motion tend to stay in motion, and the Laws of Physics decided that I should prove no exception. Out of the corner of my eye I watched Don and the wagon disappear to my left, while I flew straight ahead toward the blacktop at approximately 200 miles per hour. Bracing for impact, I put my hands out in front of me in a perfect Superman pose and prayed for a quick and painless death. As soon as my hands hit the ground they folded down to my sides while my face continued on a collision course with the unforgiving paved surface of the parking lot. In a last-second, instinctive reaction aimed at saving my beautiful, youthful smile, I arched my back so that my chest would hit the ground before my teeth did. Have you ever seen that old slow-motion crash test footage of a jumbo jetliner smashing onto the runway when its landing gear was disabled? That is exactly what it must have looked like when my fuselage impacted the tarmac. I imagine there was a shower of sparks and a plume of smoke and perhaps a large explosion, too. I can't be sure, though. No one I knew owned a video camera in those days—and even if they had, it would have been the size a Volkswagon and cost just as much, ensuring that a young kid would never have the chance to film his buddies' ridiculous stunts with it and "go viral" like kids today do. So sadly, no footage of my spectacular crash exists. After sliding on my chest for approximately three-quarters of a mile, I finally ground to a stop. I waited there at the end of the runway for a moment and listened for the sirens of approaching rescue vehicles, but I heard nothing. Apparently in shock, I stood and pretended that the horrific accident hadn't inflicted any amount of pain greater than the sting of humiliation that I was feeling for agreeing to go along with one of Don's half-witted notions. After dusting myself off I'm pretty sure I called Don something really clever like "a stupid idiot" and swore to get my revenge one day soon. Then I limped home, Blake following closely yet cautiously behind. By the time I walked through the front door in the awkward, unbending manner of Frankenstein's monster, the pain was unbearable. I lifted my shirt to assess the damage and saw that where my nipples once were, two bloody, festering wounds took their place. It took a few minutes before I even noticed that the flesh on my chin, knees, palms and backs of my hands was scraped completely raw and/or missing, too. I knew I needed to clean myself up before Dad came home (for fear that he'd do something crazy like hire a babysitter or some other such foolishness), so I took a shower to rinse off the copious amount of blood/incriminating evidence covering my prepubescent--and up till that moment unspoiled--body. Jumping in a vat of hydrochloric acid couldn't have felt worse. I think Blake was scarred for life just hearing the screams coming from the bathroom. I assumed that I would be scarred for life, too, through the magic of healing and a lifetime of clean living, I am happy to tell you that I still have two nipples and nary a scar today.

My best friend back then was a kid named Deuce Conley. James Conley, Jr. was his legal name, but "Deuce" sounded a lot cooler than "James" and less red-necked than "Jimmy" or "Junior." I'm pretty sure Hannibal had already exceeded its quota of Juniors (and Bubbas, and Cooters for that matter.) For years, Deuce and I were inseparable. He was a founding member of the Conrads and the fact that he lived downhill from the rest of the gang made for an easy bike ride to his house where we would raid his mother's kitchen virtually daily. Deuce's folks were divorced, too, so we had that in common in addition to a mutual love of baseball, video games, and staying up late watching cable television--a luxury not offered in my house. I became a fixture at the Conley house and accepted invitations to sleep-over sometimes as often as three or four nights per week. Deuce had a younger sister, who I think was named Kate, and who in my opinion seemed to be relegated to the status of Richie Cunningham's older brother in *Happy Days*; a quietly acknowledged member of the family who was not essential to any plot lines and rarely appeared or was even mentioned in any episodes. Mrs. Conley treated me like her own son, which was exactly what I needed while my mother lived out of state.

Deuce had the entire second floor of the house to himself, which afforded us the privacy we needed to read nudie mags, listen to Cheech and Chong records, and formulate plans for future mischief. Deuce was the only kid I knew at that age who had neon beer signs and posters of bikini-clad women in his bedroom--given to him by his own father! We stayed up late watching TV, and Mrs. Conley let us watch whatever we wanted, including raunchy teen movies like *Porky's* and *The Hollywood Nights*, and also professional wrestling--which pretty much made her the coolest mom in the world.

For a while, the Conleys had a pet duck named Howard, which they kept in a dog pen with a kiddie pool in it. It wasn't clear whether it was named after the lead character in the movie *Howard the Duck* or for Mrs. Conley's new boyfriend Howard who had given her the bird as a courtin' gift. Either way, having a pet duck around to play with was considerably better than the cannibalistic family of guinea pigs Blake and I had at home. *Damn you, Tiger. How could you eat your wife and children?* Before long, I was spending more time at the Conley's house than at my own home, which didn't seem to bother either my dad or Deuce's mom in the slightest. At least when I was at the Conley's, Dad could count on someone feeding me while he was at work. Kids are like stray cats: they'll hang around wherever there's food and will often play with dead rodents when given the chance, until you take them away from them.

This childhood Utopia took a strange twist when my mother decided to move back to town. With her finances in disarray, Mom couldn't afford to rent a house suitable for accommodating weekend visits by her two children, so Mrs. Conley offered her a solution: move in with her. Mr. Conley was still a regular presence in his former home, even after the divorce, and he offered to build a mini-apartment for my mother in the unfinished basement of his ex-wife's house. Mrs. Conley said that Mom could live down there and still have full use of the kitchen and bathroom upstairs. Most importantly, the rent would be dirt cheap, so my struggling mother accepted the invitation. It seemed on the surface to be a perfect arrangement. But my home-away-from-home paradise had been compromised. On one hand, I was happy to see my mother more often, but on the other hand, now there were rules to follow and I was no longer treated as a special guest. I became "the renter's kid." Immediately, unlimited skin-flick privileges were revoked. Staying up past midnight became a thing of the past. Deuce and I had to include Blake in all of our activities with the lamentable exception of a game we called "Beat the Shit out of Blake." Life at #3 Meadowvale Lane, and in the Hannibal of my youth, would never be the same again.

Later, as I entered high school and became a very moody teenager, I frequently got into heated arguments with either my mom or my dad. It was a safe bet that at any given time I was not speaking to one or both of them. Whenever I had a fight with my dad, I would pedal my bike (or later drive my car) over to Mom's (the Conley's) and seek sanctuary there. Any time my mom laid down a new arbitrary rule like "Don't drop your brother on his head" I would storm off and go back to Dad's. I eventually realized that neither place offered me the solace I thought I needed, so I cleaned out the attic/loft of Dad's house and made myself a Fortress of Solitude that rivaled those belonging to Superman and Deuce Conley.

As the years ticked by, I began to divide more and more of my time between two new pursuits. The first involved remaining holed-up in my room for hours or sometimes days on end while hosting pity-parties for V.I.P. guests including me, myself, and I. The other was hanging out with a new group of comrades who would introduce me to me a new love, a dangerous lady called Alcohol. The Conrads and the innocence of my childhood soon went the way of Deuce's little sister and Chuck Cunningham, a vague memory rarely seen or spoken of again.

The Incontinent Letterman

Beginning well before his fateful move to Hannibal, Travis Naughton has been a lifelong fanatic of the game of baseball. Over the years, he has written several stories about his enduring love affair with the national pastime. His devotion to the game hardly translated to a talent for playing it, but as he once told a reporter at a minor league baseball game before which he threw out the ceremonial first pitch, "I've never been one to let my complete lack of ability for doing something stand in the way of making a public spectacle of myself in attempting it." In typical Naughton fashion, he bounced the "fastball" over the plate on two hops after pretending to shake off the first two signs put down by the catcher. The following is his summation of his baseball career as was published as a series in a national men's magazine in the summer of 2010, under the title The Incontinent Letterman.

I started playing organized baseball when I was in the second grade. The first team I was on was sponsored by the owner of a small grocery store in a dying railroad town in northern Missouri called La Plata, *[which was incidentally the first small town Naughton lived in that was also the former home of yet another famous writer, Lester Dent of "Doc Savage" fame.]* We were the "Bombers"--an ironic name for a team of midgets who couldn't hit the ball out of the infield even if we were standing on second base. In this particular league, the coach (who happened to be my dad) pitched to his own team in order to help the kids learn to hit.

I was never a good hitter, even with my patient father lobbing meatball after meatball across the plate, but what I lacked in talent I more than made up for in embarrassing moments. I can't include contracting a horrible infestation of head lice in the category of personal humiliation because in that case, the entire team shared my misery. The cooties were apparently spread via our communal batting helmets, and as a remedy, every single one of us was required to have his head shaved before the following game. I wonder if the professional players that I see on TV these days who shave their heads bald under the guise of "building team unity" really just have an epidemic of lice spreading throughout their clubhouse.

My most infamous incident on the ball field occurred later that same season while I was standing on second base. After eking out an infield single and reaching second on an error, I realized that I desperately had to pee. As I mentioned, this was coach-pitch baseball, so my dad was standing only a few feet in front of me on the mound. As he threw pitch after pitch to the next batter, (a boy who was extremely selective when it came time to swing the bat,) the pressure in my eight-year-old bladder mounted exponentially. Not wanting to draw too much attention to my predicament, I quietly called out, "Coach!" in a voice barely above a whisper, in a feeble attempt to get my dad to turn around and see that I was in distress. I repeated this self-conscious plea for time-out three more times until eventually, the inevitable happened. Suddenly I felt the simultaneous sensations of complete nirvana and abject horror as a flood of warm liquid streamed down my legs and pooled in the infield dirt between my feet. I'm not sure if my tears were the result of the overwhelming feeling of relief I felt as my tiny yet obscenely distended bladder emptied itself or of the impending sense of doom that closed in around me as I quickly realized everyone on the field and in the grandstands would soon know what humiliating fate had just befallen me. Despair overtook me and I began to silently sob while the game continued around me. Then, like the voice of God calling out to save me, I heard a loud and concerned "Time-out!" shouted from the bleachers. In what may be the only case in baseball history of a fan calling for (much less being granted) a time-out, through my teary eyes I looked over and saw my mother rushing from the stands and across the diamond to come to my rescue. She wrapped her jacket around my waist and when players and parents asked what was wrong as she whisked me off the field she said, "He got hit by a ball." I wasn't exactly sure what getting hit by a ball had to do with wetting myself and I don't know if anyone believed her, but the lie bought us enough time for Mom to spirit me away from their befuddled and prying stares and into our getaway car, thereby allowing me to escape to our home and thus avoid any further scrutiny. For that reason alone, despite all of our later disagreements, my mom has always been my hero.

It is a well known fact that most baseball players are notoriously superstitious. Many become slaves to their own unique pregame rituals that are performed under the belief that they will help appease the baseball gods. Some guys think they have to eat the same meal before every game. Others avoid stepping on a freshly chalked foul-line for fear of jinxing themselves or their team. My pregame ritual was developed out of necessity and was far from superstitious. I found out the hard way that in addition to emptying my bladder before taking the field, evacuating my bowels was every bit as important. Once again, my mother, my hero would be called upon to save the day.

While he was an underpaid teacher, my dad supplemented his income by coaching the high school girls' softball team. I was thirteen years old by this time and I loved to hang out around the softball team's practices. Very few boys at that age enjoyed such close proximity to so many high school girls. Breasts were bouncing around everywhere I looked: in the dugout, sprinting down the base paths, tracking down fly balls. It was wonderful.

On one particular afternoon, my private Heaven turned into a very public Hell. While mulling around the practice field watching the girls run and giggle and bounce, I felt the first twinge of what I immediately recognized to be an imminent attack of diarrhea. With clenched butt cheeks, I scooted over to the gymnasium in search of the boys' locker room only to find that it, as well as the main school building, was locked. I considered using the girls' facilities, but became aware that practice was almost over and soon twenty-five high school girls would be inundating the locker room. The prospect of those athletic, adolescent beauties forever associating the unfortunate and semi-permanent new aroma of their bathroom with the image of the sheepish, ashen coach's kid stepping out of one of their toilet stalls nauseated me even further. I briefly contemplated trying to find a tree near the perimeter of the practice field to hide behind while the calamity of my colon ensued, but unwisely I decided to try to hold it. Big mistake.

Realizing the futility of my efforts to suppress the oncoming catastrophe, I decided too late to make a run for the ladies' locker room. But faster than Phil Rizzuto could say "Holy Cow!" (or "Holy Crap!" in my case,) disaster struck. I was scheduled to play in a little league baseball game shortly after Dad's practice was over and was already dressed in my uniform, ready to take the field. Let's just say that I was very thankful that my pants were gray, and not white, and…well, we'll just leave it at that. A few minutes after practiced ended, Dad found me waiting by his Jeep, red-faced, in tears, and smelling and looking an awful lot like a thirteen-year-old boy who had just shit his pants.

"Why didn't you just use the girls' bathroom, son?"

"I didn't want the team to walk in on me in there. I thought I could hold it," I said as my embarrassment crushed my waning will to live.

Dad determined that we still had time to take me home to get cleaned up and change clothes, so we hopped in the Jeep (which we thankfully had taken the top off of earlier) and sped home. When my mom saw me, she could have lectured me, she could have laughed at me, or she could have slapped me silly, (she was famous for doing any of the three on any given occasion), but instead she just threw my pants in the washing machine and gave me a tender hug. After the wash cycle and my shower ended, she tossed the clean pants into the dryer. I was so relieved that I thanked her and kissed her and told her how much I loved her. Then we looked at the clock. The game would be starting in ten minutes, with or without me, but my father, my ride, was our team's coach and couldn't be late. There was no way my pants would be dry in time to make it to the field for the first pitch. Mom said not to worry and sent Dad ahead.

It would have been easy to simply change into a different

pair of pants, but I owned no other athletic wear at all as poor as our family was, and there was no way in hell I was taking the field in a pair of blue jeans. Nothing says "inbred red-neck" like wearing jeans on a ball field. So Mom and I stood impatiently by the dryer and counted down the minutes until game time. When it was determined that I could still make it in time for my first at-bat if we left at that precise moment, she took the pants out of the dryer and we headed out to the car. They were still soaking wet, so I held them out the window to air-dry all the way to the ball park. Sure the pants were still damp when I took the field, but the misfortune that had earlier befallen them and I was completely undetectable, so I was completely happy.

I managed to get through almost the entire game before a teammate noticed a wet spot on the bench when I got up to bat. I explained it away by saying that it was sweat. The excuse was less plausible, however, when after sliding into second base and standing up with mud rather than dust caked on my uniform, I stood up and said, "Gosh, it's really hot out here today, isn't it?" The kids seemed to be none the wiser and I managed to make it through the day without further embarrassment. My parents never, ever mentioned the incident again and I began incorporating a lengthy bathroom break into my pregame routine from then on.

Years later, Wes Douglass became my closest friend on our high school baseball team and together with Andrew Phillips, we formed the nucleus of the all-important aspect of any good sports team, the benchwarmers. We loved the game but despite our best efforts, we just weren't very good. Andrew was so thoroughly uncoordinated that during practice one day, he fielded a screaming ground ball with his nose — which was obviously a bad idea. The twin black-eyes that resulted from his severely broken nose made it appear that he was wearing The Mask of Zorro. When asked later why he didn't glove the ball before it struck him in the face, Zorro answered with a swollen wink, "Because Coach told me to keep my eye on the ball."

Rather than getting too worked up about our lack of playing time, we instead chose to entertain ourselves by goofing off in the dugout. Besides seeing who could spit the shells of sunflower seeds the farthest into the field of play, we invented several other feats of skill including a contest to see who could get a mosquito to explode without swatting it. Our home field, [Clemens Field, named after Hannibal's favorite son], was situated beside a creek that served as a breeding ground for the biting pests, and all that was required to entice a mosquito to play our little game was to extend a bare arm and wait. I was particularly good at blowing up mosquitoes due to the fact that the blood vessels in my arms are so prominent that they look like garden hoses that were implanted just below the skin. If a bug was unlucky enough to land on one of my voluminous green veins, I would clinch my fist, squeeze my arm just above the bicep with my other hand, (perhaps not unlike like a heroin addict prior to shooting up,) and within a minute or two of repeatedly flexing my fist, the little blood-sucker would pop like a water balloon. Though the rest of my teammates had better batting averages than I did, none could hold a candle to my mosquito-exploding prowess. Unfortunately, Hannibal High School didn't award athletic letters for that.

Wes was a catcher and earned his varsity letter for doing nothing more than warming up the pitcher between innings while the starting catcher put on his gear. Everyone on the team knew that he lettered the easy way, but that didn't stop him from flaunting his letter jacket everywhere he went. I was not impressed, but I was, nevertheless, extremely jealous. I could not envision any scenario in which I would earn my letter. And that damned jacket looked so cool!

My singular moment of glory on the field came in the final game of the season during my junior year. In the district championship game, our small-town team, the Hannibal Pirates, was getting our ass handed to us, as usual, by a team from a large and wealthy St. Louis suburb. With two outs in the bottom of the final inning of an 11 to 1 blowout, our fate was sealed. A senior on our team named Eric Davidson was stepping in to bat for the last time in his high school career when he realized that I was the last person left on the bench who had yet to get into the game. This was suddenly important because there were only two ways to earn a varsity letter. The traditional way to qualify was to play enough innings of varsity ball throughout the season. Obviously, that path was out of the question in my case. The other route was to make an appearance in a post-season game, regardless of how brief the appearance was. Everyone on the team including Coach Harmon was aware of this rule, and it soon became obvious to everyone *but* him that I should pinch-hit for Eric so that I could earn my letter.

From inside the on-deck circle, Eric yelled across the diamond in an attempt to get the coach's attention where he stood in the third base coach's box. "Coach, put Naughton in to hit for me!" Eric shouted. Coach had a perplexed and annoyed look on his face and clearly didn't understand what Eric was saying. He yelled back at Eric saying to step in there and hit. This time Eric walked back to the dugout, took off his batting helmet, handing it and his bat to me, and yelled, "Travis is gonna hit for me!" Coach was completely confused and plainly irritated until it suddenly dawned on him what was happening. His look of annoyance changed to a look of indifferent resignation as I stepped into the batter's box. He knew that the game was a lost cause and perhaps thought that I would be the fast and easy final out that would mercifully put us out of our collective misery and help speed along the process of getting back on the bus and heading home following yet another disappointing season.

I had enough baseball smarts to know that the opposing pitcher was likely to have me pegged as a life-long benchwarmer who had never taken a swing against a varsity-caliber fast ball in his entire pine-riding life. Working under that assumption, I figured he would try to blow the heat right by me, wasting no time offering any junk balls. I decided that no matter where it was located, be it above my head or behind my feet, I would swing with everything I had at the first pitch I saw. I stepped into the box, took a moment to survey the positioning of the defense (as if I could actually hit it anywhere in particular on purpose), and said a little prayer. The pitcher reared back and delivered a scorching fastball right down the pipe, just as I had anticipated. I flexed my muscles, began my swing, and realized when I heard the sound of cowhide on aluminum that my eyes were closed as tight as a newborn puppy's. To the complete astonishment of myself and everyone in the dugout, I had hit the ball. Instinctively I ran as fast as I could, not knowing which direction the ball had traveled after it connected with my bat. As I neared first base I could hear my teammates yelling at the top of their voices "GO! GO! GO!" A split second after my right foot landed on the bag I heard the snap of the ball in the first baseman's mitt. My teammates later informed me that the "blast" had dribbled so slowly off the end of my bat that the shortstop was forced to charge the ball harder than he would have had I bunted.

"Safe!" the umpire yelled sending my teammates into a frenzy of delight accentuated with cheers of "Oh my God!" and "He did it!" and my personal favorite, the highly sarcastic yet hilarious "Everybody scores!" I had forgotten that there was a runner on third, who I managed to drive in, thereby doubling our team total in runs for the game. I looked over my shoulder into the dugout and saw eighteen of the happiest faces I've ever seen in my life looking back at me. It was by far the proudest moment I had ever experienced in the ten years since I had first stepped out onto a ball field. I knew there was absolutely no way to top it. Or so I thought.

While I was standing there delighting in my new found glory I realized there was still some game left to play. Having very little experience on the base paths, I didn't recognize the sign that Coach was giving me from across the field. His amused grin quickly changed to a look of complete exasperation after I failed to attempt a steal of second base on the ensuing pitch. This time coach shot me a wide-eyed look and mouthed the word *steal*. I touched the bill of my cap, slyly indicating that I understood, as he stood there shaking his disbelieving head. I took my lead, leaned ever so slightly towards second base, and nearly got myself picked-off when the pitcher threw over to first. I dove in head first and was thrilled to have gotten dirt on my uniform in my very first varsity appearance. My teammates roared. On the next pitch I took off like a shot and stole second without the throw from the catcher being remotely close to arriving in time to get me out. Again, the dugout erupted in cheers and laughter as I stood there sheepishly and proudly on second base with a grin stretched from ear to ear across my goofy face. On the next toss, the fireballer threw a wild pitch and I advanced to third without a throw. The next pitch was swung on and as the lazy fly ball was being caught for the final out, I crossed home plate, a wonderful feeling despite the fact that my run didn't count. I really couldn't have cared less. I had just reached the pinnacle of my baseball playing career. My complete lifetime varsity statistics:

Games	At Bats	Hits	Avg	RBI	OBP	Stolen Bases
1	1	1	1.000	1	1.000	1

The term "perfect game" in baseball is one that is used to describe a pitcher who throws a complete game without allowing any runs, hits, walks, or base runners. It has only happened twenty times in the history of Major League Baseball. In my very first appearance in a varsity uniform, I had a perfect game of my own. The fact that it would prove to be my last game ever makes the memory all the sweeter.

The following season ushered in a sad new era for our team. Old Coach Harmon retired and was replaced by a young hot-shot with a big chip on his shoulder. Coach Richard Head (as I will call him here) also happened to be the school's new head football coach. He made it obvious to everyone right away that he preferred the gridiron to the diamond. He may not have been born with the name Coach "Dick" Head, but he earned the moniker in every way. Coach Head had a policy that stated that anyone missing two practices would be summarily dismissed from the team. I thought that sounded fair, until he applied the rule to me.

We had two-a-days during spring training with one practice beginning before the school day at 6:00 am and the other immediately after school let out. One afternoon I had been running rather slowly when Coach mistook the pain I was in while suffering from a bad case of shin splints for sheer laziness. On any other occasion, his assessment might have been right. He told me that if I wasn't going to run any harder than that, then I needed to get out of his sight. "Hit the showers, Naughton." I offered a half-hearted protest but realized that I had been offered a rare chance to knock-off early, so I took it. I awoke the next morning at 7:30, having slept through the entire six o'clock practice. I went about my day at school as usual and planned to make up for my absence with extra effort at practice after school. When Coach saw me getting changed in the locker room that afternoon, he called me into his office. He said, "You know about my two absence policy, right?" I said that I did. He dropped the bomb with, "Well, you missed the last two practices, so you're off the team." I was stunned.

"But Coach," I pleaded, "I only missed *one* practice. I overslept this morning and I'm sorry about that. I know that's no excuse, but it was just one practice. It'll never happen again."

"No, you left early yesterday when you were dogging it on the run, remember? That counts as an absence. Two strikes and you're out." *And this guy called himself a baseball coach?* I attempted to argue my case, but Coach Head was judge, jury, and executioner. He walked me out of the office in front of my teammates and watched as I packed up my gear and exited the locker room.

Wes showed up at my house that evening after practice and expressed his displeasure with the situation. "Coach said you quit the team. What the fuck, man?"

"Quit? I didn't quit. He said I quit?" I was incredulous and furious and several other things that ended in "-ous."

"Yeah, he said you quit on us. Well, then what really happened?"

"That asshole cut me for missing two practices."

"But I thought you only missed *one* practice."

"Exactly."

"That really sucks, man." Wes was right. It did suck. After ten years of playing organized ball and finally getting my chance to be a starter for the varsity team during my senior year, Coach Dick Head unceremoniously ended my baseball career just days before the season started. As upset as I was, I was glad Wes stopped by. He and I had played ball together for half our lives and I was sure that the thought of enduring Coach Head's practices without me around would be too much for him to bear. Maybe he would quit. After all, he already had his precious letter jacket. But Wes was no more of a quitter than I was and I admired him for that. "What are you gonna do now?" he asked.

"I don't know. Maybe we should egg his house or something."

"Naw, we can come up with something better than that. We've gotta get creative. If you ask me, Ol' Dick Head just needs to be taken down a notch." I liked this new vindictive side of my old friend's personality.

"What do you have in mind?"

"Ever heard of Nair?"

"You mean the hair remover girls use on their legs?"

"That's the stuff. What do you say we pull the old switcheroo with the shampoo that Coach keeps in his office?"

"I'd say I like the way you think. But how do we pull it off?"

"Leave that to me. Don't you worry your pretty little head about it. Got it?"

"Got it." And with that, Wes sped off in his 1970 Olds Cutlass and headed straight for Hayden's Pharmacy for a bottle of sweet revenge. The high I felt as a result of our plan was fleeting though. I really was hurting about not being able to play ball. When my dad got home from work I told him all about my woes. First, he chewed my ass for missing that morning's practice. Second, he reminded me that the school's athletic director was an old friend of his from back in the days when he taught at the school. [He had quit teaching at HHS a few years prior.] He said he'd be happy to meet with the A.D. about getting Coach Head to let me back on the team. I was moved by the offer, but realized even if Old Dick Head reinstated me, he would never let me play and would almost certainly make every minute I spent on the practice field a living hell in the hopes that I'd quit. I told Dad that I appreciated the gesture, and he said that I was probably right about how Coach would react.

"I would like an apology from him though," I said. "He told my teammates I quit on them. I'd like a chance to set the record straight."

"I think we can do that."

Two days after my expulsion from the team, my dad and I sat down with the A.D. and explained my version of events. Mr. Locke thought about the matter for a few moments and agreed that an apology was in order. He would arrange for a team meeting to be held immediately following that afternoon's practice and said that I'd get my apology from Coach then. Unbeknownst to me, Wes had pulled off the shampoo-switcheroo during that morning's practice. Coach had skipped his morning shower that day, much to Wes's disappointment. However, following the afternoon practice, Coach showered in advance of the team meeting that he was commanded by his superior to hold. One by one, my former teammates gathered in the bleachers of the school gym. They didn't know the purpose of the meeting until they saw me come in with my dad and Mr. Locke. Soon, the bleachers were abuzz with questions and whispers until Coach Dick Head made his fantastic appearance.

Apparently in his haste to towel off and get dressed for the big pow-wow, he never bothered to step in front of a mirror. If he had, he would have surely noticed the numerous bald patches on his otherwise hirsute head. It was all I could do to not wet myself. Wes had pulled it off perfectly. His timing could not have been better. Every player on the team fought to contain their laughter as tears streamed down their bright red cheeks. Coach must have thought they were emotional over seeing their friend and former teammate again and began his speech with, "Now, men, I know many of you are upset by this situation with your teammate." *Snickers.* "I am upset about this deal, too." *Guffaws.* "I need to tell you that I owe this young man and all of you an apology." *Snorts.* "I made a mistake when I told you that Travis quit the team." *Chuckles.* "The fact is that I dismissed him for skipping practice and I should have come clean with you all from the beginning." *Giggles.* "Travis, Mr. Naughton, Mr. Locke, men; I'm sorry."

I stood to shake Coach Head's hand and I think he must have caught a glimpse of his reflection in my watery eyes because as soon as I said thank you, he wished me luck and beat a hasty retreat back to the locker room. The place exploded with laughter, including some coming from my dad and Mr. Locke. Redeemed in the eyes of my teammates, I was elevated to cult-hero status among my peers. But *my* hero was Wes Douglass, who didn't take the credit for his brilliant stunt, but instead allowed me to bask in the warm glow of my victory over Coach "Half-Bald" Dick Head. The ultimate satisfaction came with the realization that Coach Head used shampoo instead of a bar of soap when he washed his body and nether regions. For years, Wes and I laughed till we cried whenever the thought of what Coach Dick Head's reaction must have been when he looked down and saw an exposed, pre-pubescent-appearing penis peering back at him.

It was probably for the best that I didn't play that season. The Pirates went on to lose exactly as many games as they won for the fourth straight year. At least they were consistent. By season's end, Wes and Andrew were the only two seniors who didn't quit or get kicked off the team. Besides, by continuing to mess around with the Benchwarmers I might have contracted West Nile virus or malaria or something else from one of those dugout mosquitoes. Or even worse, my perfect lifetime batting average, perfect average with runners in scoring position, perfect on base percentage, or perfect stolen base percentage might have suffered. The way I see it, I hold four Missouri state records that will never be broken. In that regard, I suppose I should be as grateful to Coach Head as I am to Eric Davidson. Unlike Eric, however, Coach Dick Head won't be getting a case of beer from me as a token of my appreciation. Maybe a lifetime supply of Nair...

By his own admission, Naughton was a mediocre athlete at best. He found it humorous that Quincy College located across the river from Hannibal in Quincy, Illinois offered him a tryout for the school's ball club when he came to the campus to audition for a music scholarship. He graciously declined and focused his energies on his greatest strength — playing the trombone and baritone horn. He confessed years later, however, that he always regretted not giving baseball another shot. His only dalliance with ball and stick sports after high school was being a member of several slow-pitch softball teams. Naughton told a reporter of his dissatisfaction with playing in "those beer-drinking leagues" while attending the 2012 Major League Baseball All-Star Game as a special guest of Commissioner Bud Seilig. "Watching old men try to run bases on a softball field while tripping over their beer guts and limping from their inevitable groin-pulls and bad hammies was such a let-down after having played competitive baseball as a boy that I haven't dared to step onto a playing field since the day I realized that I had become one of them."

Tromboners, Too

I asked Dr. Naughton about his musical background during one of our conversations. A self-proclaimed "band geek" since he entered junior high, Naughton described his years in the Hannibal public schools music program as some of the most enjoyable of his life. He gives equal credit to his former band director, a Mr. Levi Buchanon and his best friend and fellow trombone player Dave Richards for making his experiences in band "some of the most fun I've ever had."

(Younger): I understand that you were a very good musician in high school. Is that as far as you went with your musical career?

(Elder): I was offered music scholarships to three different colleges coming out of high school. I guess you could say that I had a certain amount of talent. I was a pretty decent trombone player, but I actually taught myself how to play the baritone horn during the summer break prior to my senior year and received two of the three scholarship offers based on auditioning with that instrument. I was pretty proud of that.

(Younger): Do you still play?

(Elder): Not really. I played professionally for awhile in my early forties with a blues band that I formed called "The Blues Farmers." I sang and played trombone with the group until a dispute with our record label derailed our plans to record an album and the band broke up. It was a lot of fun while it lasted though."

Naughton wrote an essay about his early days as a musician that was printed in serial form back in 2009 by an underground newspaper that catered to the New Orleans music scene. The reprint of the article called Tromboners, Too *follows.*

When he wasn't trying to kill me, Dave Richards was one of my favorite people in the world. We met back in seventh grade when we sat beside one another in the junior high band. Our friendship really began as a good old fashioned rivalry with each of us striving to out-play the other in hopes of being rewarded with the title of "first chair" or "section leader" by our band director Levi Buchanan, a man whom we would both come to admire and consider a personal mentor. We played the trombone, as did Mr. Buchanan, although neither of us was that excited about it at the time, because as we saw it, playing such a ridiculous looking instrument seemed to be about the furthest thing from cool that a teenage boy could do in a band. The simple fact was that a junior high band could only use so many sax players and drummers. We were told, the world needs tromboners, too.

  Although there were a dozen or so other kids in class who were also learning the trombone, Dave and I separated ourselves from the field quickly. Natural talent and our innate competitive natures drove us to become stand-out musicians by the time we entered high school. By the time graduation loomed on the horizon, Dave had earned the Louis Armstrong award for outstanding musicianship in jazz while I was given the John Phillip Sousa outstanding musician award for excellence in concert and marching bands. Dave and I were both honored as members of the All-State Jazz Ensemble and I was named drum major of our award-winning 130 member marching band, where I was occasionally known to force insubordinate underclassmen to run laps or "drop and give me twenty." Dave ruled the rest of the trombone players with an equally heavy hand as section leader. In our minds, we came as close as anyone ever had to making playing the trombone seem cool.

  Years of sitting side-by-side every day, pushing each other to become accomplished musicians had also ensured that our friendship developed into a close, brother-like bond. Our two egos merged into one intolerable superego that demanded attention from everyone we knew. We would not be ignored. One of our favorite pastimes during rehearsals perfectly illustrated how insufferable we had become.

As we sat on the top level of the risers that filled the band room, we faced opposite the violin section. In our school, all four violin players were girls. Very good looking girls. On warm days when Dave and I wore shorts, if we happened to catch one of the members of the violin section looking over at us, we would spread our legs, pull the crotch of our shorts to one side, and flash our balls at them in order to throw off their concentration and to offer what we thought to be an irresistible invitation for sexual adventures. I realize now that this was repugnant behavior that could have gotten us suspended or arrested, but at the time, it just seemed like harmless fun. Surprisingly, rather than having us expelled from school, the girls seemed to be amused by our juvenile games. In fact, by the time high school was over, Dave and I had each slept with at least three out of the four members of the Hannibal Senior High School Pirate Pride Concert Band violin section. If only we could have earned an award for that.

Prior to befriending Dave, it would have never occurred to me--a kid from a mostly decent, mostly God-fearing family in Middle America whose most outrageous prior behavior included nothing more serious than stealing a few loose grapes in the produce section of the local grocery store--that flashing my junk in the middle of band class would actually help to get me laid. Dave probably didn't really think it would lead to sex either, but his gift (or curse) was that he lacked that little voice in the back of his head that says to most people, "This is a bad idea, we could go to jail for this," so he simply did whatever the hell he wanted. He lived his life without any inhibition, flying by the seat of his pants to the next big adventure. And I was the one lucky enough to be his co-pilot. My god, it was fun being along for the ride.

The fun we had in band paled in comparison to the good times we shared at Dave's house. His parents frequently went out of town, leaving him to fend for himself for up to a week at a time. I never understood why they did this, but greatly appreciated them for doing so. Especially when you consider that they owned a tavern in town and made a habit of keeping their home bar as fully stocked as the one at their place of business.

On a cold January day in 1989 during the winter break from school, Dave invited me over to watch some porn in his folks' basement while they were away for the weekend. I was a typical seventeen year old boy who naturally accepted without hesitation. As I had no car of my own yet, I implored my father to drop me off at Dave's so we could "rehearse" while he ran some errands around town. He obliged, and upon letting me out of his little Mazda truck in front of Dave's house said that he'd be back to pick me up in a few hours. Dave met me at the door with a sadistic grin on his face that sent alarms of panic throughout my body. Had I even the tiniest amount of good sense, I would have chased after my dad yelling and screaming "I've changed my mind! Don't leave me with this maniac! I'm too young to die!" But of course I didn't have a lick of sense and for some reason I couldn't help but go along with whatever Dave had in mind.

As soon as the door closed behind me I knew that the plan had changed. Instead of proceeding to the TV room in the basement, Dave led me into the dining room. It was there that I spied the real reason for our afternoon rendezvous: his parents' unlocked liquor cabinet. Before my eyes was a rainbow of labels and liquids, displayed behind an etched glass door set in a rich, cherry wood frame that filled an entire corner of the room. It was both beautiful and terrifying.

"Today, I'm gonna get you fucked up." Dave said this as a statement of fact, leaving no room for debate. I realized that I had absolutely no say in the matter. At once, two shot glasses were produced and filled with a clear, yet menacing liquid. "Bottoms up!"

For the next two hours the dance went like this: Vodka. Gin. *No, wait. I need a break.* Bourbon. Scotch. *If you don't drink it I'll spill it on you and then your dad will smell it.* Schnapps. Rum. *I'm gonna puke.* Repeat. My ex-girlfriend Molly stopped by during this whiskey-soaked waltz and was more than amused by the scene unfolding before her: Dave literally chasing me around with a full shot glass and me running and stumbling to get away from him. And now taking it all in was the girl who I arrogantly and naively forbade from drinking when we started dating (because I sincerely believed at the time that underage drinking was wrong. Actually, I never really stopped believing that despite my later behavior to the contrary.)

Molly was a five-foot eight, bombshell blonde with curves in all the right places, lips that would make Angelina Jolie jealous, and haunting gray eyes that peered right down into my soul. She was one hell of a violinist, my first real girlfriend, and subsequently the first person to break my heart when she dumped me after leaving for college the previous fall. A semester under her belt as a music major at a fine arts university gave her ample opportunity to re-familiarize herself with the world of alcohol consumption. And here I was apologizing to her for getting wasted and acting like a horse's ass. She didn't call me a hypocrite for getting drunk, even after all my sermonizing on the subject in the years previous, but on the contrary was very sweet and caring as I drifted closer to unconsciousness or whatever awaited me in the great beyond. She stroked my hair, held my hand, and prevented me from drinking any more Dave-forced shots. Looking back on it, she probably saved my life that afternoon. At the time, however, I was quite sure that I was going to die. Instead, my body rejected every ounce of the foul liquid sloshing around inside me at the expense of the quaintly decorated guest bathroom in the basement. Molly had a hand in dragging my nearly lifeless body down there to kneel before the porcelain god and pray for mercy. Thankfully, mercy was granted and within moments I was able to stumble unassisted up the stairs. I made my way into the kitchen where a delectable meal of bologna and ketchup on white bread was forced upon me with almost as much vigor as were the drinks. Resisting the urge to purge again, I choked down two of the horrible sandwiches before I heard the distinctive sound of a certain compact pick-up pulling into the driveway.

"Good luck," Molly offered with a worried smile. Dave was

bent over in laughter, drunk and giddy at the prospect of watching me get my ass kicked by my old man. His own father walked out on his family years earlier. It was actually his step-dad who along with his mother raised Dave, although "raised" is a strong word to describe the man's parenting style. Once, he staggered drunk into his step-son's room and proceeded to empty his bladder in the bed--with Dave sleeping in it. Dave knew not to confront his old man for fear of a beating and told no one but me about the incident. I was honored that he trusted me and felt comfortable sharing things like that with me. I guess in his twisted mind, getting me shit-faced was his way of thanking me for being there for him.

My dad impatiently honked the truck's horn as I grabbed mine (which never made it out of its case that day), and on my way out the door I managed to uncross my eyes just long enough to give Dave the old stink-eye while uttering a pathetic, yet heartfelt, "Thanks a lot, Asshole." I walked out to the truck, held my breath, and slid into the passenger seat hoping to avoid breathing in Dad's direction.

"What's that smell?" he asked no sooner than my door closed.

"What smell?" I knew beyond any doubt that I was a dead man. The odds of cheating death twice in one day were just not in my favor. My father was a Marine who fought in Vietnam and could snap my neck like a twig for making an egregious error in judgment such as lying about getting drunk in the middle of the afternoon during Christmas vacation.

"Smells like hot dogs."

He may have smelled hot dogs, but I smelled hope. *I may survive this after all.* "Uh, it's boloney actually." I cracked open my window and hoped that the fresh air would help perk me up and mask my hideous breath. "Dave made us some boloney sandwiches because we didn't know if you'd be picking me up before or after dinnertime." *Boloney indeed.*

"Oh, good. Then I won't worry about feeding you." This was

a relief to a divorced father whose idea of making dinner was ordering pizza. "Did you have a good practice session?"

"You bet," I muttered while trying not to exhale.

"That's nice," he said, and just like that, I was free and clear. I did feel guilty, though. It seemed that on that afternoon, my childhood was flushed down the toilet along with the eighteen shots of hard alcohol Dave later confessed to gleefully forcing down my throat. By all rights, I should have died of alcohol poisoning that day. I only weighed 130 pounds back then and yet I drank all of that liquor in the span of just two hours. It was the first time I had cheated death, and it was the first time that I had ever had more than a single sip of booze in my life. But it certainly wouldn't be the last time for either. I wanted to be mad at Dave for my near death experience, but the truth is that he was still one of my favorite people in the world even when he *was* trying to kill me.

Naughton wrote a follow-up article for the same publication following an overwhelming response to the first essay by the paper's readers. The contrast between the two pieces is remarkable. It was entitled Tromboners Two *and propelled the sales of the paper to an all-time high. It was later reprinted along with* Tromboners, Too *in a collection of the best essays in North America in 2010. It appears in its entirety in the following chapter.*

Tromboners Two

In the years since I agreed to sell my old trombone as a favor to my friend Dave Richards, I have occasionally felt a desire to take up the instrument again. I really missed playing in a band. Sure, I was never the lead guitar player in a rock band, but I was a pretty damned good trombone player in one of the most highly respected high school jazz ensembles in the state of Missouri. I was no Paul Stanley, but chicks still dug me alright.

As cool as I thought I was, some would say that I was a bit of a band geek. In fact, Dave and I attended band camp so many times that a photograph of the two of us was actually featured in the camp's informational brochures. While most guys wore letterman's jackets, I wore a band jacket. By the end of high school, it was adorned with 72 ribbons and medals that were awarded to me during my four years in the band program. That coat weighed ninety pounds if it weighed an ounce.

In college, as I began to shift my focus from the fine arts to the fermented arts, playing music became less interesting to me. I performed with The University of Missouri Jazz Lab Band for two years before finally packing away my horn for good. But a few years after Bethany and I got married and the fog of intoxication began to lift, I began to remember the person I had been before partying became my priority. In high school, I enjoyed being the center of attention and lived to entertain people. Case in point: my rendition of "Mary Had a Little Lamb" which I performed during the school's talent show one year.

I remember standing onstage in our school's large auditorium before a packed house of nearly one thousand students, only slightly nervous as I began to sing the children's song--quietly at first--while strumming an acoustic guitar. I had pre-tuned the strings to the proper notes because I knew absolutely nothing about playing the instrument. As the crowd began to clap in rhythm to the tune, I increased the volume of my performance accordingly. Soon, I was screaming the lyrics in the fashion of a heavy metal front man and strumming the guitar like an absolute madman. The MC of the show, who had apparently heard enough, ran out and yanked me off the stage, giving me the proverbial hook, to the resounding boos of the crowd.

As he tried in vain to introduce the next act, I could hear the crowd chanting something. They grew louder and louder until I could clearly hear that they were yelling, "TRA-VIS! TRA-VIS! TRA-VIS!" I made eye-contact with the MC as he glanced in my direction offstage and shrugged my shoulders as if to say, "What are you gonna do?" He threw up his hands in defeat and exited stage left. I triumphantly re-emerged from behind the curtain, tossed my pick into the crowd, and started slapping my hand on my guitar in synch with the clapping of the audience. "I said Mary *(slap)* had *(slap)* a little *(slap)* lamb *(slap)*..." The wood of the old six-string started to give way as I pounded it harder and harder with my fist. "Its fleece *(pow!)* was white *(boom!)* as snow *(wham!)*..." A few pieces of the guitar started to splinter-off of the face and the fretboard of the instrument began to separate from the body. "And every *(bang!)* where *(smash!)* that Mary *(thwack!)* went *(crunch!)* the lamb *(crash!)* was sure *(ker-plow!)* to go! *(ka-boom!)*" By this point I was belting out the words so loudly that I could feel the veins in my neck bulging and my face turning flush. I unleashed a primal scream and slammed the crumbling guitar onto the stage floor, sending shrapnel flying in a thousand directions, including towards the now riotous audience. I tossed the remains of the destroyed guitar into the front row, flashed the devil-horns heavy metal hand sign, and strutted off the stage knowing beyond any doubt that I was the unanimous winner of the "talent" competition. After the show, several kids came back stage and asked me to autograph pieces of the now-infamous guitar, which I gladly did.

No booze-fueled party or romantic liason could offer quite the same thrill as performing before an audience. After we graduated from college I convinced my wife (the Enabler) to let me buy a bass guitar with the goal being to work my way back into the music scene once again. I taught myself the fundamentals of the instrument and in three months time felt comfortable enough to play with a band, if one would have me. But soon my wife (the Voice of Reason) informed me at that I needed to get a job, and so I did. Eventually the bass guitar started collecting dust and when a co-worker in the butcher shop I worked in mentioned that his teenage son was looking for a used bass to buy for his garage band, I sold it to him. Once again, I found myself lacking a musical instrument and more importantly, a creative outlet. Over the next several years, I tried different hobbies like model railroading, wood-working, drawing, and writing poetry. No matter what I tried, nothing filled the void that the absence of music left in my soul.

After years of unsuccessfully searching for something to do that would replace playing the trombone, I finally realized that I simply just needed to replace my trombone. I began looking online for a cheap, used horn that I could purchase. Naturally, as I found some very cool antique horns for sale that cost more than the $50 budget the Voice of Reason had given me, I implored her to allow me to buy a nicer instrument that would have a better sound quality and sense of history than an old junker could offer. The Enabler was just about to give in, when I stumbled upon an old band friend while surfing the Internet one day.

Monty O' Brien was a year younger than me and a fellow trombone player at Hannibal High School during the late 1980s when one day he informed me that he was in search of a new horn. When my mom found a decent used car for me to buy at her dealership in 1989, she said she would pay half of the sale price if I could come up with the rest of the money. I had no job, but I did have two trombones. The first was the student model horn that my dad bought for me brand new. It was the horn that I had learned on, and it was the horn that years later Dave would pawn after I reluctantly sold it to him. My other horn was a Conn 88H professional model trombone. It was a vintage horn made in the early 1970s and had an "F" attachment trigger, and a rose brass bell. These features may not mean much to most people, but to serious trombone players, the 88H is widely regarded as one of the finest brass instruments ever made. Of course I didn't know that in high school. And even if I had, I probably still would have sold it to Monty in order to get the cash for my car. *Teenagers.*

Recently, I emailed my former band mate and asked him whatever happened to the old horn that I sold him all those years ago. He replied within a few days and said that he had donated it to our old band department after he lost interest in playing it a few years after graduating. I wondered what the odds were that the horn was still in the band room after all those years. I remembered that a former classmate named Taylor was serving as an officer in the band boosters organization at the time, so I contacted her and asked if she would do some investigating for me. She put her daughter, who was a current band student, to the task and called me the very next day with some incredible news.

"Travis? This is Taylor. We found your trombone. My daughter's best friend is a trombone player and she said that she saw your old horn lying in the back of a storage locker in the band room yesterday. She also said she's played it a time or two and that it's still in great shape."

I couldn't believe it. It had been almost twenty years since I last laid eyes on my trombone, and now I knew where it was. And, I knew I had to have it. Taylor suggested that I contact the school's new band director, Mr. Michaels, to discuss the possibility of getting the horn back.

I met with Mr. Michaels the next week and offered to purchase and donate a used baritone horn (an instrument he said the department sorely needed) and buy a brand new trombone to exchange for my old 88H that was sitting unused in his band room. He invited me to come by the school to verify that the horn was indeed the one that once belonged to me.

When I opened the worn and dusty case, I immediately recognized every scratch and ding in the delicate soft brass bell of my old horn. Warm memories came flooding back to be and to my surprise, I almost started crying. It was like being reunited with a dear friend twenty years after last seeing one another. I explained to Mr. Michaels how grateful I would be if he would agree to the exchange and he said to let him think it over for a while. *Think it over?!* What was there to think about? He would receive a brand new trombone with all the same bells and whistles as my corroded, student-abused antique plus a gently used baritone. The two instruments blew the budget given to me by the Enabler/Voice of Reason, but she didn't really mind. Bethany knew how much that old horn meant to me. Seeing the tears in my eyes, Mr. Michaels knew how much it meant to me, too. I said that I looked forward to hearing from him as soon as possible.

I could barely endure the wait. Something that had been missing from my life for all these years was tantalizingly within my reach. Not just an old trombone, but music in general, artistic expression, and a large part of my personal identity. A few weeks went by before Mr. Michaels reluctantly agreed to the deal. He explained away his hesitation with an excuse about following proper procedures, but at that point, I couldn't have cared less. I was getting my 88H back.

I drove to Hannibal to make the exchange at the school's annual band fundraiser where I ran into my old band director Mr. Buchanan who was "instrumental" (My god that's a great pun there, don't you think?) in convincing Mr. Michaels to follow through with our "arrangement" (Oops, there's another one). He invited me to crash at his place for the night and we spent the next several hours reminiscing about the old days. Seeing him again after so many years brought back a flood of memories that years of hard drinking had only managed to hide, not erase. We laughed. We cried. We talked about what happened to former band members including Dave Richards whose battle with personal demons did not end as well as mine. Mr. Buchanan was like a second father to both of us while we were in school and telling him so was twenty years overdue.

When I got back home, I discovered that the 88H still sounds as good as it ever did, and although the old horn may be a little rusty, it's not nearly as rusty as I am. I have a lot to catch up on in terms of endurance and forgotten technique. But I've already begun teaching my boys how to play it and I hope that one day when they're old enough, they will use it when they are in band. Not everyone can be a sax player or a drummer, I tell them. The world needs tromboners, too. Maybe they'll let their old man play with them someday. It would be pretty cool to finally be in a band again. Maybe the Enabler will let me buy a tour bus…

His wife, the Voice of Reason, never did let him purchase a tour bus, but she did allow him to form a blues band and tour the Midwest off and on for two years until the group disbanded. Travis Naughton the Bluesman credited Bethany the Enabler for helping to reignite his love affair with music after it lay dormant for nearly two decades. He told me how grateful he is that she still indulges his whims even after all the years they've been together. Fans of Travis Naughton the Author are grateful for his two decade search for a new creative outlet to fill the void left by his break from music that eventually led him to become a writer.

Remember When I Asked Your Mom to the Prom?

As Dr. Naughton became more comfortable sharing personal stories from his past with me, I asked not about what led to his parents' divorce – deciding that story has been told countless times by the millions of other children of divorce in this country--but instead how his father and stepmother came to be a couple. I was very glad I did. His candor and trademark racy wit rewarded my choice of inquiry.

On the rare occasions when his parents Butch and Donna Naughton went out for a night on the town, they would usually hire high school students from Mr. Naughton's social studies classes to babysit young Travis and his younger brother Blake. They looked forward to these evenings for reasons Travis related to me:

For two pre-pubescent boys who were beginning to become interested in the opposite sex, what could have been better than having an attractive teenage girl at our beck and call? Well, I'll tell you: Having *two* attractive teenage girls at our beck and call, that's what. Susan and Rhonda were best friends and students in my dad's history class and accepted the babysitting gig under the condition that they be hired as a team. Blake and I took a liking to this arrangement immediately. The girls were a great deal of fun to be around and they seemed to genuinely enjoy spending time with us. And they both had ample, pert teenaged breasts that I simply could not take my eyes off of. When the girls asked us what we wanted to do for fun, the answer always had something to do with creating an opportunity to see down a blouse or to "accidentally" brush up against a tight, wool sweater. Our favorite game to play was "Chicken," which for most people was typically played in a swimming pool but was easily modified for our living room. It involved the girls giving us "piggy-back" rides and running into each other while Blake and I tried to dislodge the other from his "mount" in the hopes that we might fall on or under the heaving bosoms of one or both of our shapely babysitters. By the age of ten, I had seen and felt more boobs than many boys twice my age. I couldn't have been happier. Unfortunately, my parents were anything but happy, as I would soon find out.

On a beautiful, sunny day in the spring of 1983, Butch told the boys to hop in the family car for a ride to their favorite park [Huckleberry Park]. As Travis recalled, his father was quiet on the way there and when they had arrived, he walked his sons over to a swing set and launched his opening salvo. "You know your mother and I love you both very much." Travis was old enough by then to know exactly what his dad was going to say next. "But sometimes mommies and daddies fall out of love with each other..." Before the word "divorce" was ever uttered, Travis broke into angry, heartbroken, and uncontrollable sobs that Blake, who was only a kindergartner at the time, couldn't grasp the cause of.

Looking back on it, Travis now knows why he took the news so badly. Because his family moved so often, (he attended five different schools in the five years from kindergarten through fourth grade), he had made no meaningful, long-term friendships with anyone outside of his family. His closest friends were his parents and his brother. Suddenly his father explained that Donna would be moving away, thus breaking up what Travis described as "our gang." His mother's reasoning for this was that she believed it was better for boys to be raised by their father who could teach them about being a man. "What a crock of shit" was what Travis thought, and for the better part of the next decade, he blamed her for ruining his home life. "Thankfully, I came to my senses in time to make several years worth of wonderful memories with her before she died," he told me. "But at the time, as a ten year old whose world was just turned upside-down, I didn't think things could get much more screwed-up. I didn't know how wrong I was."

After Susan and Rhonda graduated, they moved on to college. In the meantime, Butch and the boys moved on, too, to yet another house;

this time, just across town and just across the street from Susan's parents' house. Naturally, like all college students, Susan came home to visit her folks on the occasional weekend or whenever she needed to do laundry. So the Naughton boys still saw her fairly regularly. Before long, Travis noticed that whenever she was in town, Susan was at his house more often than her own. He claims that at first, this didn't bother him too much, "because she didn't wear a bra half the time." But eventually, the shine wore off and he grew tired of competing with her for his father's attention. Travis and Susan were only seven years apart in age, and at times it felt to him "like I suddenly had an older sister who was now Daddy's favorite." Their relationship was still a cordial one, until one fateful evening after which it became painfully apparent that Susan was anything but a sister.

Susan was home for the summer and as usual had spent the better part of her day at the Naughton house. As the hour grew late, the boys were sent to bed for the evening. Travis still recalls hearing the familiar, muffled sounds of his dad's and Susan's voices coming from down the hall as he drifted off to sleep. Sometime later, he heard what sounded to him like someone howling in pain. Half-asleep, he sat up in bed and strained to hear the sound again. "Butch!" a woman's voice cried out, obviously in distress. Naughton described the ensuing moments in a passage from his memoir Rude, Crude, and Socially Unacceptable:

My heart leaped from my chest as I leaped from my bed and cautiously opened the bedroom door. Tip-toeing toward the family room, I bristled in fear when a loud moan echoed down the hallway. The gravity of the situation became crystal clear to me as I became fully awake; the old man was murdering the babysitter. As I reached the end of the hall, I prepared myself to rescue the damsel in distress. I knew it was up to me to save Susan from the death blows being dealt her by my enraged father. I rounded the corner and as I opened my mouth to shout, "Stop! You're killing her!" I saw a scene that years and years of heavy drinking did nothing to erase from my memory; my father's middle-aged, naked body nearly crushing Susan's nude, lithe form into oblivion. For a moment, I stood transfixed as the haunting image of their two bodies becoming one burned itself permanently into my retinas.

Had they been an abstract painting, instead of merely two horny people going at it on my couch, any admirer of fine art would probably have appreciated the stark visual contrast between the two body types gyrating before me. The art critic would have said something like, "See how the crude, savage features of the Beast play against the smooth and unspoiled contours of the beautiful Maiden's flesh? Such beauty! Such horror! I *must* have it. I shall hang it in my den!" But to me as a young boy, the sight of my dad screwing the babysitter on the sofa that he and my mom had bought together for our happy family's home just a few years earlier was simply too much to bear.

It would be fair to say that I reacted badly to this new turn of events. A voice in the back of my mind reminded me, "If you don't have anything nice to say, don't say anything at all." I would like to think that it was my mother who taught me those words of wisdom, but really that doesn't sound like her at all. (She was famous for her utter inability to bite her tongue. In front of a large crowd of parents and children, she once threatened to kick the hind-end an umpire at one of my little league games when he refused to eject an opposing pitcher who hit me with a poorly aimed fastball.) At any rate, I decided that I would give Susan the silent treatment as a way of punishing her for trying to replace my mom, or for trying to steal my dad's affection, or perhaps for wasting her youthful good looks on an overweight, divorced, forty-something father of two. In my forever scarred yet naïve mind, I failed to recognize that the arsenal of juvenile, passive-aggressive behaviors I planned to aim at derailing the budding romance of two consenting adults, who were blissfully unaware that they had been seen mid-coitus by an emotionally damaged twelve-year-old boy who was still smarting from his parents' recent divorce, would have no effect on "fixing" the situation whatsoever. Nevertheless, it was the only plan I could come up with at the time, so I went with it.

It is not an exaggeration to say that I went weeks and sometimes months without uttering more than an occasional grunt to my dad's new girlfriend. At one point I decided that silence was not a strong enough weapon, so I ratcheted things up a bit by refusing to make eye contact with her--ever. By the time we moved into yet another house before I entered the sixth grade, Susan had become a permanent fixture, although she wouldn't "officially" live with us until she and Dad were married a few years later. By the time I reached high school, merely avoiding eye contact had lost its luster, so I began holding my hands up to the sides of my head in a manner reminiscent of a horse wearing blinders in order to avoid seeing anything in its peripheral field. My tunnel vision technique apparently pushed Susan past her breaking point one day when she was vacuuming and cleaning our house.

"Why do you act like an asshole whenever I'm here?" she asked. I was happy she noticed.

"Why are you such a bitch?" I replied. Clever, I know.

"I didn't say that you *are* an asshole. I just said you're acting like one."

"Well, you're still a bitch." And I left, having just made the most well-reasoned, thought-provoking, and perfectly-articulated argument in the history of modern intellectual discourse. I proceeded directly over to Dave Richard's house where we held an impromptu therapy session over a few dozen drinks. This would be the pattern I would follow throughout high school.

When Dad and Susan started making wedding plans, it became clear that Blake and I were expected to attend the ceremony. Blake was always friendly to Susan and had no problem wishing the newlyweds the best. After my new girlfriend Molly had just been hired to work with my soon-to-be step-mother at a local restaurant, they became fast friends. Molly suggested that she and I should go to the wedding together and oh, by the way, "grow up and be nice to Susan." But it was a tall order; like asking Donald Trump to be nice to Rosie O' Donnell. I did lighten up a little, but it didn't help matters when I went out with my friends and had to endure their constant ball-busting about my new step-mother.

Roosevelt Crane, a friend who was easily twice as heavy and seemingly twice as tall as I was, relished any opportunity to get under my skin, knowing full well that I would never be able to physically shut him up. He paraphrased a line from the movie, *Bill & Ted's Excellent Adventure*, "Hey Trav, remember when I asked your mom to the prom?"

"Shut the fuck up, Rosie. She's not my mom." But of course he didn't shut-up. All of my friends loved teasing me about having a parental figure who had graduated in the same decade as us, but they also liked to point out what an idiot I was being for treating her the way I did. I knew they were right, but I inherited my stubbornness from my beloved mother--my *real* mother, so I continued to distance myself from Susan for years.

It would take a few months of Marine Corps boot camp, the birth of my half-siblings, and a few other life-altering/life-threatening events for me to gain enough perspective and maturity to finally accept the fact that my dad and Susan really were meant to be together. Susan is a good wife and a good mother to my younger brother and sister and I wish to go on the record right now by issuing this public apology for my previous, immature behavior. Susan, I'm sorry I acted like such an asshole.

But just for the record, Dad: I saw her boobs first.

Naughton's accounts of the events of his formative years give a candid glimpse into the origin of many of his quirks that he is now celebrated for. His famous sense of humor, his infamous temper, and finally his ability to forgive but never forget (qualities that make him a beloved writer) are all traits that he owes to his life in Hannibal. It boggles the mind to ponder "what might have been" if Samuel Langhorne Clemens and Travis Alexander Naughton had grown up somewhere else. I asked Dr. Naughton what he thought was the source of the writing genius that sprang from both his and Twain's experiences in that otherwise ordinary river town. He said, "I don't know. It must be something in the water."

Hail to the Chief

Since his first appearance on Jimmy Kimmel Live *promoting his bestselling book* Stay-at-Home Rollercoaster, *Travis Naughton has been a world-wide celebrity. Kimmel remarked after the show finished taping, "That guy was one of the funniest guests we've ever had on this show. Honestly, the way he ripped apart Dane Cook, [who also appeared on the same broadcast], I thought I was going to wet myself." Naughton went on to appear on the program twenty-three more times before Kimmel announced his retirement and married long-time on again/off again girlfriend Sara Silverman. Cook never appeared on the show again.*

Naughton delighted audiences at every morning news show, evening talk show, and shock-jock radio show appearance he made. His knack for self-promotion is the stuff of legend. In one day, he taped appearances on all three major networks' morning programs plus Live with Regis and Kelly *and* The Late Show with David Letterman. *He still managed to appear at three book stores in New York between tapings that day and signed an estimated 2,500 copies of his book. Soon enough, Naughton's manager convinced the author to go hit the lecture circuit, although by his own admission, he didn't need much convincing.*

I asked the author when he first developed his panache for public speaking.

(Elder): My first experience in speaking before an audience was at a high school debate club event in which each participant selected a controversial position to defend and then gave a speech supporting his or her opinion. I chose to speak out against year-round school. I thought it was a crime against humanity and childhood to keep kids in school all year. Imagine what it would have done to the likes of Tom Sawyer.

(Younger): Who won the debate?

(Elder): I did, of course. Although I don't recall receiving any prize money. I'll have to see about collecting that.

(Younger): Were there any other moments that you recall from your youth that gave you the confidence to become the fearless public speaker you are today?

(Elder): There were a few more occasions in my high school days in which I really seemed to have the crowd eating out of the palm of my hand. A pair of student council speeches I gave comes immediately to mind.

Naughton wrote about these unforgettable and almost unbelievable early appearances on his blog back in 2007, nearly twenty years after they happened. The memories were obviously still quite vivid in his mind and in the minds of several of his former school chums that I was able to interview who witnessed the twin spectacles.

During my senior year of high school, I was a co-editor of the school's yearbook, co-drum major of our award winning marching band, and president of the student council. I wasn't necessarily the Big Man On Campus, but I certainly had the biggest ego. I made a conscious choice to get involved in as many extra-curricular activities as possible in order to make myself look better on college applications and to get my photo in the yearbook more than anybody else. (I succeeded at both.) Of course my "something-point-five" grade point average (to borrow an expression coined by Rosie Crane when running for senior class president) was all that was really necessary to gain acceptance to my college of choice, the University of Missouri, which was rated at that time as one of the top ten party colleges in the nation by a major men's magazine.

Being a member of student council during my junior year

inspired me to make a run for the office of president. The girl who ran against me was a straight "A" student, with striking good looks and a reputation for excelling at everything she tried. On paper, there was no way that I could defeat Rebecca White. But life is not lived on paper, although it was in fact cheap copy paper that contributed significantly to my election. I used my dad's primitive Apple II computer to print out campaign materials such as flyers, banners, leaflets, and business cards. My opponent distributed nothing. I plastered the halls with propaganda and slid a business card that read, "Naughton for President: Representing <u>Everyone</u> at H.H.S." into every hand I shook. My opponent hoped that her impeccable reputation alone would be enough to sway voters, but I truly did represent a far wider variety of kids in our school than Rebecca ever could have, despite the fact that she was a genuinely wonderful human being. I hung out with rednecks, preppies, punks, metalheads, jocks, you name it, while Rebecca never strayed too far from the Izod-wearing, tennis playing, college-bound crowd that she was so much a part of.

On the day that we were scheduled to deliver our campaign speeches to the assembled student body, I was chosen to speak second, after the eloquent and beautiful Rebecca. Was I worried? Hell no. As I imagined, Rebecca gave a straight forward, "Here's why I would be a good president, so please vote for me" speech. It was well written and executed as I knew it would be. But it was also boring and predictable. That's where I knew I had the advantage. Travis Naughton is anything but boring and predictable.

When it was my turn at the podium I began with, "Friends, Romans, and Countrymen- lend me your ears…" I looked down at my notes in mock embarrassment, crumpled the sheet of paper, and tossed it over my shoulder onto the stage floor. I began again, "Four score and seven years ago…" The audience began reacting exactly as I had hoped, with laughter. I wadded up the second sheet of paper and tossed it into the crowd. "I have a dream today," I began again. "A dream that one day…" More laughter. Another discarded page of my speech. The crowd was eating it up and I sensed that it was the time to deliver the goods. "Fellow students, if

I am elected President of the Student Council, I promise to work with school administrators toward the goal of acquiring a jukebox to be placed in the cafeteria so that we can enjoy music instead of the sound of our digestive tracts. (I paused for the applause.) I promise that I will work to have vending machines installed in study hall. (My voice began to soar as the din in the great hall rose.) I promise to negotiate preferred parking for seniors. (The crowd was electric.) And I promise to represent *everyone* at Hannibal High School. Thank you very much!" A standing ovation erupted from the congregation. The noise was like that at a rock concert. Triumphantly, I started to return to my seat and noticed a look of utter defeat in Rebecca's eyes. I thought she might even cry. Part of me felt a twinge of guilt for destroying her so, but it was just a small part. The election took place immediately following the speeches for the other offices. The results were to be given over the school's P.A. system later in the day.

When fourth period began, Rebecca and I were both seated at our desks in English class when the principal, Mr. Wilder, began his announcement. "Your attention please. The results of this morning's elections have been tallied." He announced the winners of the lower offices first. "And finally, in the race for president, the winner is: Travis Naughton." I was naturally elated and I wanted to stand up and yell, but I quickly realized that poor Rebecca was sitting just two desks to my right with her face buried in her hands. I turned to say something to break the awkward, silent tension in the room but as I made eye contact she stood up, eked-out a feeble "Congratulations," and sprinted out the door, leaving a defeated trail of tears behind her. I felt genuinely bad for her. I realized that until that moment she had no idea of what it felt like to fail at something. Rebecca was simply not used to dealing with disappointment. Of course after she left, everyone in the room congratulated me and confessed that they voted for me. I later found out through a kid who worked as an errand boy in the school office that I had won by a ten to one margin. I was called into the principal's office that afternoon and the subject of my campaign promises was broached.

"So what's this about a jukebox and soda machines?" Mr.

Wilder began.

"Don't forget the primo parking spaces for seniors."

"Of course." He paused for a moment, making it appear that he was actually considering my propositions, but I was pretty sure that the former football coach and Marine just liked watching me squirm uneasily in my chair. "I don't see why we can't work something out. I'll be in touch."

I was flabbergasted. Could it be that the school's principal was really going to make my pie-in-the-sky campaign promises anything more than a cheap ploy to get myself elected? I'd believe it when I saw it.

When school commenced again the following fall, I was floored to see a brand spanking new jukebox sitting in the brand spanking new cafeteria that was completed during the summer break. I was stunned to see a snack machine and two soda machines in the room used for study hall. I was thrilled that as a senior, I was able to park my 1979 Chevy Monte Carlo in a row of parking spaces within thirty paces of the school building's front doors. To my amazement and to the delight of the entire student body, all of my campaign pledges were kept. The real beauty in all of it for me was that I was required to make no additional effort beyond making my initial dubious promises in order to accomplish these objectives. My BMOC status was beginning to emerge and would continue to grow throughout my senior year. But my next speech, delivered as the incumbent, lame-duck student council president would be forever remembered as one of the greatest spectacles in the history of Hannibal High, and would complete my metamorphosis from band geek to living legend, if only in my own mind.

In the spring of 1990, student council election time came around again as it did every year. And as usual, tradition dictated that the out-going president give his farewell address to the student body before introducing the new candidates. In hopes of building upon the favorable response to my speech given the year prior, and knowing that since I had nothing to lose in terms of trying to get re-elected, I decided to go out with a bang. Literally. I planned to stage a fake assassination attempt, with myself as the target. All I needed was a little help from my friends.

To look presidential, I would be wearing my Sunday best suit. I would also need a "Secret Service" detail, all dressed in suits too, with the additional touches of dark sunglasses and ear buds. Rosie Crane and Chris Stevens were the biggest bodies in our crew, so they would be flanking me on the stage as I delivered my speech. My baseball teammates Wes Douglass and Andrew "Crash" Phillips, (Crash being aptly nicknamed for his propensity for being involved in auto accidents,) would be walking up and down the aisles, keeping a wary eye on the crowd. And Dave Richards would be the trigger man, hiding in the audience, waiting for his opportunity. To be as convincing as possible, we would need guns, so we purchased five black cap-guns and painted the safety-orange ends black to make the weapons look more like real pistols. Then we meticulously rehearsed how it would all do down.

On election day, I walked backstage and peeked through the curtain at the gathering masses. There were slightly more than one thousand people in the auditorium that day, and only six of them had an inkling of what was to come in the next few moments. At 10:00 am, Mr. Wilder stood before the audience and introduced me one last time to my constituents. I stood up and from their hiding places in the shadows of the stage's wings, Rosie and Chris emerged to escort me to the podium. I saw Crash and Wes enter the room from the rear exits and watched as they began patrolling the aisles. They even pretended to speak into microphones concealed in their cuffs. The crowd could readily tell who the guys in the suits were supposed to be, and a general sound of recognition and amusement bubbled up from the seats. I began my speech.

"Mr. Wilder, Distinguished Members of the Faculty and Staff, my Fellow Students; One year ago, you the students of Hannibal Senior High School entrusted me with the responsibility of serving you in the capacity of Student Council President. I can only hope that I lived up to your expectations--"

"SIC SEMPER TYRANNIS!" Dave's voice rang out from the

middle of the crowd. He leaped from his seat, pulled out his weapon, and began firing shots in my direction. Instantly, the half-asleep congregation erupted into chaos. As Rosie and Chris grabbed me and whisked me off the stage safely away from the shooter, Crash and Wes converged upon Dave and returned fire. They grabbed him by the wrists and dragged the would-be assassin's "lifeless" body up the entire length of the center aisle and out the back of the auditorium. I watched from the wings as students and teachers dove for cover between the rows of seats while several panic-stricken kids crouched frozen in fear with tears and looks of horror obscuring their faces. From the time I began my address to the time Dave was dragged out of the room, no more than thirty seconds had lapsed. By the time everyone realized it was all just a terrifying and perfectly executed hoax, the six perpetrators had made a clean, triumphant getaway.

It bears mentioning that in 1990, no one I knew had ever heard of a real school shooting. Nearly a decade would pass before the massacre at Columbine High School in Littleton, Colorado took place. When we pulled off our caper, it was as innocent as any fake murder could be. If Mr. Wilder had entertained any notion of punishing us, he hid it extremely well. Of course we would have never dreamed of attempting such an act in this new world in which we now live, but on that spring day nearly twenty years ago, it was just about the best goddamned school prank ever pulled off by anybody, anywhere.

I must concur. And so marked the beginning of a lifetime of outrageous public appearances that solidified Travis Naughton's standing as the world's most sought after speaker. However, twenty some years would pass before the self-anointed "second most interesting man in the world" (presumably following only the man in the Dos Equis beer commercials) would have his demons in check enough to allow his ascension to world-wide fame.

I'm a Drinker, Not a Fighter

By Naughton's own admission, Lady Liquor was his first true love. "But she could be a real bitch," the seventy-six year old laughs as he thinks back to the wilder days of his youth. The circle of friends that he ran with in high school was apparently quite the bunch of hell raisers. Naughton, or "Naughty" as his friends called him then, fit right in.

(Younger): About how often did you and your buddies go out drinking when you were in high school?

(Elder): Oh, I'd say that we went out and tied one on at least two or three nights every week.

(Younger): Really? And yet you were still able to get by in school and get accepted to college?

(Elder): Get by? Hell, I was a two-year member of the National Honor Society, although I'm pretty sure taking two or three band classes every semester helped my G.P.A. a bit. I was a fairly functional drunk back in those days. I kept my drinking pretty well hidden from my folks and still managed to participate in several extra-curriculars at school without anyone knowing how out-of-control I was on the weekends.

Naughton wrote about this period of his life in his novel Burning Couches:

With a small block V-8 and rear wheel drive, my '79 Monte

Carlo was a squirrelly, but fun car to drive on winding country roads--especially when I was drunk. As an unemployed and penniless high school student, I paid for the car with the money I got from selling the nicer of my two trombones to an underclassman who wanted to upgrade from his student horn. That was just one of the many choices I would grow to regret as the years went on.

As we pulled off of a blacktop highway one night and onto the gravel road that led to the Dunes, a favorite party spot on the Mississippi River north of town, Chris Stevens never let off the gas. He was driving my car because by that point I was already so wasted that there was a very good chance I would have driven us straight into the river. Rather than slow down as we turned off the paved road, it seemed that Chris actually sped up, (he was intoxicated, too), even though the loose gravel made for quite a wild ride. That same loose gravel kept flying up and hitting the sides of my car, scratching the hell out of the metallic flake paint job that had caught my eye the first time I spied it at my mom's dealership. When I suggested that Chris slow down, he told me, "Don't tell me how to drive. You're drunk. Just shut up and let me do the driving."

I said, "It's *my* goddamn car, so I *can* tell you how to drive it. Slow the hell down."

"And I said to shut the fuck up and let me drive," Chris snapped back through gritted teeth. We went back and forth like this all the way to the party. When we finally got out of the car, I grabbed a case of beer and started walking down the road from where we parked to where everyone was gathered. I kept jawing about Chris's driving skills, and he kept warning me to shut my mouth. I guess he reached some kind of breaking point because the next thing I saw was a cloud of dust kicked up by the beer that had flown out of my hands. Chris had blindsided me with a shove in the back, sending me sprawling across the road and leaving me face down in the dirt. Before I had a chance to get back on my feet, he started kicking me in the ribs again and again until all I could do was curl up into the fetal position and wait for the cavalry to arrive.

Help never came because we were far enough from the light of the bonfire that no one saw what was happening just a hundred yards or so off in the dark. Chris eventually wore himself out or lost interest, scooped up the beer, and walked down to the party. I staggered to my feet, dusted myself off, and followed a safe distance away, still flapping my gums about his lack of motoring etiquette and his newly earned title of cheap-shot artist. Dave and Rosie stepped in between us, and after I explained my version of events and Chris did little to dispute my account, we agreed to stay away from each other for the rest of the night.

Before going our separate ways, I said, "You know I would kick your ass in a fair fight," although there was little no to chance of that ever happening.

Chris said, "Anytime, big man."

"Tomorrow on the golf course. Noon." (I think it's a federal law that all showdowns have to take place at noon.)

"I'll be there." And with that the party resumed and everyone had a great time for the rest of the evening. Our scuffle was nothing out of the ordinary to the rest of the party-goers that were there that night. A Hannibal party was like a hockey game; you didn't feel like you got your money's worth unless there was a fight.

The next morning I was awakened by a pounding in my head and a pounding on my door. It was Dave, coming to escort me to the golf course. "You can't be serious, Dave. That was just the beer talking."

"Listen, Trav. Rosie called me a little while ago. He and Chris are headed over to the number three fairway as we speak. They wanted me to make sure you didn't chicken out. Get dressed and let's go."

"Come on, man. I'm no fighter. Chris knows that."

"I don't know, man. He's pretty wound up about last night.

If you don't show up, you can bet your ass that he'll be over here in no time--if that's the way you want it."

"No. I'll go. Just give me a minute." I had no desire to fight anybody, much less one of my best friends. I'd known Chris since we were in the fourth grade. He was one of the first real friends I'd made when my family moved to Hannibal. Prior to that, I didn't have a single friend that I had known for more than one year. The idea of ending the longest lasting relationship I'd had with anyone outside of my family made me sick to my stomach. The sour beer from the night before did nothing to help, either.

A short while later, Dave and I arrived at the prescribed location at the town's only public golf course. It was a cold spring morning with a slight mist falling from the sky. No golfers would be out in such weather to interrupt our business. When Rosie arrived with Chris, I had to do a double-take to make sure my eyes weren't playing tricks on me. Chris was dressed exactly like I was. I mean *exactly*. We were both wearing our fathers' green jungle fatigue jackets from their days in Viet Nam. We both had faded blue jeans on and were wearing boots. Tied around our right fists were red bandanas that were there to protect our knuckles from being sliced open on the other guy's teeth. To any casual observer or unsuspecting golfer, it would have been one of the most ridiculous looking scenes imaginable. After realizing how silly we both were being, I started laughing. Chris, however, failed to see the humor in the situation. "You ready?" He asked in a manner that indicated whatever answer I gave would be irrelevant.

"Look at us, man. This is a stupid. I don't want to fight you. Let's just forget it, okay."

"No chance. You called me out, remember? You said you'd whip my ass in a fair fight. Well here I am, pussy. Let's see what you got."

Pussy? *Really?* I couldn't believe it. Chris was deadly serious. There would be no way to worm my way out of the mess I was in. "Okay, *friend*," I said as sarcastically as possible. "Let's do this." But before we were turned loose on one another, our "corner men" had to pat us down for weapons. Apparently Dave and Rosie had discussed the ground rules on their way home from the Dunes the night before. It became obvious that they had actually been looking forward to our little "battle-royale" ever since I threw down the challenge at the party. They took their jobs seriously as they each diligently searched Chris and me for hidden weapons. The scene was so surreal that I just stood there and tried to force myself to believe that it was all really happening. My Extreme Hangover--Beer Edition did nothing to help the situation either.

Suddenly reality, and Chris's left fist, hit me square in the jaw. *Game on.* I shook off the initial blow and circled around Chris while he searched for another opening. As he came back in close, I ducked a left hook that would have surely killed me had it connected, and threw my right arm around Chris's neck. I squeezed with all my might and found myself controlling my flailing opponent with a deep headlock. With my left hand, I fired uppercut after uppercut into Chris's face. I landed at least six or seven blows before he finally managed to wrestle himself free.

"Wrestle" being the key word, because Chris was a member of the school's wrestling squad, and he knew exactly how to end the fight at any time. We danced around for a few more minutes and then he made his move. He lunged at my legs for a textbook takedown and had me laid-out flat on my back before I had any chance to react. Before his fists started raining down on me while I lay pinned helplessly under his weight, I somehow managed to "belly-out" as grapplers call it, rolling face-down on the ground. Like the previous night, I found myself once again curled into a defensive position, waiting for my friends to intervene. Again, they opted to watch and laugh as I employed my vaunted fetal defense. Chris then proceeded to pummel the back of my head relentlessly. Only after his fists started to ache from hammering them repeatedly into my skull did he at last roll off me, utterly exhausted. I lay there for a while, half expecting him to resume, but mercifully, he did not.

Our corner men helped us to our feet, dusted us off, and inspected our wounds. Blood trickled down Chris's face from a nasty gash above his left eye. I suffered a giant knot on my noggin and a gaping wound to my ego. When Chris and I reluctantly shook hands, I noticed that we were both still sporting the red bandanas. The irony was that neither of us had landed a significant blow with our "protected" fists. The knuckles on our left hands, however, looked like freshly ground hamburger.

Dave broke the silence. "Are we all done here?" Chris and I nodded. "Good. We still have a case and a half of beer left over from last night."

"Road trip?" I asked.

"Road trip," Chris agreed. We called Crash Phillips right away.

Despite the fact that Crash liked to drive as fast as Richard Petty and had probably wrecked more cars than the NASCAR legend, he was always our first choice for a driver when we hit the gravel roads. We didn't have a death wish, but instead we figured that since Crash had survived all of his accidents, we would, too.

One evening after my mom got home from work, she said to me, "I pulled one of your friends out from behind the wheel of his totaled car today."

"Oh my god! Who was it?" I asked.

"Frankly, there was so much blood on his face that I couldn't tell. But the paramedics said he was 18 years old, so I figured you would know him. He pulled out in front of a semi-truck and it hit him right in the driver's door. That boy's lucky to be alive. You kids need to use your heads out there when you're behind the wheel."

Crash did use his head. He used it to stop the force of the eighteen-wheeler as it flattened the side of his car. Mom was wrong about one thing, though. Crash didn't pull out in front of *a* semi. He pulled out in front of *two* semis. From his hospital bed, he could not explain how or why he failed to notice the big-rigs approaching as he pulled into traffic. He did explain that he was a little disappointed that the lacerations on his forehead did not clearly reveal an impression of the "Mack" logo from the hood ornament of either of the trucks.

A frequent destination on our road trips was a cabin on stilts near the banks of a tributary of the Mississippi River that we called "The Love Shack." A sophomore had informed us that his uncle had this little cabin down by the river that he never used and if we let him hang out with us he'd show us where it was. Always on the lookout for a new place to party, we enthusiastically agreed.

When we first laid eyes on the cabin, all of us fell head over heels in love with the place. It was just beautiful. Faded paint flaked from the weather beaten siding. The stilts seemed to lean at a slight angle, giving rational people reason to worry about the cabin's structural integrity. Driftwood deposited during previous floods was piled up beneath the deck. After climbing a flight of rickety wooden stairs, we peeked in the windows of the delightful little domicile. The kid, Ryan was his name, told us that the kitchen window was always unlocked and so we boosted him up to the sill where he slid right in and unlocked the front door for us. As the door opened, so, too, did a wonderful world full of new adventures. Inside, there was a modest kitchen that would play host to countless hours of drinking games. There was a living room complete with a wood burning stove to keep us warm in the cold evenings while we made out with our dates on the exquisitely tacky old furniture. There was a small bathroom with a toilet in it that only flushed by pouring buckets of water collected from the kitchen sink into the tank. And there were two bedrooms ripe with possibilities for a bunch of horny teenagers. More than one of us got misty eyed as we took in this magnificent scene.

During the course of our senior year, while we used the cabin as our unofficial party headquarters, we were meticulous about the way we cleaned-up after ourselves, and our intrusions were never detected by Ryan's uncle. To this day, every time I hear that old B-52s song on the radio, I can't help but smile like the cat that ate the canary.

From what I can remember, my final year of high school was

one of the best of my life, despite having my hair set on fire by Chris after I passed out at one of Dave's "my parents are gone again this weekend" parties and nearly getting arrested for a graduation party gone terribly wrong that I hosted at my dad's place on the one and only night he and Susan had ever left me the house to myself. Gee, I really don't see why they thought they couldn't trust me.

After returning home from a romantic weekend away with his new wife, I thought my old man would wring my neck after he received a call from the landlord, who was also our next-door neighbor, informing him of my beer-bash and subsequent near-arrest while he was gone. But to my surprise, Dad didn't kill me, although I'm sure it would have been a case of justifiable homicide. He knew that his beloved Marine Corps would soon take care of that task for him. My "don't give a shit about anybody or anything" attitude was fixin' to get adjusted one week later, when I shipped out to sunny San Diego for the kind of summer camp that had me wishing I were still a non-drinking social misfit who enjoyed whiling away his summers among the geeks at band camp rather than with a bunch of bloodthirsty warriors intent on crushing my soul for the good of my country. But that, as they say, is another story.

Secret Squirrel

As he alluded to at the end I'm a Drinker, *Naughton was destined for a stint with the United States Marine Corps. After realizing late in his senior year of high school that he didn't have the money to attend college (a problem he probably should have been aware of due to the inescapable fact that he hadn't worked a day since a three week period of employment at a burger joint in the summer following his sophomore year), he decided to follow in his parents' footsteps and enlist in the Marines. His plan was to be in the Marine Reserves, which would help pay for his college tuition and prove his worth to his parents.*

(Younger): Weren't you worried about having to go to war someday? Were you prepared to die for your country?

(Elder): When I decided to enlist, I did ask myself, "What's the worst that could happen?" But the prospects of being sent to war, having to shoot someone, or getting killed never really entered my mind.

(Younger): But the Marines are usually the first to see action in a conflict. Surely you were aware of that fact.

(Elder): It had been fifteen years since the U.S. left Vietnam. The Cold War had just ended. I never seriously considered the possibility that I would be called to fight. My attitude was that I was only going into the Reserves. Really, I just liked the idea of only having to work two weeks in the summer and one weekend a month. Plus the uniforms looked cool.

Naughton wrote about his military experience in his memoir Rude, Crude, and Socially Unacceptable. *Although his account is humorous at times, it becomes clear that he enlisted for nobler reasons than "cool-looking uniforms."*

I could hear my heart pounding in my chest above the roar of the engines of the Boeing 737 as it taxied to the terminal. The plane sat there for a torturous few minutes while the boarding platform was moved into position and the flight crew prepared to open the hatch. A wave of fear and panic caused me to shudder as I contemplated what awaited me once I disembarked. I wanted to cry out for my mommy, but she had already done her time in the Corps and would show no sympathy to her whiny offspring.

The "Fasten Seat Belts" sign was turned off and an announcement was read over the intercom: *Ladies and gentlemen, on behalf of everyone at Southwest, we would like to thank you for choosing our airline and we hope you enjoy your stay here in beautiful San Diego.* Not likely, lady. *For those of you who flew into San Diego for Marine Corps boot camp, the captain has asked me to remind you that this was a one-way flight and if you do not de-plane immediately the cabin's oxygen supply will be turned off. Once you lose consciousness, your lifeless body will be handed over to the United States Marine Corps to be disposed of as they see fit. Thank you and have a nice day.*

I was told that a Marine would be waiting for me when I arrived, and I knew as soon as we made eye contact that I would be forfeiting my freedom to this stranger and his Marine Corps. As soon as I stepped into the terminal, I saw a sharp-dressed man in uniform holding a sign that read: *Naughton.* Against my better judgment, I said, "That's me," and the Marine said to follow him. The welcome wagon was a little reserved, there wasn't a marching band waiting to play in honor of my arrival. But at least I wasn't doing push-ups in the airport. I followed the Marine to a bus, which had about forty other nervous young men on it, none of whom were making a sound. The bus drove purposely through the black night for only a few short minutes. I could see a sign on the front gate of the barracks that welcomed visitors and new recruits to Marine Corps Recruit Depot San Diego blur past the windows of the olive drab school bus. A few anxious passengers began to mumble excitedly to no one in particular until the bus came to an abrupt stop. Immediately three very intimidating and extremely boisterous Marines climbed on board and began shouting orders.

"Get up! On your feet! Get off my bus! Hey hello there, who are we? I said get your ass off my bus! Move! Move! Move!" Frozen in fear, no one wanted to be the first one off the bus. A very angry looking Marine with horrendous breath bent down, stared straight in my face, and yelled, "I said to get your ass off my bus, now GO! GO! GO!" I shot to my feet and sprinted out the door. To my complete horror, I was the first recruit to step off the bus and into Hell. "Go stand on my yellow footprints!" I thought this may have been a trap, so I scrambled to get away from my tormentor only to find two more waiting for me. There was nowhere to hide. "On the yellow footprints--NOW! Stand at attention, you little puke! Don't you eyeball me! Look straight ahead!" The still of the night was shattered with the chaos of four drill instructors shouting at forty boys scared completely shitless. I did what I was told and felt a slight reprieve when the D.I.s shifted their attention to the other hapless recruits. But the break would not last long.

The first place that we were led to was the base "barbershop." This consisted of nothing more than a half-dozen old men shaving everyone's head bald with the same type of electric clippers that my friends had used on me back home during my going away party. While I was in line, my wretchedly uneven haircut drew the ire of two of the drill instructors standing near me. "Ooh, what do we have here? Somebody thought they could cut their own hair, huh? You wanted to deprive my barber of doing his duty, is that right? You think you can do a better job than a barber in my Marine Corps, is that it?

"No sir."

"You shut your mouth! Don't you talk to me! Are you out of your Gosh-damned mind?" (It is worth noting that as verbally abusive as the drill instructors were, I never heard one of them take the Lord's name in vain. Ever. Now that's what I call discipline goddammit.)

"No sir."

"I said shut the Hell up! Now you get up there and let a Marine cut your gol-darned hair, you understand me?"

"Yes sir."

"I can't hear you!"

"Yes sir!"

"No. No. No. Come here. What's your name, recruit?"

"Private Naughton, sir."

"PRIVATE?! Private? You're out of your god-danged mind aren't you, boy?"

"No sir."

"Yes you are. You sure as hell are. You ain't no *private* in my Marine Corps, you hear me? You aren't *in* my Marine Corps yet, you got that?" I didn't quite get it but I said that I did to please this rabid Marine who was foaming at the mouth and getting madder and madder by the second. "Until you graduate after thirteen weeks of the hardest military training on God's green earth, you will refer to yourself as 'recruit.' Do I make myself clear?"

"Crystal."

"What!?"

"Yes sir."

"I can't freaking hear you. Wipe that sand out of your clit and act like you've got a set when you answer me. Do you understand?!"

"YES SIR!" I was catching on. Marines like shouting. I mean they really like it. If you're not yelling back, they're not happy, so from then on I bellowed every time a Marine spoke to me, even when I probably shouldn't have, like when I was sitting in the base's dentist's chair or a doctor's office, but I wasn't willing to take any chances.

I got the few remaining hairs on my head shaved off, was issued a sea bag with some articles of clothing, two pair of boots, and a grey sweatshirt. All of the "first phase recruits," guys who were in the first third of their training, wore these sweatshirts to indicate to everyone on base that they were the new meat. It was like wearing a bull's-eye on your back at a shooting range. Drill instructors could spot those sweatshirts from a mile away and would pounce on a newbie at the slightest provocation. Sneezing while wearing a grey sweatshirt could get you killed and the murderer wouldn't even be court-martialed. It was considered standard military procedure or something.

Our newly formed platoon would undergo further processing for the next day and a half and by the time my head hit the pillow the following evening, it was the first time I'd had a chance to rest in over 36 hours. I have never slept more soundly in my life, which made the tossing of a 55 gallon steel trash barrel across the squad bay of our barracks at 0500 hours the next morning all the more jarring. For the first few days of boot camp, we went for medical check-ups, took aptitude tests, purchased toiletries and essentials at the PX, and got used to our harried, yet highly controlled schedules.

On the fourth day, we were introduced to the men who would be our drill instructors for the remainder of boot camp. The largest and most intimidating of these four individuals was Sgt. Hayden. He was a six foot two, 220-pound mass of muscle and anger. He was cruel beyond words, and dumb as a post. I hated him with every fiber of my being. Next was Sgt. Tucker, a five-eight, 160 pound black man with a sense of humor as sharp as the pain he inflicted while doling out punishments for even the slightest indiscretions. Sgt. Boland was a cross between Barney Fife of Mayberry and Goofy of Disneyland. He simply did not scare me in the slightest, and he proved to be my lifeline several times during my time in boot camp. He was as close to a friend as I could ever hope for in a D.I. Finally, our senior drill instructor was Staff Sergeant Greico. He was only about five foot six, maybe five-seven, but weighed about 180 without an ounce of fat on his frame. He was a solid brick of humanity who spoke calmly and never felt the need to yell because he didn't have to shout to be intimidating. This was a man that no one would dream of fucking with. He had my respect from day one.

A typical day of training involved a great deal of pain. Beginning with a painfully early wake-up, five minutes to "shit, shower, and shave" which usually resulted in pain of some sort or another, excruciating physical training (PT), breakfast, some painfully boring history of the Corps, more torturous PT, lunch, more classroom training while fighting the urge to nod off (an offense punishable by death), more PT, dinner, more PT, a painfully thorough cleaning of the barracks, and then sweet, merciful sleep. I slept like a rock but was further pained by having to frequently wake up in the middle of the night to report for a duty called "fire watch" where the overnight guards on duty were supposed to watch out for guys sneaking off to smoke, kill themselves, or go AWOL. I became convinced that Satan and his eternal fires of Hell could not match a Marine Corps drill instructor's capacity to inflict physical and mental pain. Somewhere back home, my jarhead parents were laughing their asses off.

The days went by quickly and within a few weeks I began to see my physical self transforming from boy to man. My mental fitness was growing, too. I realized that no matter how much they yelled, the D.I.s were probably not going to kill me. Hell, they rarely even touched me. The days of being beaten to a pulp by a combat-hardened grunt were replaced by a hands-off form of mental abuse by men professionally trained to destroy an individual's sense of self in favor of a commitment to his Corps. I understood that the mind games played by the D.I.s were just intended to weed out those recruits who were mentally weak, and to my surprise, I found that I was not one of them. I began to enjoy my training. I added ten pounds of muscle in the first six weeks of boot camp. But the muscle between my head was what got me noticed by my superiors. I quickly advanced to the head of the class, so to speak, and was honored to be named a squad leader within the platoon. I started to believe that I was destined to succeed in the Marine Corps and in life. I had finally found something besides drinking beer or tooting the trombone that I was actually good at. I knew I was on the right track when Staff Sergeant Greico called me into the duty hut (his office) one afternoon while the recruits were reading their "Knowledge" (a book filled with Corps history, lists of ranks, and other information useful to a Marine.)

"Sir, Recruit Naughton reporting as ordered, Sir!" I quickly learned never to use the words "I" or "you" when speaking to a superior. It was an awkward way to speak, but it beat doing push-ups.

"Come in." I stood at attention before his desk. "At ease, Naughton. Son, do you love my Marine Corps?"

"Sir, yes Sir!" I shouted at the top of my lungs, although we were just a few feet from one another in the small, quiet office.

"Dial it down, Naughton. Tell me, why do you want to be a Marine?"

"Sir, Recruit Naughton's mother and father were both in the Corps, Sir. The recruit wants to make them proud and wants to serve his country, Sir!"

"Ooo-rah. That's a damn-good answer. I want you to do a special favor for me. Ever heard of the 'Secret Squirrel' cartoons?"

I couldn't imagine why a senior drill instructor in the fiercest fighting unit in the entire world would want to talk about cartoon rodent spies with a nobody like me. Still, I was intrigued. "Yes Sir."

"Good. I need someone to be my eyes and ears around here. I need someone who will tell me when shit is going down that shouldn't be. You understand?" My blank look answered for me. "If you see anybody doing something that can get someone hurt, then I want to know about it. You think you can handle being my

Secret Squirrel?"

"Sir, yes Sir." At this point, he could have asked me for one of my kidneys and I would have gladly given it. *Would you like part of my liver while we're at it, Sir?*

"I don't care who it is, if you see something that's not right you tell me about it, understand?"

"Sir, yes Sir."

"Very well. You're dismissed." I turned and walked back to my rack and sat on my foot locker to absorb what had just taken place. On one hand, I was being asked to spy on my fellow recruits and, from what I gathered, my drill instructors, too. I didn't want to rat anyone out, but I liked that the senior drill instructor trusted me with a secret mission. I was honored, yet apprehensive about taking on this new duty. I hoped I would never have to report anything to SSgt. Greico. But as I soon learned, Hope ain't nothin' but a town in Arkansas.

Anyone who has ever been to San Diego in the summer knows that it is literally hotter than Hell. When the temperature reached 100 degrees, we were ordered to sit down immediately, take a moment to rest, and drink water from our canteens, or 'water bowls' in Marine speak. I guessed that the Corps had learned about heat stroke the hard way, probably many, many times over and wanted their recruits to survive boot camp (a novel concept) so we may live to fight another day.

On one such occasion, Sgt. Hayden ordered us to sit and drink until our water bowls were empty. Then, he stood us up, marched us back to our squad bay, made us refill our water bowls, and ordered us to drink until they were empty again. Then, for reasons I'll never know, he made us refill the thirty-two ounce containers a third time. "Drink." Now, if you have ever tried to drink three quarters of a gallon of liquid in less than ten minutes, then you can imagine what happened next. The men started throwing up left and right. When they did, Sgt. Hayden made them get another refill and start drinking again. Guys were sprinting to the head, puking, refilling their water bowls, puking again, and so on. *Drink, run, puke, refill, repeat.* After about ten more minutes of this nonsense, Sgt. Boland entered the room and then Sgt. Hayden quickly, but reluctantly ordered us to put away our water bowls and square away the squad bay. I was within moments of vomiting myself, and was very happy to see Sgt. Boland unwittingly save the day. Later that evening, I knocked on the door of SSgt. Greico's duty hut. "Sir, Recruit Naughton requests permission to speak, Sir."

"Come."

"Sir, does the Staff Sergeant recall making Recruit Naughton his 'Secret Squirrel', Sir?" When you refer to yourself as a secret squirrel, especially while wearing a combat uniform, there's simply no way to command or expect even a shred of respect from anyone, especially a hardened Marine. I felt small and childish and wanted to crawl into a hole and die as soon as the words left my mouth, but at least I'd had the good sense to keep my voice down.

"Yes I do. What is it, Naughton?" I was greatly relieved that he had remembered our arrangement and somehow managed to not burst into an immediate fit of laughter when I asked the ridiculous sounding question. I went on to explain the "water bowl incident" of that afternoon. I conveyed to SSgt. Greico my concerns for the health of my fellow recruits when they were forced to drink until they vomited on such a hot day. His face showed that he was bothered by this, too, and he thanked me for being courageous enough to come forward. I was proud to do the right thing by looking out for my buddies' well being, but I was also scared out of my mind that I had just taken the bait in a sadistic trap set to see if I would squeal on my superiors. I had a fitful sleep that night while I fretted over what the next morning would bring.

The following day, Sgt. Hayden made us sit and drink when the temperature reached 100 degrees. "Get out your water bowls," he commanded with a tone that implied that failure to comply in a timely fashion would result in an untimely death. "Drink *slowly*," he continued. "We don't need anybody getting sick, understand?" There wasn't even a hint of concern for our well being in his raspy voice. In fact, he sounded downright pissed that no one would expire from water poisoning or excessive regurgitation on this, an otherwise great day for dying.

"Sir, yes Sir!" I wanted to smile as I shouted my reply, but knew not to push my luck. It was one of the proudest moments of my time in the Marines.

There were other good times, too, like when I conquered the obstacle course (and my fear of heights). Sgt. Boland was supervising the recruits climbing an apparatus called the "Stairway to Heaven," a fifty foot tower made out of utility poles that resembled a colossal ladder that's "rungs" became progressively farther apart near the top. This design forced short guys like me to literally take a leap of faith in order to grab hold of the top rung. I was terrified. But I amazed myself when I safely reached the top, where I stopped to catch my breath and to give one of the vertical supports a bear hug of relief and an unabashed kiss. I looked down at the ground and saw Sgt. Boland laughing at me in spite of himself. I thought for sure he would make me pay for that, but instead, he hid his smile from the rest of the platoon and yelled for me to hurry up and get my ass back down on the ground.

One day after asking me where I was from, Sgt. Boland revealed that he and I grew up only twenty miles apart. Ours were rival high schools, and he enjoyed giving me a good-natured ball-busting at the expense of my former baseball team every chance he got. He asked what my parents did for a living and I told him they had been in the Corps and that my mom currently sold cars in Hannibal. He asked if it was at Ed Gates Chevrolet by any chance. I said that as a matter of fact it was. He said, "So did your mother sell my dad that piece of shit Chevy that he's been fixing since the day he drove it off the lot?" As sweat beaded up on my forehead, I asked him what year his father had purchased the truck and was relieved to be able to honestly tell him that my mom had been working at a different dealership at that time. He could see the relief on my face and I recognized a look on his that said, "Lighten up. I'm just fuckin' with you." That's what drill instructors do. And they do it very well. I would have never believed anyone had they told me that I would enjoy a quasi-friendship with a D.I. while in boot camp, but it was clear to me that Sgt. Boland was actually a pretty decent guy under that gruff exterior. These feel-good moments were few and far between in boot camp, and sadly could not negate the dark moments that were to come.

On one Saturday morning, our platoon was scheduled to participate in a series of physical competitions against other platoons in what was called a "field day." Joining us for this event were four D.I.s from the infamous Parris Island MCRD in South Carolina. Officially, we were told that they would be on hand simply to observe the techniques of our D.I.s. Unofficially, I thought they were just there to make us twice as miserable as our own four drill instructors could. I knew that the movie "Full Metal Jacket" was based on recruit training at Parris Island, and anyone who has seen that film will forever remember what happened when R. Lee Ermy's character pushed Private Pyle past the breaking point. I still haven't forgiven myself for telling my girlfriend to watch the movie once I shipped out. "That's exactly what I'll be going through this summer while you're here sitting by the pool living the good life." I doubt she has forgiven me, either.

We marched across the base to the space designated for the competition to be held, where we began to stretch and prepare for battle. As I psyched myself up, I noticed that the butterflies in my stomach felt more like a swarm of killer bees. Sharp pains doubled me over and soon I realized that I needed to make my way to a toilet double-time. Sgt. Tucker was giving us our instructions for the events and I patiently waited for him to stop speaking before asking for permission to use the head. But he rambled on and on, the biggest fan in the world of his own raspy voice.

Sensing the eminent evacuation of my bowels I stood and interrupted, "Sir, Recruit Naughton requests permission to make an emergency sitting head call, Sir!"

"You gotta be gosh-danged kidding me! You did *not* just interrupt me."

"Sir, yes Sir. It's an *emergency*, Sir!" Had there not been all those witnesses, I am certain that I would have been summarily executed on the spot.

"Go," was all he said. He was mad as hell, but seeing the pained expression on my increasingly ashen face brought him to the wise conclusion that he didn't want to be anywhere near me if I had a blowout. I ran as fast as anyone trying to keep from shitting his pants has ever run. I ran all the way across the base and into our barracks. I rounded the corner and as my eye spied the head, four sets of drill instructors' eyes spied me.

"Well, hello there you," one of them barked. "Where the hell do you think you're going?" (The written word just doesn't convey the animosity of the actual spoken words, but trust me, it was there.)

"Sir, the recruit needs to make an emergency sitting head call, Sir." The cramps in my gut were like an officer's sword slicing me open.

"I highly god-dang doubt it. Get back to the field day, you," one of the D.I.'s ordered.

"Sir, no Sir!" I countered as I ran into the head, (restroom in the civilian world,) ignoring the death-stare being shot at me by the enraged D.I., and then I proceeded to destroy the nearest toilet. I had just disobeyed a direct order, but I didn't care. I'd managed to not shit myself, which was a major triumph at that moment. About five minutes later, my victory was quickly forgotten as I emerged from the head. Four of Parris Island's biggest badasses surrounded me like a group of hungry gators back home in one of their Carolina swamps.

"Boy, we're gonna gol-danged play now. Push!" the tall one said. I dropped and started doing push-ups.

"On your feet!" The second chimed in. "Jumping jacks. Go!"

"On your back. Move!" the third ordered. "Crunch!"

Let me just say that doing sit-ups fast enough to make a Marine Corps drill instructor happy while suffering from intense abdominal cramps is about as pleasant as say, shitting oneself in front of a few hundred people who are busy enjoying a friendly game of tug-o-war on a Chamber of Commerce weather, southern California day. As I was forced to switch between push-ups, sit-ups, jumping jacks, and squat thrusts at a break-neck pace, I thought that maybe I should have just gone ahead and filled my drawers. Who would have wanted to mess with me after that? But then again, these sickos would have probably just made me run five miles in my soiled britches for the fun of it. I gave my best effort to please my tormentors, but eventually collapsed in a sweaty, smelly heap in the middle of the squad bay.

"Stand up," the last of the four sadists ordered. He stared at me with utter contempt. I knew not to make eye contact. After another few seconds he realized there was nothing left to do to me. I was completely spent. "Get out of my sight."

"Aye-aye, Sir." I hobbled back to the field exercises and was told to sit out as punishment for leaving my platoon. It was the best punishment I ever received in the Marines. It was nothing compared to the punishment my knees would take over the remainder of my stay in San Diego.

Early in 1989, the Corps began issuing a new type of combat boot to its recruits with a higher heel than the previous model had. This caused many people to develop a condition called iliotibial band (ITB) syndrome, a severe form of tendonitis. I was one of those people. The band of muscles and tendons running along the exterior of my legs became extremely tight and rubbed over the bones in my knee, which inflamed the bursa sacs, and caused cartilage damage which caused severe pain in both of my knees. The full extent of this pain was realized after a long forced-march along the beach at Camp Pendleton, in the seventh week of my training. When Sgt. Hayden woke us the next morning, I threw my legs over the edge of the top bunk as I always had, except this time, both stuck straight out, neither bending at the knee even as gravity pulled on them. I sat there for a second, wondering what was wrong, and then Sgt. Hayden hollered at me to get down. So I jumped out of bed, hit the ground straight-legged, and fell flat on my face. He yelled at me to get on my feet, but I couldn't stand. My knees were locked and would not bend. Disgusted with me, Sgt. Hayden gave up and ordered me to go to the medical unit to get checked out. Once there, the doctor diagnosed my condition and matter-of-factly predicted that if I didn't allow enough time for my knees to heal, I would end up with debilitating arthritis in both knees, effectively rendering my legs useless at the ripe, old age of eighteen.

"How long will I need to rest before I get better?" I asked.

"Well, it could be a few weeks or even a few months before you'll notice an improvement. I'm afraid you will have to halt your training until you are medically able to perform," the doctor said.

"Doc, I'm in the 84-day reserves," I explained. (This was a special program for college bound recruits in which I only had 84 days to complete boot camp before heading off to school.) "I can't afford to take any time off from training."

"I'm afraid you have don't have much choice. Either you rest and wait until you are able to perform, or you can file for a medical discharge. The problem with that option is that it sometimes takes several months to determine if this type of condition is permanent. You would have to remain here in the medical rehabilitation platoon (MRP) until such time that the medical review board certifies you as permanently disabled or until you become well enough to resume your training, which in my opinion won't be for several weeks at best."

"But I have to finish my training before school starts this fall. If not, I'll wash out."

The sympathetic look in the doctor's eyes told me all I needed to hear. If I intended to attend college in the fall, I would not do so as a United States Marine. I was heartbroken. That's not a strong enough word. Devastated. I had become "gung-ho" as the Marines say while in boot camp. I really did love the Corps and I wanted desperately to become a Marine. Also, after all of the stupid stunts I'd pulled in high school, I yearned to make my Leatherneck parents proud of me. The thought of letting them down destroyed me.

Senior Drill Instructor Staff Sergeant Greico called me to his duty hut that afternoon. "Naughton, I regret to inform you that you are being dropped from active training and placed into the Medical Rehabilitation Platoon. I know this is disappointing, but after you heal up you can rejoin another training platoon and pick up where you left off."

"Sir, Recruit Naughton requests permission to speak directly, Sir."

"Go ahead."

For the first time since boot camp started, I looked a drill instructor square in the eye. I explained my predicament and ended by stating, "Sir, if you drop me to the MRP, I'll lose my chance to become a Marine."

"You said before that your folks were both in the Corps, is that right?"

"Yes Sir."

"Well, I know that they're both very proud of you for enlisting. You don't have to prove anything to them or me or anyone else. You have done an outstanding job here and have nothing to feel bad about, you understand me?" I began to cry. SSgt. Greico gave me a few minutes to compose myself before sending me back out to say a brief goodbye to my fellow recruits. I will always have the utmost respect for him for the kindness he showed me in a notoriously unkind environment.

On my way to the MRP it occurred to me that I was facing the possibility of sitting idle for a maddeningly indefinite amount of time, waiting for a medical discharge that may or may not come. I would possibly have to miss the beginning of my first semester of college waiting for the paperwork to go through. I decided that I wasn't willing to do that just to collect a disability check every month. I shared this decision with the powers that be and they explained to me what an entry level separation was. In a nutshell, in exchange for putting my ass on the first airplane home and not having to spend one extra minute twiddling my thumbs waiting for a medical discharge, I would have to agree to an entry level separation or ELS. By signing on the dotted line, I agreed to not hold the United States Marine Corps or the Veterans Administration responsible for any injuries or lasting conditions I may have incurred while in boot camp. As a Marine in the admin office put it, "It's like you were never here." *Tell that to my knees.*

All these years later, my knees still ache, but being lucky enough to have avoided serving in the first Gulf War, I should be grateful for only having bad knees instead of having been mutilated or killed in action. It's rumored that the combat engineers unit in which I would have served was ordered to bury enemy forces alive in their trenches with the runway-building bulldozers that I would have been trained in operating. I guess having a pair of bum knees can be a blessing when you look at it that way. Besides, had I gone to war, I would have missed out on some killer parties in college. I guess war really is hell, isn't it?

It is obvious when talking to Dr. Naughton about his brief stint in the military that he was extremely disappointed by his failure to become a Marine. He confided in me that he felt like he let down his parents--and himself--and that for years afterward he tried to mask his pain by cracking jokes and by cracking open the bottle. It wasn't until years later, under the loving care of his wife Bethany, who was a healer--an occupational therapist to be exact--that he began to get past the pain in his knees and his self-loathing soul.

It has been said that every good artist suffers for their art. A bluesman is just another singer if he hasn't experienced the deep-down blues at some point in his life. The same must be true for great writers. Luckily for his readers, Travis Naughton suffered just enough to produce some of the most memorable examples of prose ever written.

Going Kerouac on Everyone's Ass*

*Explanation the character Dale Doback gave in accounting for the twenty-two year gap in his employment history on his resume in the movie *Stepbrothers*.

Travis Naughton, the son of a former car dealer, has felt drawn to the open road since his earliest memories. When he was very young, Travis's family had a Volkswagen Bus that they took on a driving vacation from Missouri to California and back again. His parents took turns at the wheel while he and his brother relieved the hours of monotony by playing road sign bingo and "making incursions into the DMZ that separated Blake's seat from mine." Having since taken many long distance trips with his own children, Naughton says, "I cannot fathom how my folks maintained a shred of their sanity without the aid of portable DVD players or hand-held video games to keep us kids occupied." But in the 1970s, there wasn't much else for children to do on long road trips besides watching the landscape streaking past the windows and having an occasional slap-boxing bout in the back of the vehicle.

"Of course no one wore seatbelts in those days and it was simply unheard of to use child safety seats. Somehow, we managed to survive our trip out west, although when my father stood in the back of the van with his balding head protruding from the sunroof so that he could get a clearer photograph of the Golden Gate Bridge, my native Californian mother was so mortified that she almost tossed him into the San Francisco Bay."

A year or so later, as his mother Donna was driving the van to drop Blake off at day care, she hit an icy patch on a bridge and lost control of the vehicle. The van slid across to the other side of the road, spun as it ricocheted off the guardrail, and rolled over two or three times. Naturally, neither occupant was wearing a seatbelt. As Donna's nose smashed into the windshield (shattering both), blood and glass sprayed everywhere. Her left leg hit the steering wheel with such force that for the rest of her life she had an indentation on her upper thigh that she proudly referred to as "my dent." Four-year-old Blake was thrown from the back seat through the opening in the windshield made by his mother's face. Donna crawled out of the vehicle to come to her child's aid and held him in her arms as they waited for help to arrive. She bled so profusely from her broken nose all over her youngest son that by the time an ambulance arrived, the paramedics initially feared Blake was the one bleeding to death. At the hospital, doctors credited the boy's Spiderman ski mask for lessening the impact of his skull hitting the pavement and possibly saving his life. Travis wrote about the incident many years later in his memoir:*

The aftermath of the accident was far harder on me than it was on my brother. The x-rays were inconclusive, but it was generally accepted that Blake had suffered a hairline fracture of his skull. In no uncertain terms, my parents warned me that if I harmed so much as a single hair on Humpty Dumpty's eggshell-fragile head, I would be the one in need of medical attention. Of course I continued to beat the snot out of Blake whenever the opportunity presented itself, (no eight-year-old possesses the inner strength necessary to turn the other cheek when his younger brother insists on relentlessly agitating him,) but I always had to pay to play. My mother was the undisputed head of discipline in our family and when you add to that fact the overwhelming sense of guilt she felt for nearly killing her baby in the crash, what you have is something akin to a mother grizzly bear protecting her cub in the wild. Mom used her big bear paw to slap the shit out of me on many occasions, sometimes for no other reason than, "I'm sure you had it coming for something I don't know about." I had a red mark on the side of my face so often that people swore it was a birthmark. It was so bad at times that I had to caution her, "Mom, wait! Today is school picture day!" It is a safe bet that throughout my childhood at any given hour of any given day a handprint was present on one or more of the four cheeks on my body.

Ours was a family of nomads. It seemed that we never stayed in any one place long enough to answer the question, "So where are y'all from?" with any degree of certainty. In addition to spending the first five years of my elementary education in five different schools, I spent the first seven years of my life living in seven different towns. My first ten years were spent in ten different houses. I don't think we were on the lam or travelling with a circus or anything, but it just wasn't in my parents' nature to get too comfortable. I suppose I inherited that trait from them, so I should be excused for having lived at fifteen different addresses during the seven years it took me to graduate from college. Moving is in my blood. It came as no surprise that when I was introduced to the idea of college road trips, I immediately fell in love with the activity.

My college roommate and old high school friend Roosevelt Crane and I started our own fraternity in the fall of 1990 while we were freshmen at the University of Missouri. Our collection of misfits was a blend of the frats depicted in *Animal House* and *Revenge of the Nerds*. We became an officially recognized Greek organization and celebrated our legitimacy by partaking in all the usual fraternal activities including hosting rowdy parties, selling dope out of the basement of our house, and of course going on the occasional road trip.

We drove from our fraternity house in Columbia, Missouri to Iowa City, Iowa; Carbondale, Illinois; Rolla, Missouri; and on the evening before an apocalyptic earthquake was predicted to strike in southeast Missouri, we spent seven hours on the road to get to New Madrid in time for the anticipated moment of Armageddon. The R.E.M. song, "It's the end of the world as we know it" came on the radio as we neared our destination, which seemed pretty appropriate as the cataclysm grew near, so of course we had to pull all three of our cars over so we could get out and dance in the moonlight on the side of the highway. What else would you do when the end is so near? I found a phone booth nearby and called my mother at three in the morning. "Hey Mom, guess where I am?"

She was less than thrilled with the early wake-up call, but relieved that the answer did not involve any mention of jail or prostitutes. Later, when we pulled into town we discovered a media circus awaiting us. To our surprise, we became instant celebrities. Several of us were interviewed by reporters from various radio and television stations and newspapers with the overriding question being, "Why did you and your friends come here today?" To which we replied that if the world was going to end, we wanted to be right there in the middle of it all drinking beer and going out with a laugh. Obviously, the experts were wrong in their doomsday prediction, but we weren't disappointed. After all, we were on *Good Morning America*.

In the summer of 1993, Rosie Crane and Travis Naughton decided to go on an epic road trip to Mexico. Neither had ever ventured beyond the borders of the United States. In fact, in all of his 21 years, Crane had never even left the Central Time Zone. He had left college by then however, having been dismissed for failing to earn a passing grade point average in any of his first three semesters in school. The two friends had each just recently procured their first credit cards and were armed with a combined $1500 worth of credit cards at their disposal. Rosie arrived at Travis's house on a Saturday afternoon in June and immediately they encountered their first problem. Naughton recalled their conversation during one of our interviews:

(Elder): Rosie asks me "You got any duct tape? The shift linkage broke just as I pulled onto your street." I asked him what the devil that meant. I knew next to nothing about cars. He says, "It means we can't shift gears. But don't worry, it's done this before." Somehow, that didn't deter my inclination to start worrying. I went and fetched a roll of tape and warily handed it to him. Then he asks, "Do you have any rubber bands?"

(Younger): Oh, that doesn't sound good.

(Elder): Nope. I asked him if he was serious and he said he

was. I said I would see what I could find but knew this didn't bode well for the trip. The last thing we needed was to be stranded in Mexico because our rubber band and duct tape repair job didn't hold up. But I found four or five skinny rubber and bands from some old newspapers and gave them to him. I watched helplessly and with a certain amount of admiration as Rosie wrapped a length of tape around the connection between the two linkage pieces, then a rubber band around the joint, and then another length of tape. He repeated this process until all five rubber bands were used, basically creating a five layer thick bandage on the linkage. Then he says, "Get in the car and try shifting gears."   (Younger): What kind of car was it, by the way?

(Elder): It was a tarnished silver, 1984 Plymouth Horizon with about a million miles on the odometer. Duct tape already held both of the front seats together and some old baling wire was holding the radio in place. The back tires were bald as hell. But I tested the shifter and sure enough, it worked beautifully.

(Younger): Please tell me you didn't drive all the way to Mexico in that old heap.

(Elder): I'd been nervous about traveling to a country where neither of us spoke the language even before the condition of the car started to concern me. Now I was sure that we needed to pick a less remote and slightly safer destination. I told Rosie that I was thinking that maybe we should try for Canada instead of Mexico.

(Younger): What did he say?

(Elder): He snapped at me. "Canada?!" he says. "Hell no. I'm not going anyplace where people don't sit on couches." Well I didn't know what the hell he was talking about, so I took the bait and asked him what do they sit on if they don't have couches? He says, "Chesterfields. Damn Canadians. They're too good to sit on couches like you and me. I won't go."

(Younger): Was he serious?

(Elder): As serious as Rosie Crane could ever be. I was

confused by his logic, or lack thereof, and asked if there was anywhere else he would want to go?" He said, "Vegas." I consented immediately. We had our new credit cards, an atlas, and now that we were 21, we could get into casinos. We decided that we would keep a journal of our trip, which we called *Rosie and Travis's Excellent Adventure*.

(*Younger*): An homage to the movie *Bill and Ted's Excellent Adventure*?

(*Elder*): Precisely. And just like the burned-out simpletons in the movie, Rosie and I were about to embark upon a journey that neither of us were even remotely prepared for. We got out the map and came up with a half-assed plan. We would drive the southern route to Vegas, stopping at Dave Richards's parents' new house in Arkansas, where he was staying that summer. Then we would take the northern route on our way back home so that we could see the mountains of Colorado and tour the Anheuser-Busch brewery in Ft. Collins. A finer plan had never been hatched.

I have included some of their original journal entries below, as it was written during the odyssey, without correcting the countless grammatical errors and a confusing disregard for tense agreement. Years after the trip, Naughton corrected most of the spelling errors, enhanced some sections with some added commentary, and noted the author's name (in italics and parentheses) in order to add clarity to the raw travel log. These alterations were the first step in a series of revisions that ultimately became the backbone of his notorious, yet still unpublished road manuscript – an excerpt of which is included after the following peek at the journal. In 2013, negotiations were held with a major motion picture studio to produce a movie version of the epic road trip, but after disagreeing over whether to base the film on the campy original journal versus the far edgier road manuscript, the project was killed by Naughton himself. From the journal:

Day One, 2:50pm *(Travis)*: We've just purchased supplies and pulled out of Columbia. $1500 worth of credit, a cooler full of beer, and some cans of soup. We're set! Rosie wants it noted that we've already repaired the vehicle once. (You can fix anything with duct tape.) The odometer says 134,039 miles right now and we will keep track of our mileage. Here are a few goals for this trip:

1. Gamble in Vegas

2. Tour Budweiser brewery in Ft. Collins, Colorado

3. See Dave Richards in Arkansas

4. ~~See an ocean~~

5. Survive.

3:03: The can opener broke. Haven't eaten all day.

5:00: Lebanon, Missouri: Rosie and Travis bicker over what color can opener to buy.

5:01: Situation resolved.

5:10: Dinner served. Cream of mushroom soup and baked beans, straight from the can.

8:04: Rosie is rambling incoherently.

8:05: Rosie stops at flashing yellow light. "I'm so embarrassed."

8:21: Made it to Arkansas. Debated taking a picture. Decided, "Fuck it."

8:31: Arrived at Dave's already in a drunken stupor.

(Looking back, I am still amazed that we were able to make it out of town, much less to Arkansas. By the time we got to Dave's, we were both fairly hammered, and had more or less forgotten that the car was being held

together with duct tape and baling wire. Dave was happy to see us, and of course his parents were conveniently out of town during our visit. We spent the rest of the evening catching up with him and getting blitzed on Coors Light. We invited him to tag along on the rest of our trip, but he declined, which was probably a wise choice on his part.)

Day Two, 6:30am *(Travis)*: On the road again. Of course no one knows how we woke up so early, but we're off to an early start--for Vegas! Rosie needs Rolaids. We get into a dispute as to our exact whereabouts. Rosie keenly observes, "We're in Arkansas!" I told him, "No shit? We've only been in Arkansas for the past ten hours, dumbass." We have taken note that there are no gas stations in this god-forsaken, one-horse, po-dunk state. Oh, wait. Nix that. Found one. Interesting side-note: it was decided last night that neither of us will bathe until someone says, "Hey you stink." *(Jesus, did we ever stink.)*

7:03am: The car smells lovely.

7:31: *(Rosie)*: Puked all over my shirt. Travis took the wheel. In that order.

8:15: We stop in the Ozarks to do some exploring. I puke again. The tongue is a bastion of bad breath.

8:15: More breakfast. We bicker once again over the color of the can opener.

9:54: *(Travis)* Stopped at restroom/information center. Teased the locals. Rosie insulted their governor. He really knows how to hurt people.

11:52: Rosie is yelling at other motorists. He's starting to scare me. Especially when he's speaking in tongues.

1:39 *(Rosie)*: Oklahoma is so red. I think Travis is hallucinating. He claims bees are stinging him. He whines a lot.

1:52: Rosie and Travis take cologne bath with sample found in magazine.

2:08: Almost to Texas. Spotted a herd of camels.

2:32: We've made it to Texas. Everything really is bigger.

3:10: Stop to refuel in Shamrock, Texas. Bought snacks, which consisted of BBQ chips (because we're in Texas), beef jerky (because we're in Texas), and Lone Star beer (because we're in Texas). The beef jerky was like shoe leather--tasty, Texas shoe leather. The chips and beverages were much bigger than we get up north.

3:21: Top Ten Things NOT to do in Texas:

    10. Ask them to speak English, not Texan.

    9. Remind them that Alaska is bigger.

    8. Defame Hank Williams, Jr.

    7. Ask to compare "pipelines."

    6. Ask if "Bocephus" is a type of a cow.

    5. Disparage animal husbandry.

    4. Comment on the chaw stuck in someone's teeth.

    3. Ask if the Alamo is where one rents cars.

    2. Defame Hank Williams, Sr.

    1. Show people that thumb trick.

5:45 *(Travis)*: Rosie and Travis enter New Mexico. This marks the first time in his life that 21 year old Roosevelt Crane has left the Central Time Zone. "I feel enchanted," Rosie quips.

5:47: Dinner served. Cold ravioli and mushroom soup. Yummy.

6:18: Travis makes a polite request, "Rosie, take the knife out of your ear."

The journal continues in this choppy and disjunctive, yet lively and humorous fashion for another thirty-two pages. The travelers even had the foresight to leave blank spaces on some pages to allow room to affix snapshots of the places they visited throughout the trip, and where no photo corresponding to a description existed, stick figure illustrations were sketched on the page. Crude as it was, the journal is considered by Naughton to be his first book, and his very favorite of all that he has written over the years. However, admirers of his work would argue that his unpublished, novelized manuscript based on the journey (sections of which were mysteriously posted to the Internet — some say by Naughton himself in a publicity stunt) is the true masterpiece. An excerpt follows.

It's still raining. Land of *Dis*enchantment if you ask me. This wasn't mentioned in the visitor's guide. Had it pictured all wrong in my head I guess. The dry-desert sea of sun-baked stone and wind-whipped sand sadly set adrift without a beach to settle upon, home to coyote-sharks swimming through the Great Cactus Reef that I had envisioned must simply be a figment of my peyote imagination--or the propaganda of the state tourism commission. There's thunder and lightning and hail in *this* New Mexico. Thank god we didn't take *my* car.

Rosie pulls over at a roadside trinket tent to have a pow-wow with some real live Indians (the first he's ever seen in his sheltered life) and to let the tempest pass. Nice folks. We make small talk with a boy around sixteen who asks us where we're from. He's a beautiful, sweet kid. Impossibly black Indian eyes. I want to reach out and touch his hairless Indian face. I want to ask if he has any more hair on his balls than he has on his face he's so smooth. He wants to know where we came from and we say we're from Missouri, which he says he's never heard of. Then I say we're from St. Louis, by the Big River. "Oh," he says. "Is that near Salt Lake City?" We laugh, but not in a mean way. We just say yes and move on. I'm not sure if I'm more impressed by his ignorance or his indifference. Either way, he's a real sweet kid. Later in the car, Rosie says he thinks it's a reflection of the shit school system on the reservation, but I say it's refreshing that the Navajo Nation ain't forcing their children to memorize the map of their oppressors, their would-be conquerors. Maybe they're still free after all. Except our new friend has to sell this beaded necklace to this White Man for two dollars just so his family can eat tonight. Rosie says he hopes our contribution could be counted as reparations, but I tell him I doubt it. I mean, didn't the White Man give beads to the Indians when he "bought" Manhattan Island? Now all these years later, the Indians are selling them back to us. Rosie says, "So you're saying we're even now, right?" Something like that, Rosie.

Stop in Grants, NM to eat at a Mickey D's. Rosie says, "You know their ketchup packets work just like ours." He wakes up in a brand new world about every five minutes. A 300 pound newborn. Decide to ditch the campground scene and sleep in a motel so we can take real showers. No vacancy. Rosie says, "It's those damn Shriners," but I don't see any go-carts or mini-bikes parked out front. We keep driving and take a wrong turn in the inky moonless midnight. We flip a bitch on a dead dirt road somewhere and Rosie screams like goddamn Jamie Lee Curtis when our headlights catch a pair of cattle in the act of bovine union about ten feet in from of the car. I laugh till I piss myself. We really need showers.

Find a Days Inn somewhere in Arizona. *Arizona?* What the fuck happened to New Mexico? I take a shower. By the time I get out, Rosie's already hooked on some Mexican soap opera and says he might bathe later. God I hope so. He smells just like the car; a couple-dozen empty beer cans, a half-dozen half-eaten cans of ravioli, baked beans, and cream of shit soup, sweat-soaked piles of dirty clothes fouled by two guys who've been driving and sweating through the desert and haven't bathed in two stinkin' days. Bear in mind, that within minutes of leaving Dave's diggs earlier that morning all the way back in Arkansas, Rosie ralphed all over himself--while he was driving. He's worn that puke-stained shirt all goddamned day. I doubt the hottest hotel shower in the world could remove the lingering stench from his wretched goatee and fat rolls but he has to try. I am mostly pleased with the results of my scalding, even though the tiny motel shampoo bottles offer but a temporary reprieve from the olfactory bombardment I've endured all day in that miserable little car. In the morning, we'll find ourselves right back in the putrid Plymouth, and I am fairly certain that the Car Cleaning Fairy won't have found us here in the middle of the motherfucking desert.

Day Three. 7:12am. On the road again. The desert sun is already getting to Rosie. He breaks into an insta-sweat. He's already soaked his clothes and I'm sick to death of seeing his man-tits showing through the tired fabric of his thread-bare Liquor Guns & Ammo t-shirt. We just left the motel five minutes ago and he's already whining about needing a drink. Christ I'm tired of hearing Big Boy bitch. Stop for water and supplies. My mood improves as we stumble across the greatest find in the history of western civilization; Natural Pilsner beer. Available only in certain markets, aside from a free sample at the Budweiser brewery in St. Lou, this full-calorie cousin of Natural Light (the only beer from our favorite brewery that we can afford) has eluded us for years. I think Rosie might be weeping.

After trading with the natives and restocking our beer supply, Rosie gets the car stuck in the middle of the desert. The heat is unbearable. We're gonna die out here and I'm pretty pissed about it. Less than an hour after he made me stop for beer and water at a convenience store, Big Baby makes me stop for food at an inconvenience store, a fucking grocery store. Then, as he's pulling out of the lot, he high-centers the car on a parking curb. Big Bitch says he'll die of heat stroke if he has to get out and push, but he's spared by simply removing his 300 pound carcass from the car, which tips the vehicle back to the drive wheels. I take the wheel again and drive off without further incident. Rosie thanks me by cracking open a beer and raping a bag of pretzels in my ear. Jesus I need new friends.

Stop at Meteor Crater and polish off the first twelve pack of Natty Pilsner. It shouldn't be possible for cheap beer to taste this good, but Christ it's hot here. Is it just me or did the crater just get bigger? I hear myself threatening to steal the tires off a stranger's car. What kind of 'shrooms were in that cream of mushroom soup anyway? We find out it costs money to see the big hole in the ground, so we decide not to give the greedy bastards the satisfaction. We can see the parking lot and that's good enough for us. A pack of school kids surrounds us and start gnawing at our legs. Rosie says we should split and for once he's making some sense. We head for the Painted Desert with the hopes of seeing the coyote catch that prick roadrunner once and for all.

...It's noon. We stop at another roadside Indian souvenir stand to visit with the natives. One guy asks if we have any girls with us. We tell him no, but Big Boy tried to buy some at the crater. And we when we say we're heading for Vegas, the Indian says, "You'll be getting laid every night!" Everybody laughs, except for his old lady. God I really dig those Indians.

...We make it to the Grand Canyon. I can't wrap my head around the overwhelming beauty of the place. The rainbow of rock and the fathomless eternity of the sacred expanse humble me, destroy me. While taking in the unimaginable spectacle, Rosie says, "I wonder how much beer it can hold."

...Rosie's crossed into his second new time zone in two days. Now we're following the ever-moving Joads in their jalopy. They hold us up in traffic for eight sweltering minutes. Rosie's getting hungry and cranky and we're awful close to Donner Pass.

...We make it to Vegas at last. Tits and ass and blackjack and liquor and a thousand Elvises. Viva Las Vegas! Neither of us has any business being in a Vegas casino. We're young, drunk, and stupid and fried. We take a cab from the Howard Johnson's we're staying at to Circus Circus. We play the slots while we take it all in. The bells, the flashing lights, the trapeze, the other drunks. We watch some pros play the live games until we muster the liquid courage to belly up to the tables. We're so fucking clueless that we actually pay for our drinks all night until we finally wander over to a craps table where the waitress politely informs us that the drinks are in fact complimentary. By this point, we've already blown half our wad on booze. Nevertheless, we decide to sit in at a five dollar blackjack table and we're both busted within minutes. We take cash advances on our credit cards at the ATM and lose all that by the time we call it a night. We stagger out to the lobby to call a cab and are a little stunned to see the sun rising over the desert. The sun never seems to set here and our brains have been thoroughly cooked by it. When we tumble into the taxi, I realize I have no money left at all, but Rosie has just enough to cover the fare. I take stock as the cab takes us back to HoJo's. After driving three days straight to get to Vegas, we only saw one casino, never saw a single Elvis or a pair of titties, and lost every penny we had. Rosie says this is his first time riding in a cab. I remind him he rode in one last night. "No shit?" he says. No shit, Rosie.

We load up the car and start crossing the Mohave Desert. Jesus it's hot. By noon we realize the car has less than a gallon of gas left in the tank. Just when all hope seems lost and Rosie starts eyeing me like he eyes a country ham, we stumble upon Glendale and its one and only Heaven-sent filling station, the last one for ninety miles. I'm so happy I could kiss Rosie, but he's still awful hungry and won't stop licking his lips. Rosie decides to play "Burn Out" after we take off. It's the opposite of "Freeze Out," the game in which you roll the car windows down in winter and try to impress your buddies while driving around in the cold until somebody pusses-out and begs for mercy. In Burn Out, we roll up the windows and turn the heater up to full-blast. The radio weatherman says the temperature is ninety degrees north of here, so we figure it's got to be ninety-five or a hundred wherever the hell we are. The cabin temperature must be one-ten, one-twenty already. Both of us are sweating the remnants of Vegas right out. I start to feel faint. I hope Rosie doesn't, since he's driving. It's gotta be a hundred and thirty in here now. Delirium's setting in. Rosie says he sees a forty foot Jesus on a cliff face. He leans over and whispers in my ear, "Do you believe in spontaneous combustion?" I can't answer that.

I think we're in Utah. We could boil water in this car right now. Rosie says, "God bless cottage cheese." I don't know why. We don't even have any cottage cheese. Then he asks, "Did you ever put on a bra and squeeze your ass real tight?" I think maybe I should drive for a while.

...In Golden, Colorado looking for the Coors Brewing Co.

We plan on returning two Coors Lights that we acquired by accident from Dave Richards in Arkansas. Being loyal to Missouri-based Anheuser-Busch, we'd rather not be seen with (much less drink) Coors, so we are kindly returning the strays to their birthplace, still iced-down. Now that's classy. We stop to eat and ask for directions to the brewery. After we bicker over the map like an old married couple, Rosie says, "I need a taller friend," for at least the third time of the trip.

Eventually, we find the brewery, which is already closed to tours for the evening, and drop off the two Coors Lights along with the following note at the shuttle-bus stop in the visitor's parking lot:

"To Whom It May Concern at Coors Brewing Company,

We were given these Coors Light beers by a 'friend' by mistake. Being lifelong Budweiser drinkers from Missouri, we were naturally appalled by the discovery of these inferior cans of swill which ended up in our cooler. We have decided that the only proper way to dispose of these items is to bring them back to the place that made them. They're still cold, and perhaps drinkable to someone who has not developed a taste for good beer, so feel free to give them to whomever you think will appreciate them.

Sincerely,

Roosevelt Crane & Travis Naughton"

...On our way to Ft. Collins. We're headed for the AB brewery. After taking the tour of Heaven and sampling some beer fresh from the source, we tell our tour guides about bringing the Coors beers back to the Golden brewery. Clearly impressed by our loyalty, and after everyone else on the tour clears out, they allow us thirty minutes in the sampling room instead of the usual fifteen. Happiness is losing track of how many free beers you can pound in a half-hour.

We thank our hosts and stumble out to the car…

(Younger): Clearly, you have written a very good Kerouac-style road book here. Why have you never published it?

(Elder): No matter how good it is, it will never be as good as *On The Road*. I like the way my manuscript reads, but I'm just not convinced the world needs another Jack Kerouac. He's a literary icon. A beat hero. You can't improve upon perfection.

(Younger): Years later, you wrote about your continuing obsession with the open road from the perspective of a father and husband in your book *Stay-at-Home Rollercoaster*. The road still calls out to you doesn't it?

(Elder): I've never stopped taking road trips. I'll drive for hours to drop in on friends and family or to just clear my head. It's as important to me as breathing. Lately I've been trying to convince my wife to let me buy a recreational vehicle. Minivans are nice, but we need to spread out sometimes what with kids and grandkids and all. "Wouldn't we be more comfortable in an RV?" I ask the Voice of Reason. "It doesn't have to be fancy or brand new," I tell her. "It could be an older, relatively small model that would fit nicely into a parking space at any campground or parking lot at, say…a Mizzou football game for example." *[Hosting tailgate parties is another of Naughton's obsessions.]* The Enabler says she'll think about it, which is as good as a yes.

I Want To Be Near The Beer

"In hindsight, spending my first three semesters of college as Rosie Crane's roommate was probably not a very good idea, despite--or perhaps more accurately because of--the amount of fun we had together." During those three terms when the pair roomed together, Crane never managed to achieve a passing grade point average, (which ultimately resulted in his dismissal from the university,) and Naughton only exceeded a 2.0 GPA in the second of the same three semester stretch, which was just enough to avert expulsion. Naughton credited his old friend Crash Phillips for his lack of effort: "Crash always said, 'If it's an easy 'A,' then it's an even easier 'C'.' How could I argue with that kind of logic?" Fellow high school chum Wes Douglass lived just down the hall from Travis and Rosie in the same dormitory, and he, like Rosie, was soon kicked out of school for failing grades. Naughton wrote about his time in college with Rosie in his memoir Rude, Crude, and Socially Unacceptable:

Being Rosie's roommate was a great way to meet new people. Almost nightly after we first arrived on campus Rosie would become quite intoxicated and wander off from our dorm room forcing me to play a drunken game of Marco Polo in order to track him down. On many occasions, Rosie would be passed out on a complete stranger's floor or bean bag chair by the time I found him. I always said "sorry" to the inconvenienced residents of whichever room Rosie was currently occupying, but soon I realized that apologies were completely unnecessary. People fell in love with Rosie the minute they met him, even when he was drooling on their freshly washed and folded pile of laundry. Roosevelt Crane was a bigger-than-life figure, standing six feet four inches tall and weighing close to 300 pounds. He was goofy and relatively harmless, and he entertained rather than annoyed most of the people he met. I was the Spade to Rosie's Farley, and the way we played off of one another won us scores of friends everywhere we went. Our antics were not inhibited in the slightest when after donating blood Rosie received a written notice from the American Red Cross that alerted him to a possible problem with his liver (no doubt due to his heavy drinking habit). Crane rolled up the document and deposited it into a freshly emptied bottle of Jack Daniel's to keep for posterity. The party must go on.

At home football games, Rosie always brought his "A" game. Our tailgate parties typically started at least three hours before kick-off, which meant that the first beer was drawn from the keg by nine or ten in the morning. The only time I ever saw Rosie's cup empty was when the keg ran dry. By the time the games ended, we had been pounding beers for over six hours, making the post-game mass-exodus from the parking lot a wildly entertaining spectacle. Usually Rosie would harass the opposing team's fans, despite the fact that in those days the Missouri Tigers lost eight out of eleven games each year for five straight seasons. We weren't there to support the football team anyway. Half the time, Rosie didn't even know who the hell we were playing. It didn't matter. Rosie was the real attraction. Several times after games I saw him grab a stack of white paper napkins, walk into the line of cars stuck in bumper-to-bumper traffic, and accost the trapped and unsuspecting drivers while exclaiming, "Jay Leno is the Antichrist! Dave Letterman is the new Messiah! Would you like some literature, sir?" God, the looks on those poor people's faces!

When we moved into our "fraternity house", which was originally a four bedroom, single family home that had three additional closet-sized "bedrooms" cobbled together in the basement (to better accommodate the thirteen of us who agreed to cram into the squalid, condemnable dwelling in order to keep the rent affordable for each man), Rosie and I naturally decided to share a room, and just as predictably, we were relegated to the dank confines of the basement. Where our closet should have been, our room had a water heater in it. There were no heating or air conditioning vents. A window similar to what you'd see in a jail cell in an old cowboy movie was our only proof that an outside world existed. Two other unfortunate schmucks were cellar dwellers too, although they each had rooms to themselves. Rosie and I had just enough room for our two twin beds, two dressers, and two or three piles of dirty laundry on the floor. Our TV sat on Rosie's dresser and our electric typewriter on mine. We put our mini fridge full of beer between our beds—in the middle of the room--and sat our extra cases or twelve packs on top. It was a dark, smelly pit in the bowels of the house, but it was our dark, smelly pit. And our room would soon become a refuge from the freakshow taking place upstairs. A few of our fraternity brothers sold pot and coke, several more tripped acid with frightening regularity, and a couple were homosexual--all of which was both fascinating and frightening to Rosie and me, two relatively innocent kids from a small, relatively innocent town.

What our room lacked in amenities we made up for in ingenuity. To turn our light on and off, without getting out of our beds (because we were just that lazy,) we rigged up a system of pulleys with twine and thumbtacks. The string ran from the light switch along the walls toward our beds and was wound around tacks stuck in the drywall. If we wanted to turn the light on, Rosie would pull the string by his bed, if we wanted lights-out, I would pull mine.

A similar system was used to operate the TV, which did not have a remote control. The set was turned on by pulling a knob on the front panel. It was equipped with a feature called "auto tune" which allowed the TV to search for a channel when first turned on. So we rigged up an innovative system that included a tennis ball suspended from the ceiling by more twine. When a person pulled the string, it would draw back the ball, which had a second string attached to it that was connected to the on/off pull knob on the set. The second string pulled out the knob, the TV would turn on, and it would automatically find a tuned-in channel. To turn the TV off, we would pull the string and when the ball was pulled back far enough, we'd let it go, sending the ball in an arc downward toward the TV where the ball pushed in the power knob and turned the set off. To change the channel, we would call out to a housemate and have them change the station for us. But if no one else was home, we settled for watching the one station. (Did I mention we were lazy?) The engineering majors in our house were amused by our designs, and I suspect they were also secretly impressed with our ingenuity. If only we had applied that kind of energy toward our studies.

Because of the campus wide ban on kegs in fraternity houses, we decided to construct one more engineering marvel in the basement. To hide our stash, we built a false wall that hid a 16-gallon barrel of beer along with an ice bucket and related accessories. The wall was built with two by fours, dry wall, and paint and was mounted on hinges so that all we had to do gain entry to the secret room was to swing open the entire, seamless unit. It was beautiful, and Rosie and I managed to impress the engineers once again. Admittedly, having all of this hidden beer in the house may have contributed significantly to Rosie's eventual expulsion from the university and my increasingly frequent and disturbing habit of having Errant Urinary Events, or EUEs.

The first of these EUEs happened on a Thursday night after "Dollar Pitchers Night" at a favorite bar of ours. ALERT: If the only way to keep track of how many pitchers you've consumed in one evening is by counting how many one dollar bills are left in your wallet, then you might have a problem. And you definitely don't need to go back to your house and open the false wall in your basement to start sucking off the three day old keg that's hidden there. But Rosie and I did it anyway. We both eventually passed out, and sometime in the middle of the night I apparently woke up needing to relieve myself. Rosie woke briefly amid the noise I was making and watched as I stumbled blindly out the door, presumably toward the bathroom. He informed me the next day that I got up a second time that night, too, much to his dismay.

Evidently, he awoke to the soothing sound of flowing water, not unlike that of a small waterfall one might stumble upon while strolling through a scenic meadow in springtime as the melting snow from a breathtaking alpine landscape meanders its way toward the sea. He looked up to see by the soft light of the half-moon shining though our tiny prison window me emptying my bladder in his dresser drawers. "Travis!" Rosie shouted. "You're pissing on my clothes!"

"Shut the fuck up Crane," was my response, according to Rosie.

"Travis! You're pissing on my clothes!" he tried again.

"And I said shut the fuck up!" Then I calmly turned and stared straight ahead as if I were standing at a urinal and finished saturating Rosie's socks, shirts, shorts, etc. while he sat in bed powerless to stop me. The next day as he told me all of this, all I had to do was look inside and smell his dresser to know that he was telling the truth. I was as mortified as Rosie and promised to wash all of his laundry immediately. Rosie trudged off to class and I bagged up all of his sopping-wet clothes and prepared to head to the Laundromat. As I walked out my door, Dan Huston, the guy who lived across the hall from us, stopped me.

"Where are you going?" he asked.

"Uh, I'm doing some laundry. Why?"

"Well while you're going that way, I wonder if you would mind taking some of my stuff, too. Of course I don't imagine you can fit my carpet in a washing machine, can you?"

"Probably not. Why do you ask?"

"Because you soaked it last night. Yeah, I talked to Rosie this morning and he said you got up *twice* last night. Betcha didn't know that, did ya? Turns out you pissed in his drawers *after* you pissed on *my* door. Yeah. You see, *your* piss ran under *my* door and soaked *my* carpet and some of *my* clothes I had lying on *my* floor."

"Yeah?"

"Yeah." I believed Dan, but I had absolutely no recollection of waking up either time that night. I didn't know what to say so I quickly gathered up Dan's damp laundry and left without saying another word. By the time he and Rosie were back from class later that day, their laundry was folded and put away (after a thorough cleaning of Rosie's dresser and Dan's carpet.) I swore to anyone who would listen that somebody at the bar must have slipped something in my drink, but I knew that was highly unlikely. The fact was that I was losing control over my drinking habit (and my bladder apparently.) At the end of that semester, Rosie flunked out of school—which was unfortunate for him, but probably life prolonging for me.

Before Rosie and Wes got booted from Mizzou, we had the bright idea to procure fake identification cards, which were made by another friend of ours from high school (who shall remain nameless for obvious reasons), to make getting our hands on beer even easier. According to my fake I.D., my name was Travis B. Keller. I resided at 967 Turner Avenue, Madison, Wisconsin 52302. I was born on 9/25/69. Wes Douglass lived at 679 Tanner Avenue. Rosie Crane lived at 796 Tannery Avenue. As long as we remembered to never use our I.D.s at the same time, we had nothing to fear. (Unfortunately for a couple of girls who also had purchased I.D.s from the same guy, they forgot this cardinal rule. Megan Rose of 976 Banner Avenue and Morgan Ross of 679 Bonner Avenue, both of Madison, Wisconsin had their I.D.s confiscated and were summarily barred from the premises of a particularly popular Columbia nightspot.)

I used my fake I.D. only when absolutely necessary, like at a St. Louis Cardinals baseball game or when a regular college I.D. wasn't enough to get past a doorman. During my sophomore year, after Rosie flunked out of school, I shared an apartment with a fraternity brother from Chicago named Clark Heinrich and when he suggested that we take in a Cards-Cubs game one evening, I jumped at the chance. I already had tickets to a game the following day with my dad and grandma but since I expected that they might frown upon seeing me illegally purchasing alcohol, I figured I had better go with Clark and his brother Ed if I wanted to drink beer at the ballpark.

There are few things in life more thoroughly entertaining than watching a Cards-Cubs game from the bleachers while downing as many beers as possible before last-call. Crash Phillips always told me, "A beer an inning keeps the Redbirds winning."

Therefore it was my duty to get drunk and help the home team win. Clark, Ed, and I went to the game that night and as we were taking our seats, unbelievably, I ran into Crash himself. I shouldn't have been surprised. Where else would Crash be when the hated Cubbies were in town? Why wouldn't he make the eight-hour round trip from Kansas City to St. Louis to catch a ball game? I used my I.D. to buy several rounds that night, until one extra-diligent beer vendor decided to scrutinize it. I showed him the tremendous stack of empty beer cubs in my hand as proof that none of the other vendors had a problem with selling to me, but he still was not convinced. He called in a supervisor who glanced at the card and then at me. I presented my stack of empties as evidence and when he told his subordinate to "Go ahead and sell it to him," the entire population of drunks in the left field bleachers erupted into cheers. By the seventh inning stretch, I was feeling pretty good about myself, emboldened both by my beer buying success, and by the excessive consumption of such. A message flashed on the scoreboard encouraging those in attendance to report any "unruly fans" to the nearest usher if someone was acting rudely or inappropriately. Naturally, I should have been the first person on anyone's list to get booted, so I decided to launch a preemptive strike of my own. I had noticed a few innings earlier a Cubs fan that was located on the level of seats above us spilling his beer over the edge and onto some unsuspecting Cards fans in the bleachers. He had a mouth even more obnoxious than mine and when an usher walked by, I stood up and shouted, "Unruly fan!" while pointing him out. Again our section of bleachers erupted into applause as we watched the furious Cub lover being removed from his seat.

    I don't even remember who won the game. It really didn't matter. I was riding the high of my newfound bleacher hero status and suggested to my friends that we go bar hopping in downtown St. Louis. I was feeling bulletproof and invincible armed with my fake I.D., and Clark and his brother were both over twenty-one, so they were both game. We hit several bars that night until the law of averages finally caught up with me. At one club, a doorman was armed with a book that showed all of the fifty states' I.D. cards. Clark and Ed had already made their way into the establishment when the bouncer stopped me. "Got any I.D.?"

"Of course." I waited with an impatient look on my face that implied, "I have used this I.D. all over town tonight, you just let my friends in ahead of me, and besides--don't I look like I'm twenty-one?" But I didn't look twenty-one. I looked like I was about fourteen. I still get carded to this day, even at the grocery store while I'm pushing a shopping cart with two kids in it.

"Do you want to know what's wrong with this I.D.?" the hulking doorman asked, with an amused grin on his face.

"Um, okay," I said, knowing that the jig was up.

He then proceeded to show me the side-by-side comparison of my fake I.D. and the real one depicted in his book. They weren't even close. I don't know where my buddy came up with his artwork for the background, but it clearly wasn't from a real Wisconsin driver's license. The doorman sensed my guilt, embarrassment, and fear and said, "But this is a pretty good try. Have a good night somewhere else." To my astonishment, he handed back my I.D. rather than confiscate it for his trophy collection. I thanked him profusely and we headed to another bar.

At the next place, Clark hooked up with a woman who was as drunk as all of us put together. She invited us over to her house for a nightcap, so we gave her a ride home and as we were getting out of the car, Clark said, "You two wait here. I'll be back in a little while." There would be no nightcap for Ed and I. Clark was looking to score, and he certainly didn't need us getting in the way. So we waited. And waited. And waited. And passed out. I awoke to a bright light and a pounding in my head.

"Hey you two. Wake up in there." It was one of St. Louis's finest. Apparently passing out in the backseat of a car in the downtown area was the sort of thing that is frowned upon in those parts. "Which one of you was driving?"

I was relieved to not have to lie. "Neither one of us, officer. Our buddy who was driving is in that house with a girl. He told us to wait out here, if you know what I mean."

"Well, alright then. Just move it along as soon as he's done."

"Oh, yes sir. Have a nice night officer."

"You, too."

And we were having a nice night. When Clark finally returned to the car, Ed said that he wanted to see the Gateway Arch. He had never been to St. Louis before. That sounded like a fine idea to us, so we drove straight over. I staggered out of the car and up the steps that led to the base of the monument while the brothers Heinrich followed closely behind.

"Wow. I didn't realize how big it is," Ed observed. He was clearly impressed. "And it's so smooth and shiny. I just want to rub myself all over it." That seemed like a fine idea, too, so we all three rubbed ourselves all over the iconic structure. To a passing tourist, it might have appeared that we were gang-raping the Jefferson Westward Expansion Monument. But really, we were just three over-served college guys who were harmlessly dry-humping an arch. Nothing out of the ordinary there. I still have aluminum stains on the white sweatshirt I was wearing that night, and it still makes me smile every time I wear it.

Somehow we managed to make it back to Columbia in the wee hours of the morning, and a few hours later, I started driving to my dad's house to meet up with him and my grandma for that day's ballgame. Halfway there, I became very drowsy and pulled off the highway for a quick cat-nap. I awoke an hour and a half later and when I tried to start the car, I realized that I had left my headlights on. The battery was dead and so were my chances of making it to the ballgame. I hitched a ride into town and called my dad, who was not amused in the slightest. My grandma, it turned out, was a huge Cubs fan and had never been to a game in person. Having waited for me as long as they did, it was now too late to make it to the game. Grandma never did get to see her Cubbies in person. I have lived with that guilt ever since, as well I should.

Grandma-guilt was still not a strong enough deterrent to keep me away from my pursuit of perpetual intoxication, though. Being a beer drinker became a large part of my identity in college, which obviously was not good for my grades, my liver, or my relationships with the members of my family. I amassed a beer can collection that made people gasp in awe upon viewing it for the first time. Wes Douglass and I even brewed our own beer for awhile, as if there wasn't enough already being produced by the world's major brewers to keep us satisfied. Basically, I was the guy at the party who was a hellofalottafun to drink with--for a while, but whom you could always count on to invariably puke, piss, or pass out at the worst possible time and/or place. Chicks dig that, right?

While I worked at Westgate Foods, a small grocery store in Columbia, a new brew pub was opening up across town and I thought it would be fun to work there. I had the nerve to tell my boss that I had to leave work for an hour or so to interview for a different job. I realize now just how unprofessional that was, but at the time, I really didn't give it a second thought. When I arrived for my interview, several people were already waiting in line ahead of me. Most people might use the time spent waiting to rehearse their answers for the interviewer's questions, but not me. I thought it would seem more real or honest if I just winged it. So I did.

Interviewer: "Mr. Naughton, what position are you applying for today?"

Me: "Well, sir, I would like to work in the brew house."

Interviewer: "I'm sorry, but we already have a brewmaster and he likes to work alone. Is there anything else that interests you?"

Me: "Yes, I would like to be a delivery driver. I have a chauffer's license."

Interviewer: "We don't plan on selling our beer outside of the premises, so we won't be needing a delivery driver. Does anything else sound appealing to you?"

Me: "Well, maybe bartending."

Interviewer: "Do you have any bartending experience?"

Me: "No."

Interviewer: "We're only hiring experienced bartenders right now. We may need a bar back, though. Would you be interested in keeping the bar stocked and perhaps learn how to tend bar while you do that?"

Me: "Um, not really."

Interviewer: "Alright then. Why don't you just tell me where you want to be?"

Me: "I want to be near the beer."

Interviewer: "Right. Well, thanks for stopping by."

Me: "You're welcome."

I was gone from the grocery store less than an hour. When I returned, I put on my apron and resumed my chicken-frying duties. "Well, how'd the interview go?" my boss asked, seeming to be genuinely interested.

"Oh, they said something about not needing a brewmaster, so I said 'Nevermind, man.'"

"Huh. That's too bad."

I wasn't going to let a little disappointment like that come between me and beer. Instead, I redoubled my efforts in the pursuit of unending inebriation. During one stretch, I showed up for work with a hangover twenty-four days in a row. A concerned co-worker stopped me in an aisle and said, "Hey, Fish. You don't look so good, man. Maybe you should go easy for a while."

"Did you just call me 'Fish'?" I asked.

"Yeah, because you drink like one." He had a point. And I kind of liked that nickname, but sadly, it didn't catch on. Instead, my boss started calling me "Colonel Sanders" when I transferred to the deli and started manning the chicken fryer. All these years later, many of my friends from the old Westgate days still call me "The Colonel."

By the end of his sophomore year, Naughton continued his downward spiral. He wound up quitting the fraternity that he co-founded (blaming the demands of his work schedule at the grocery store). Although its membership peaked at around forty members, no amount of everyday Joes could make up for the organization's loss of Roosevelt Crane and Travis Naughton. In another year, Theta Xi fraternity would cease to exist on the University of Missouri campus. Within one more year, Travis Naughton would cease to exist on the University of Missouri campus as well.

The Not-So-Cratic Method

After Crane left school, Naughton bounced around from apartment to apartment, from roommate to roommate, never staying at any one address for more than nine months. He lived at a total of eight different addresses in Columbia during his post-Rosie college years. It was during the semester that he lived with Clark Heinrich that he finally decided to settle on a major and get somewhat serious about earning a degree. Clark was a philosophy major who had no plans to teach philosophy or use his degree toward getting into law school (like many people in that major do.) He explained that it was just the fastest way he could think of to get a degree and get school over with. Naughton said, "That sounded good enough for me."

Upon further investigation, Travis discovered that he had taken enough high school mathematics to exempt him from having to take any college math classes if he were to pursue a degree in philosophy. That sealed the deal. Clark was right, it seemed. Philosophy appeared to be Travis's ticket for getting through college as painlessly as possible, so after previously declaring himself a political science major and then a history major, and being told at one point that his poor grades during his first two years in school disqualified him from becoming an education major, he formally declared himself a philosophy major. A lover of wisdom. The irony was not lost on Naughton.

(Younger): How did it feel to call yourself a philosopher?

(Elder): Instantly I felt better about myself. People always think you're smart when you say you're a philosopher. I signed up for classes and impressed myself with the schedule I came up with. During my first semester as a philosophy student, all four of my classes were within my major and were held back-to-back-to-back-to-back in the same building, on the same floor, on the same side of the hall every Tuesday and Thursday--leaving every Monday, Wednesday, Friday, Saturday, and Sunday open for working part-time, sleeping-off hangovers, and playing disc golf. How smart did I feel? *Philosopher smart.*

(Younger): It would seem that attending classes was almost an incidental part of your week. Did this pose any problems for you?

(Elder): There was a fatal flaw to my plan. Often I would be just as hung-over on Tuesdays and Thursdays as I was any other day of the week, which made it difficult to roll out of bed for my first class in the morning. Rather than getting up in time to at least try make it to my second, third, or even fourth class of the day, I would usually just stay in bed whenever I missed the first. Eventually, I only showed up to class to take exams.

(Younger): How'd that work out for you?

(Elder): Let's just put it this way; My professor in Existentialism, who had assigned my first three exams a letter grade of "D," noted in the margins of my third test when he handed it back to me, "Consistency at this level is not a virtue." He had a policy that his students could drop their lowest test score, which gave me a sense of hope until I did the math and realized that because an "A" would be impossible to achieve on my final exam due to my complete lack of understanding of the subject, there would be no way to get any final grade in the course other than a "D." Therefore, I opted to not even bother taking the final.

(Younger): You must have felt somewhat embarrassed to look your professor in the eye as he handed back your test.

(Elder): I was. But I was happy at least to never have to step foot in Dr. Alexander's classroom again—or so I thought. You can imagine my horror a few years later when I was compelled to enroll in his senior seminar course in order to fulfill my graduation requirements. If you can, try to visualize the expression on the permanently grim face of a German-born, humorless professor who learned the English language by reading an unabridged dictionary cover-to-cover during the boat ride to America when he was a boy as he recognized me when I walked into his classroom. When our eyes met, I felt like throwing up.

Studying was obviously very low on Naughton's list of priorities in those days. In addition to taking twelve hours of classes, he was also struggling to keep a dying fraternity going while working thirty or more hours per week at Westgate Foods. There simply wasn't much time left to study. Of course he spent what little free time he did have killing brain cells. But Naughton's heavy drinking was not the only brain cell killing habit he picked up during his college years. In his book Reason for Leaving, *the author wrote extensively about his experiences with a new circle of friends and a new Lady Love named Mary Jane. (Years later, Hollywood bought the rights to a screenplay Naughton wrote called* Paper or Plastic, *which was based on the section of the book dealing with his time in the grocery business, and produced a comedy that paid tribute to films such as* Car Wash, Empire Records, *and* Waiting *about an eccentric group of co-workers. The film was nominated for awards including best comedy or musical and best original screenplay.) The following is an excerpt from* Reason for Leaving:

We called ourselves the Westgate Dudes from Westgate Foods. Tony Lipper, his roommate Ted Miller, Clete "Buddha" Roberts (so nicknamed for his uncanny resemblance to the Enlightened One), and Robin Westgate, the store owner's son, and I worked and played together 24/7.

Tony was a scrawny little shit, about five foot six and 120 pounds soaking wet. What he lacked in stature he made up for in personality, which drew me to him from the first time we worked together. He was a talker, and in the short time I had been employed at the store, I was sure that I had heard his entire life's story. He had been in the Marines before enrolling in college and one of his favorite stories to tell about his time spent overseas involved an exotic dancer he saw perform in Thailand while he was taking some R & R. I won't attempt to duplicate his style of storytelling, but I will say the tale involves this girl picking up a stack of quarters that Tony had placed on the stage and then firing them back at him, one-by-one; all without ever using her hands, or toes, or mouth. Let your imagination work that over for a minute. He loved to share that visual imagery with complete strangers just to see their reactions, even in the check-out line of the grocery store.

  Columbia had a recycling law on the books back then that charged a five-cent deposit on every can and bottle sold in city limits. Once emptied, they could be brought back to the store for a refund. Behind our dingy little store, a building so filthy and worn-out that a customer once dubbed it "the only place in town you have to wipe your feet on the way out," there was a recycling area that we called "the bottle room." It was an open-air patio, with a chain-link fence surrounding it, and a crude tin roof that kept recyclables, and dope-smoking employees, literally high and dry. It is no exaggeration to say that during the time I worked at Westgate Foods, many, many pounds of weed were smoked in the bottle room. Whenever the announcement, "I need help in the bottle room, please," came over the intercom, any and all of us who didn't happen to have a customer in their check-out line would convene in the back to smoke a bowl or two or three. And I mean all of us. Only the girl at the customer service desk abstained, but just until she got home from work. I can't recall a single day that went by that pot wasn't being smoked at that store during the two years I worked there.

  As you can imagine, working the evening shift at "The Gate" rarely felt like work. It was never a busy store, as there was a major competitor in the area that offered a better selection, lower prices, and a building that didn't appear to be on the verge of collapsing. The slow pace suited us fine, although I don't know how the owner stayed in business. I swear that some customers shopped there just to hear the crazy things that came out of our mouths while we were stoned. I'm sure most of them didn't know we were high, but our blood-shot eyes and foul-smelling breath had to have tipped off more than a few savvy people. The gems that spilled from Tony's mouth while he stood at his register made working "up-front" emmensely entertaining.

"Hey, Travis," Tony yelled over to me from his check-stand while we both had a line of customers in our lanes at least six people deep. "I was thinkin' about what to do after work tonight."

I cringed, but curiosity forced me to ask, "Oh, yeah? What do you have in mind?"

"Well, I was thinkin' that after we do a couple bong-hits at my place, we should go hit the bars. What do you think?"

Instantly, twelve complete strangers were all staring at me, not at all sure if they really just heard what they thought they heard, waiting for my response. I smiled sheepishly, and couldn't say anything but, "Sounds good to me." Several of the customers giggled, the rest looked away and pretended not to notice, but everyone present understood perfectly that the shopping experience at Westgate Foods was far and away a much better value than anything Mega-Mart could offer.

On another occasion, Tony was ringing-up items for a cute, but grumpy-looking college girl who was dressed in baggy sweatpants, a wrinkled t-shirt, and flip-flops.

"How are you this evening?" Tony asked with a broad smile on his face, as he always did.

"Fine," The girl replied, although her irritated tone betrayed her lie. Tony swiped her items over the scanner: tampons, a pint of Ben & Jerry's, and a National Enquirer.

"What, no Midol?" Tony blurted-out, picking up on the reason for the young woman's foul mood. Miraculously choosing to spare his life, she paid for her items and left the store bearing a murderous scowl on her face, without saying another word. I admired Tony not for the things he said, but for the fact that he was unafraid to say them. He showed me that being yourself and not giving a rip about what anyone else thinks is essential to finding happiness.

Tony seemed to be majoring in the pursuit of happiness, a discipline I dedicated myself to as well, although I had been failing miserably at it as my drinking spiraled out of control. I decided that to find happiness, all I needed to do was whatever Tony did. He and Ted introduced me to the game of disc golf not long after I starting working at the store. If ever a sport was invented for potheads in college, this was it. There was no need for an expensive bag of clubs. No greens fees or cart rentals. No memberships. Just one or two specialized plastic discs and a bag of weed were all that were required. I fell head-over-heels in love with the game right away.

Before long, I was playing eighteen holes once or twice every day. We played every hole as a par three, regardless of what the actual par was. We did this, we told people, to challenge ourselves. Really, it was just easier to remember that the par on any particular hole was always three throws, especially when we were stoned. But, as stoned as we were, the three of us came to excel at the sport. Our preparation involved nothing more than smoking a bowl on the way to the course. No warm-ups were needed. No two-a-day practices. No riding the bench hoping for a chance to get into the game. This was the sport for me.

Half-way through a round, we'd pass another bowl around to sustain us through the back nine, and many times we realized we weren't alone. It would be a safe bet to state that half the other players on the course were high, too. One guy that we ran into virtually every day actually lived in his car, which was always parked in the lot adjacent to the course. Disc golf wasn't just a hobby, it was a way of life.

I become so good at the game that I routinely played eighteen holes under par. That is quite a feat when you consider some holes were over 400 feet long, through trees, and near busy roads and a swimming pool. And once, I scored a hole-in-one on Hole #13, which required making a blind throw over a wide stand of trees. I threw the disc vertically, watched with anticipation as it disappeared over the tree tops, and heard the most beautiful and distinct sound in the world: the sound of chains, suspended from a hoop on top of the metal pole and reaching to the middle of the wire basket, rattling as my disc landed dead in the center of the target. Tony and Ted witnessed the feat, but to date have never themselves managed to duplicate it. It is my claim to fame alone, having never met another player who has aced that hole. I lived for the game and during any given week, I spent more time on the disc golf course than I did on any of my philosophy courses.

When we were indoors, our game of choice was darts. Normally, there was no real threat of bodily harm when we tossed the sharp-tipped projectiles across the room, even when high, because we did everything while we were high. I guess you could say that we were "high-function" stoners. Darts became more of a thrill-sport when we added psychedelic mushrooms to the mix of pot and booze. During one party, I was so out of it that I was flagged by Referee Ted for "intentionally grounding" my darts when I could no longer aim at the board and instead threw my darts to the floor near his feet.

That night was the first time I had ever "gone 'shroomin'" as Buddha Roberts called it. I don't remember much of the experience except for a period of time that I spent sitting in the backyard, looking up at the starry sky and watching the trees as they "breathed" in and out in rhythm with my own breathing shortly after I sang a bizarre rendition of "Mack the Knife" and ran out the back door in a complete hallucinogenic freak-out. I've been told that the performance really brought down the house.

I drew the line on taking drugs there. Marijuana and mushrooms were God's own creation, so I had no problem with utilizing the gifts provided to man by nature. But I never used anything that had to be processed by man, like cocaine, heroin, acid, or meth. That invisible line in the sand may be the only reason I'm still alive today. That and perhaps the love of a very special woman.

It was around this time when Mr. Naughton met the future Mrs. Naughton. Their love story is well documented, as are most aspects of the famous author's life, and are discussed at length throughout most of his writings and the remainder of this biography. In 1992, Travis's childhood friend Cliff Joseph was dating a girl named Charla; a tall, slender brunette who Travis says, "...was so beautiful that I couldn't for the life of me figure out why she was with my short, obnoxious friend Cliff." While Travis was at Cliff's apartment one day watching an MU basketball game on TV, Cliff mentioned that Charla had a sister named Bethany; a twin sister, he added.

"I asked Cliff if they were identical and he said they were. Then he asked me if I would like to see a picture of Char's sister. Naturally I said yes. Like most men, I had fantasized about twins since I felt the first tingling of adolescence in my loins. Cliff produced a photo of Bethany, who was every bit as gorgeous as her sister, and mentioned that she would be coming to town in a few days to visit her sister." *[The two women attended colleges in different towns at the time.]* "He asked me if I'd like to meet her. I said yes."

Naughton wrote about this first encounter in a book he dedicated to his grown children in 2028 called How I Love Your Mother:

> I was a five foot, seven inch tall, recently-turned twenty one year old drunkard who was too busy partying to even think about having a girlfriend. She was a six foot tall, eighteen year old goddess with legs that climbed to Heaven who was pure and good and deserving of much better than me. Yet the instant we met, we were both hopelessly enchanted with one another. Throughout the evening, we could not take our eyes or hands off each other. I remember that I had on a pair of blue jeans with a hole in the left knee that her right hand seemed to be drawn to like a moth to flame and she would smile the most beautiful and coy smile whenever her hand found its mark. Her smile was so natural, so comforting that it warmed my heart whenever I saw it. As the evening wound down and Cliff and Charla went to bed, I asked if she would like to crash at my place for the night.
>
> She said yes.

Opportunities for me to sleep with good looking college girls were so few and far between that I rarely passed up a chance whenever one presented itself. But when I looked into those trusting eyes, I softly kissed her goodnight instead of succumbing to temptation. The next morning, I awoke to tender kisses on my neck. "Good morning, sunshine," I said. She smiled. Her dimples devastated me. The curves of her long, lithe body ignited a fire deep within me that has not gone out to this day. I asked her if she could stay awhile longer.

She said yes.

Later that morning, when she stood in my doorway preparing to say goodbye and return to her life at another college in another town, I asked if we would ever have another chance to be together.

She said yes.

Bethany attended a small, all-female college in a small town twenty miles from Columbia. Twenty miles may as well have been twenty thousand. I was too busy going to bars with my friends to make the trip to Fulton to see her. She came to see me a couple times over the next few months and we went out and had a wonderful time when we were together, but because of my juvenile selfishness and my infatuation with self-destruction, I started losing interest in making a long-distance romance work. I stopped returning her calls. Eventually, she must have realized that I wasn't worth the effort, and she stopped calling me.

I ran into Bethany now and then after she transferred to Mizzou the next year, and she always managed to smile as big as she did that first night when we met, but I was always too drunk or self-involved to pull my head out of my ass far enough to realize what I was missing. Of course, Bethany couldn't wait forever for me to wake up, so naturally she moved on with her life. Our paths crossed again one semester when we both wound up taking the same theater appreciation class. I sat beside her and asked her how she was doing. She said she was great. She was living with her sister and her new boyfriend.

"You mean Charla's new boyfriend?" I asked.

"Nope. Mine," she said with her patented smile gracing her lovely face. Only then did I notice that her smile was not as naive and care-free as it once had been. It was the smile of someone who'd lived a little more life. It was more mature. It was, perhaps, the smile of someone who had been hurt once by someone she loved.

"What's his name?" I asked, pretending not to be jealous.

"Tom."

"Tom, huh? Does he treat you right?" I was being sincere.

She said yes.

"Does he make you happy?"

"Yes he does."

"Well that's good." I looked away, not knowing what else to say, and noticed that Bethany had a hole in the knee of her jeans. I remembered the night long ago when it was the hole in the knee of *my* Levi's that precipitated our first moments of intimacy and I started to become flooded with feelings of regret. Needing to break the awkward silence, I grabbed my ink pen and wrote "Hi Tom" on the part of her leg that was visible through the fraying tear in her jeans. She laughed and to my surprise, did not wipe off my note. I knew right then that she had forgiven me for hurting her before. I also knew that somehow, I would find a way to win her back. After class, I asked her if I could give her a ride home. She explained that she could walk home in less time than it would take for us to make our way over to the parking garage my car was in and drive her across campus. I asked again anyway.

She said yes.

I gave her rides home almost every day after that. We attended a play together (which was a requirement for the class we were taking.) We ran into one another at a few parties. But as charming as I tried to be, Bethany was committed to Tom, and she made it clear that I had missed my chance.

(Younger): After you realized that Bethany had moved on, how did you react?

(Elder): I decided to fully embrace my bachelorhood. Basically, I gave up on finding love because I knew that I was such a mess in those days that I wasn't fit for any woman to love me. I sought solace in a bottle, but no matter how many I emptied, none contained what I was looking for. As a philosopher, I should have been able to recognize the folly of my decision to drink myself to death. I was, as Jean-Paul Sartre put it, condemned to be free. Free to do whatever I chose, no matter how self-destructive those choices were, or what the consequences. Hey, maybe I *did* learn something in college after all.

(Younger): But you managed to earn back Bethany's love eventually. How did this come about?

(Elder): That, my young friend, is a long and crazy story. I could tell it to you, but I think it would be easier if you would refer to the chapter *The Lord of the Fruit Flies* from my memoir. It describes the time period that preceded our reunion. If you have seen *Paper of Plastic*, some of the story will seem familiar to you. Then our reconciliation is described in detail in *How I Love Your Mother*.

The Lord of the Fruit Flies

"The best part is that there's no security deposit and we don't have to sign a lease." When Chris Stevens uttered these words, I should have recognized them as a warning sign that the place he had found for us to live in was perhaps not fit for human habitation. (It is a matter of public record that I have trouble reading warning signs.) Instead, I agreed that the dilapidated three bedroom house was indeed an ideal place for four college guys to live. The plan was for me, Derek Herr, and Cyrus Flemback to occupy the three bedrooms while Chris inhabited the "luxury suite" that was the basement.

Upon first inspection, the run-down ranch house seemed livable. The carpets were slightly stained, which didn't bother us, we never planned to keep them clean anyway. The appliances all worked, although our seldom used oven doubled as a condominium for a sizable colony of mice. Here's some free advice: Always bang on the range top before turning on a burner. It is as hard forget the smell of singed mouse and ramen noodles as it is to remove it from one's house. After that unfortunate incident we set traps on top of the stove and heard the eerie "snap" of a sprung trap at least once per night for a solid week.

Chris's room in the basement was where things got really dicey. On the plus side, he was the only resident of the dwelling with his own bathroom. Never mind the fact that the toilet was not connected to a water source and was strategically situated in the middle of the unfinished subterranean living space without so much as a wall or modicum of privacy surrounding it. When someone wanted to flush it, they had to fill a plastic bucket with water from the sink upstairs, carry it back down the steps, and then pour it into the tank- a process that was second nature to those of us who had enjoyed the creature comforts of the Love Shack back in the high school days. I can assure you, however, that this process was mostly bypassed in favor of the "Someone will get around to flushing it whenever people can smell it upstairs" method. After a while, Chris went one step further in the laziness category by simply urinating in a plastic gallon jug half-full of fruit juice. Whenever anyone was brave enough to venture downstairs at one of the frequent parties we hosted, they were always cautioned, "Don't drink the juice." The most vexing feature of the basement was a room filled entirely with old doors. There were dozens of them, and for the life of us, we couldn't figure out why they were there. Not until Rosie Crane dropped by for a visit, that is.

One would think that in a house full of college students, a certain amount of time would be set aside for studying. I can remember opening a textbook on exactly two occasions during the year we lived in that house. One of these times was during finals week, when Derek came up with an ingenious idea to add an incentive to our studying process. He procured a large bottle of whiskey and a twelve pack of beer-- study aids if there ever were any-- and suggested that for every chapter we reviewed in our respective books, we would do a shot of Jack and chase it with a can of Bud. We studied a lot that night. *A lot.* The next morning, as I lay comatose in my bed, Derek walked into my room. "Hey Trav, don't you have a final going on right now?" One bleary-eyed glance at the clock confirmed that he was correct. I scrambled to get dressed and jumped in my car, still wiping the sleep from my eyes. Unfortunately, we did not live on or anywhere near campus. On the contrary, we lived about five miles outside of town, so when I finally walked into the lecture hall and asked the professor for my exam, I was 40 minutes late to a final with a one hour time allotment. And yet, I was still one of the first students to hand in the test. Surprisingly, I passed with flying colors, if you can count a "C-" as flying colors.

The occasional study session aside, the primary focus of our household was throwing parties. These gatherings frequently lasted well into the night, and on one particular evening at least one of the neighbors in our primarily family-populated subdivision took issue with the level of noise we were making. As we were gathered around Chris's Toyota truck, which was parked in the driveway beside the house and was on that night, outfitted with a large plastic sheet lining the inside of the bed that contained approximately 500 gallons of water for our "First Annual Cold-Tub Party," a man approached our group, Louisville Slugger in hand.

"Ya'll better shut the hell up 'cuz I got a boy that's fixin' to bowl in the state tournament tomorrow mornin'."

"Did you just say 'fixin'?" asked an amused friend named Clint.

"Boy, you better watch yer mouth," the irate bowling dad warned.

"What's the bat for, man?" Clint asked, fully aware that he was asking for trouble.

Apparently the overzealous parent understood that the odds of one bat defeating fifty drunks were not likely to turn out in his favor, so he retreated to his home. A few minutes later, a sheriff's deputy rolled up.

"Is there a problem, officer?" I asked innocently.

"Well, we got a complaint from a neighbor about the noise, but honestly it doesn't seem like you're being all that loud to me."

"We like to keep it pretty low-key, sir. Oh, by the way, did the gentleman who called mention that he threatened us with a baseball bat?"

"No he did not. I'll probably need to go and ask him about that. Well, you folks keep it down and have a good night."

"You, too, officer." As the deputy pulled away, I picked up the bag of weed that I had stashed on top of the nearest tire of the Toyota that I was leaning against throughout our conversation. Clint and I retreated to a small equipment shed in the back yard to get stoned while we contemplated the sorry existence of the poor kid that had to bowl to please his bat-wielding father.

That tool shed became known as "The Smokehouse" for obvious reasons. It contained a bench seat out of an old school bus and some assorted junk left over from the previous tenants. Because none of my roommates smoked dope, I often took my pothead friends out there to get high. The first time I brought Tony Lipper over to the house, Chris was sitting in a recliner in the front room watching the Playboy Channel. He was also biting his toenails, which was not an uncommon sight at our house.

"Chris, this is Tony. Tony…Chris." I still wonder to this very day why I felt the need for formal introductions while such a stunning display of vulgarity was at play.

Chris looked at Tony, spit a severed toenail on the middle of the floor, and said, "Hey."

"Good to meet you?" Tony muttered in disbelief, clearly questioning his decision to befriend me.

"Let's step out back," I said. Tony gladly complied.

"Dude, what the fuck was that?"

"I've seen worse around here," I said. And it was true. Chris was known for two other stomach-turning habits: He liked parading around the house naked after taking a shower (no matter who was in the house at the time) and he never took a dump with the bathroom door closed. Ever. He couldn't stand to be alone that long, so he always left the door open. This was especially unfortunate because in our little house, the bathroom was adjacent to the living room. Therefore, when you were sitting there watching TV or visiting with guests, Chris was just a few feet away in the bathroom emitting sounds and odors the likes of which you would think very few humans were even capable of. You may wonder; how could anyone love this beast? But love him I did. And I wasn't alone.

Chris married a beautiful woman about a year later and I

was his Best Man at the wedding. I was a little disappointed that he didn't want a bachelor party, but the night before his wedding proved memorable nevertheless. Several of us went to a bar to listen to a cheesy local rock band where the bride-to-be and her friends happened to be as well. We contemplated leaving for a few minutes, but ultimately decided we were too drunk and lazy to go anywhere else. As we partied and danced, we noticed several patrons watching intently a news report on the TV mounted above the bar. Apparently, some guy named Al Cowlings was driving a white Ford Bronco around the streets of L.A. with a dozen cops following him, while none other than my childhood idol, O.J. Simpson, who was suspected of murdering two people, was riding in the back. Any bachelor party can have strippers, but I'll bet not very many can boast that they were centered on watching the Juice on the loose.

Our rapidly disintegrating domicile earned the nickname "The Fruit Fly House" because none of us ever washed dishes until every last plate, bowl, and glass was dirty. Even then we usually only washed what we needed to get through the next meal. A swarm of flying insects was omnipresent in our kitchen. It got so bad that at one point we actually paid a friend of ours to come clean our house for us on a weekly basis. She did a pretty good job, but was so disgusted by what she witnessed that she never returned after the first week. We couldn't blame her. Cy remarked, "I can't believe she agreed to come out here in the first place. She knows *us*. What the hell's wrong with that girl?"

Things really got out of hand whenever Rosie came to visit. He had dropped out of college by that point and only occasionally made it back to visit his friends in Columbia, but he always made the most of his time at The Fruit Fly House. Because we lived outside of city limits, we could legally have open fires in our backyard. It didn't matter that we had only one tree with limbs to burn. We had a whole room full of doors in the basement. Rosie didn't consider it a party unless there was a bonfire, so once he discovered our door stockpile, he was delighted. Every weekend when he visited, Rosie could be counted on to keep the home fires burning for us. It became such a common occurrence that Cy once remarked, "Rosie, I can tell when you've been here even if I've been out of town. Do you know how? Because there's always a fresh pile of door knobs and hinges in the back yard."

All good things must come to an end, and by the time the school year wound down and we ran out of doors to burn, it was decided that we should abandon the Fruit Fly House and look for new accommodations. After we moved everything out, Chris and I remembered too late that we had forgotten to clean out the refrigerator before the power was turned off. Knowing we didn't have a security deposit to forfeit, we decided to just leave the mess for the landlord to deal with. Unfortunately for me, Chris sold his waterbed to Buddha Roberts, who recruited me to help him remove it from the basement. I was wrong when I previously held the belief that there was no smell on earth worse than that of Rosie's car or Chris's ass. The smell of the rancid shrimp that had been decomposing for the better part of a week in the unplugged refrigerator in the already pungent Fruit Fly House was far and away the worst odor I have ever encountered in my life. Buddha and I both took turns dry-heaving as we scrambled to carry the bed upstairs. He could try for the rest of his life to repay me for helping him that day, but he'll never succeed.

A few days later, Chris and I felt so badly for the landlord that we bought a case of beer, a bottle of bleach, and some garbage bags and headed back to the house to clean out the fridge. When we turned onto our street, we spotted the poor son of a bitch's car parked in the driveway. We couldn't bear to face him, so we just kept on driving until all the beer and feelings of guilt were gone. From there, Chris moved in with his fiancée. Cy leased one half of a small duplex, having sworn-off roommates for the rest of his life. Derek and I tried and failed to find lodging apart from one another, and out of desperation rented a horrible, fake wood-paneled apartment in the basement of a house near campus.

The location of our apartment was the only positive thing it had going for it. We could ride our bikes to school, which diverted the money that we would have spent on parking to our beer fund. Two small windows were our only glimpse of the outside world, but neither opened to allow fresh air in to replace the stagnant air trapped within. But we made a go of it. Things were going along fine until one morning while I was taking a shower and I felt something brush up against my foot. With shampoo streaming into my eyes, I was just able to make out what it was that was swirling around in the ankle deep water: human excrement. The drain had backed up and because we were in the basement, the raw sewage that clogged the pipes began to float up the line and into our shower basin. The most troubling thing for me was the realization that the feces that I was bathing in was likely not my own. Our upstairs neighbors were four college guys who had probably clogged the pipes earlier in the morning as they shit, showered, and shaved before leaving for class.

Here's a riddle for you: Where do you wash the shit off your feet when your shower is full of shit? That's the question I posed to our landlord who unflinchingly informed me that it wasn't his problem. I said that it most certainly was and that he needed to get our sewer pipe unclogged as soon as possible. He declined. I reminded him that he was in fact a licensed plumber. He countered with, "Check your copy of the lease. I'm not responsible for anything outside of the house. The sewer main is outside of the house. It's your problem, not mine."

I called the city utility people to come take a look and they told me that a tree root had grown into the sewer pipe in our back yard. The gentleman I talked to said they would bill the landlord and then he asked me, "Do you like rabbits?"

"You mean as pets or cartoon characters?"

"No, as food."

"Yes I do as a matter of fact." I was lying; I had never eaten rabbit in my life. But I felt that I needed to play along since he was going to stick my jackass landlord with the repair bill.

"Well, I raise and butcher my own rabbits. I sell 'em for five dollars apiece, cleaned and delivered. I can bring 'em by this evening. How many do you want?"

"Um, I guess two?" Dear Jesus what was I agreeing to?

"I'll be back at about six o'clock."

"Can't wait." And like clockwork, he showed up at six on the dot. The carcasses were still warm to the touch.

"How's that for fresh?" he asked proudly. I just hoped that he washed his hands between the time he snaked-out my sewer line and the time he field-dressed those tasty little varmints.

I brought the meat to work with me that night where I cooked it on the store's grill located behind the building. Stepping out back to tend the fire, I was reminded of the time when I was almost shot by one of Columbia's finest while he was investigating reports of a break-in next door. The cop incorrectly identified Westgate's back door as that of the one belonging to a pharmacy that was in fact, one door over. I was taking out the trash for the night and with my hands both full, I kicked open the unlatched door. The door swung open as it usually did, but stopped with a thud as it struck an object. "Police! Keep your hands where I can see 'em!"

As my eyes adjusted to the darkness outside, I saw a police officer leveling his 9mm handgun at my chest. He was standing a mere three feet in front of me and was adjusting to the bright light coming from within the store himself. Just then, his partner stepped from behind the door, her weapon drawn and ready to fire, too. It was her that the heavy steel door had smashed into when I kicked it open.

"I take it you work here?" the male officer asked as he began to realize that I was not a burglar.

"Yes sir," I answered with both arms and two bags of trash stuck high in the air. He allowed himself a sigh of relief and both he and his partner holstered their weapons. "Would you like to come in and sit down for a moment?" I asked.

"Yes, thank you," he said. We sat at the break table in the

stock room and exchanged nervous and relieved laughter. The cop explained that for a moment he thought I was a thief with two bags of loot in my hands trying to make a break for it when I kicked the door into his partner. It was by the grace of God that he did not fire his already-drawn weapon at me in self-defense. At that range, he could not have missed. We sat there for a few minutes and I noticed that he was shaking as badly as I was. I apologized to his partner for hitting her with the door and as soon as they both had collected themselves, they said goodnight and set out to catch the real bad guy.

"Thanks for not shooting me," I said as they left, without a trace of sarcasm.

After enjoying the lagomorphic feast, Robin Westgate invited several of us over to his house after work for a game of croquet and multiple bong hits. Robin's croquet course was not just a few metal wickets stuck in the ground in a hap-hazard fashion. He had engineered an elaborate croquet park complete with outdoor lighting, water hazards, sand traps, rolling hills, doglegs, and the most finely manicured lawn in all of central Missouri. It was his pride and joy and he and his wife took great pleasure in sharing it with their friends. He came up with special ground rules that were unique to his park; regulations that still mess me up to this day whenever I play the game with people unfamiliar with Westgate Rules.

Unique is a great word to describe Robin. As the owner's son, he had to invent creative ways to get out of work. Just calling in sick would not cut it with his old man. On two occasions he called to tell the manager on duty that he would be unable to work his shift because he had shit his pants on his way to the store. No one knows for sure if he really filled his drawers or not, but for the life of me I can't figure out why anyone would lie about shitting himself to get out of work when there are a million other less humiliating excuses he could have come up with. Then again, I don't know why anyone would admit it if they really had done such a thing.

That night at Robin's, Tony and I got a little out of hand.

Okay, we got a lot out of hand. We at least had the good sense not to try to drive home and instead opted to sleep it off on the couch, or in Tony's case, the bathroom floor.

"Hey Trav, do you by chance remember what you did in the kitchen last night?" Robin asked the next morning.

"Not at all. What, was I cooking? I didn't start a fire or anything did I?"

"You pissed in my dishwasher. You actually opened the door and pissed all over the dishes my wife had just washed."

"Oh, man. I am so sorry. I've been known to sort of sleep-piss sometimes when I'm really wasted. Is Angie mad?" Of course she would be mad. Why wouldn't she be mad? I was sure she'd never let me come back to their house again. So long croquet park.

"That's the best part. She's not mad at all. She was glad that you at least picked a place to go that had a drain. She just added some more soap and re-ran the load after I told her about it. She was still laughing about it when she came back to bed."

"I'll never be able to look her in the eye again."

"Don't sweat it. It's Tony she's mad at."

"Why, what'd he do?" I wasn't sure I wanted to hear his answer.

"Well, he's still passed out in the bathroom downstairs if you want to see for yourself."

Morbid curiosity led me into the basement where I immediately sensed what Robin was referring to. The smell of vomit permeated the air. I cautiously peeked into the bathroom. It was a hell of a sight, probably better suited for the scrutiny of a crime scene investigator, not a guy with a hangover. Judging by the direction of the spray pattern, Tony must have started at the sink located on the left side of the room before he eventually found the toilet on his right. The sink, the outside of the toilet, and a large portion of the tile countertop in between were covered. From across the room, I saw Tony's scrawny body sprawled out across the floor. I hollered at him to wake up, afraid to go anywhere near him. Within a few moments he sat up and began to take note of his surroundings. I could see that Tony was shaken by what he saw. He asked, "What the fuck happened in here?"

What happened was that Tony received a loud and clear wake-up call to get his life in order. A few days later, he checked himself into a treatment facility for alcohol addiction and has not had a single drink for almost eighteen years now. Eventually, he went on to earn a doctoral degree and is a currently a professor at a major university. My wake-up call would have to wait. I still had beer to drink, a shower full of feces, and an asshole of a landlord to deal with.

When the landlord received the invoice for the city's services, he told me and Derek that we could either pay the bill in full or vacate the premises. "You've got one week." Well a week was more than enough time for Derek to find a new place to live, but I had no money, no prospective roommates, and no leads on an affordable place to move in to. One week later, as I sat on the couch watching cartoons, the landlord walked in without even knocking. "What the hell are you still doing here?" he asked.

"Watching Bugs Bunny. What the hell are *you* doing here?"

"I came to clean out the apartment. I told you to pay up or get out. You didn't pay, so you need to get the hell out."

"An eviction takes thirty days. The way I see it is that I've got three more weeks."

"You've got till the end of the day." He was a hulking Neanderthal, and I knew not to push my luck. I also knew that I had nowhere else to go. Reluctantly, I packed up my meager belongings and moved into a rented storage unit for the next few days until I decided to make some drastic life changes. The first decision I made was to withdraw from the university. My heart just wasn't into it, and besides, it's hard to study when you're homeless.

The Westgate Dudes could see that I was nearing rock-bottom when we attended a costume party days before I loaded up my truck and headed to northern Iowa to live for a while with my dad and Susan where they had recently relocated.

At the Halloween party, I masqueraded as a doctor. My white lab coat and apron were splattered with real blood from the meat department of the grocery store. Tony was Bob Marley complete with dreadlocks, black face make-up, and a fat bag of dope. Buddha was dressed as a homeless man wearing filthy, stained clothes. He had a blacked-out tooth and carried a hand-lettered cardboard sign that read "Homeless and thirsty. Wouldn't work if you put a gun to my head. Need money for beer. God bless." Ted went as Captain Jean-Luc Picard from Star Trek, but when his bald cap loosened, it wrinkled and looked like a shriveled-up testicle so we took to calling him Jean-Puke. Throughout the evening, I "prescribed" medications for my fellow party-goers.

"Nurse Marley, this man needs a bong-hit," I would say. "Nurse Buddha, give this man a shot of nitrous oxide, STAT!" "Jean-Puke, hurry up with those mushrooms." That night I smoked dope, tripped 'shrooms, inhaled laughing gas, and drank half a bottle of Jagermeister. By the end of the evening I was standing on the balcony of some poor girl's apartment yelling "Fuck you Mizzou! Fuck you world!" at the top of my lungs. I was the exact opposite of Leo Dicaprio standing on the stern of the Titanic. I was a college drop-out living in a storage shed who in addition to recently letting the girl of his dreams slip away, had failed at becoming a Marine, been kicked off the baseball team, couldn't keep a struggling fraternity going, and could barely recall how to play the trombone anymore. If someone at the party had been playing "The Limbo" on the stereo, I think I could have finally provided the answer to "How low can you go?" once and for all.

All it takes to start getting your head screwed on straight is to live on a hog farm in northern Iowa during the frigid winter months with your dad, his wife (who used to be your babysitter), and your two-year-old and three-year-old half-siblings while knowing absolutely no one in the area and only being able to find work in a factory that threads washers onto bolts for eight hours a day, every day, and to have no access to drugs stronger than cough medicine and then having a huge, drunken fight with your father on the night you arrive at his house after you had already become convinced that life couldn't get any worse--a fight that will lead to you not speaking to your father for the entire three months that you live in his basement and will strain your relationship for years to come. Really. That's all it takes. Although I wouldn't recommend it to anyone.

After a few months living in exile, I decided it was time to get my life in order and return to Columbia. I called the owner of Westgate Foods and asked for my old job back. I slept on Tony and Ted's couch for a few days until I found a cheap apartment to rent with the few dollars I managed to save while working in the fastener factory. It was spring, and life began anew as it always does when the air warms and the days grow longer. I felt invigorated and before long was feeling more like the positive, happy person I used to be before my downward spiral began. Not long after I got back into town, I was happy to get a phone call from Crash Phillips. That one phone call changed my life.

The story is picked up at this point in How I Love Your Mother:

"Hey Naughty," Crash said, "I ran into somebody the other day at a party back home that asked about you."

"Oh, really? Who was it?" I expected it to be Dave, or Wes, or Rosie.

"Bethany Lemon. She asked if I had heard from you lately. I told her that you had just moved back to Columbia and she said to tell you 'hi.'"

"Huh. Did she say anything about me?"

"No, but if you want I can pass her a note in study hall."

"Smart ass."

"If you want to get in touch with her, I can get her number from Cliff's little sister Kim. She and I were in a class together last semester. I think she and Bethany lived together a while back." Crash had just moved to Columbia and I was glad he was living close by again, but I was much more excited that Bethany had asked about me.

"Yeah, get her number. That would be great. Thanks, man."

I had the number the next day. I dialed the phone, not exactly sure what I was going to say if she answered.

"Hello?" a familiar, sweet voice answered after the second ring.

"Is this Bethany?" I asked, nearly choking to death with nervous excitement.

She said yes.

"Hey, it's Travis Naughton. How are you?"

"I'm good, how are you?" I could hear that she was happy to hear from me.

"I'm good. Andy Phillips called me and said he ran into you the other day and well…he told me 'hi' from you, so I wanted to call you and say 'hi' back." I cringed as the awkward words tumbled from my mouth.

"Hi," she said, and I could hear the smile on her face.

"Would you want to get together sometime to hang out or something?" I said while trying not to sound too anxious or desperate.

She said yes.

It was decided that I would come by to take her out the next evening, on a Saturday night. Sometime toward the end of the conversation, it occurred to me that she was home alone talking to me on a Friday night. "What are you doing right now?" I tentatively asked.

"Talking to you."

"Would it be alright if I came by right now?" I was pushing my luck, but I couldn't help myself.

She said yes.

I arrived a little while later with flowers and a bottle of wine. When she opened the door and I saw that tall, beautiful girl with the warm smile, all of my nervous energy was displaced by a sense that I was finally where I belonged. Bethany invited me in and we sat beside each other on the couch, the way we first had years earlier at Cliff's. In no time, we found ourselves entwined in a loving embrace that has not ended in all the years since.

There was one slight problem however. Bethany, Charla, and Tom all still lived together. Char was out of town that night visiting her new boyfriend Doug, who would later become her husband, and Tom was staying at his parent's house on the east coast somewhere for the summer. The way I saw it, I had three months to make Bethany forget she ever knew anybody named Tom. Over the course of the summer, we fell deeply in love and I knew that when Tom came back to town, he would have to graciously bow out of the picture and move out of the two bedroom apartment. But when I mentioned this to Bethany, she said that Tom's name was on the lease, too, and if he didn't want to move out, then she wouldn't force him.

"I don't understand," I said. "There are only two beds for your sister, you, and Tom to sleep in. Plus, I plan on sleeping over as often as possible. (My new apartment was almost as bad as the Fruit Fly House.) So how exactly is that going to work?"

"Well, Tom and I both paid for the bed, so I couldn't make him sleep on the couch."

"Yes you could. You and I aren't going to sleep on the couch while your ex-boyfriend is sleeping in your bed in the next room."

"That's how we were living by the end of the last semester. He even brought his new girlfriend over sometimes."

"And you didn't think that was weird?"

"Not really."

"Well I think it's really freaking weird. I could never live like that. Listen, I love you and if you really love me, you'll make him move out."

"Well, he has as much of a right to live here as I do. The best I can do is to ask him if he will sleep on the couch, but I won't make him leave."

"Well, *I'll* make him leave."

"No you won't. Please don't say anything to him. He's a good guy and I know it will all work out fine."

"Don't you think it'll be a little awkward having him around while we're having sex in his bed?"

"I don't want to talk about it anymore. We'll just deal with it when he gets back."

At the time, I was really upset about her apparent insensitivity to my insecurities. But after a while, I realized that Bethany's refusal to throw a perfectly nice person out on the street simply because she wasn't in love with him anymore was one of the qualities that best demonstrated her sense of compassion and her capacity to put other people's well-being before her own. I also realized that after the way I had unceremoniously blown her off a few years earlier, I had no right to demand anything from her. Nevertheless, I really couldn't bear the thought of sharing an apartment with my girlfriend's ex.

When Tom arrived just before the fall semester was set to

begin, Bethany told him that she and I were in love. To my great relief, he did choose to bow-out graciously and agreed to move out immediately. I almost felt a little sorry for the poor bastard, but the possessive jerk in me didn't trust him for one second around my new girlfriend, so I made sure to be at the apartment when he came to get his things. I sat on the couch and watched wordlessly as he gathered up his belongings and told Bethany goodbye. He and I exchanged nods of acknowledgment and a forced handshake and never crossed paths again. I had been hoping for a lavish changing of the guard type ceremony with a marching band or the minting of a commemorative coin, but settled for his quiet and hasty departure. The potential crisis of the relationship-killing living arrangement was averted and Bethany and I settled into a healthy, loving life together that has endured through situations far more awkward and uncomfortable than meeting her live-in ex-boyfriend.

From time to time I allow myself a moment to think about how far I've come since the day I first met Bethany. Since that fateful evening, I dropped out of college, got evicted, cheated death once or twice, somehow managed to win back the love of my life, got married, finished my degree, became a parent, finally made it to Mexico with Rosie Crane, held a memorial service for a pygmy goat, and started writing this book. I hate to imagine what my life would have been like had I not met Bethany. (Thank you Cliff.) I might never have finished school. I might have been stuck in a filthy grocery store frying chickens for the rest of my life. I might not have had kids (human or goat). I might not have lived past the age of 25. Thank goodness that when I asked if I could come over to her apartment that night she said yes.

And when I asked her to forgive me for breaking her heart: she said yes.

And when I asked her to marry me: she said yes.

And when I asked her if she'll still love me when I'm old and fat: she said no, because she won't let me get fat.

And when I said that I don't deserve someone as wonderful and loving as her: she said yes I do.

Who knows how or why life turns out the way it does? All I do know is that I am without a doubt the luckiest guy in the world. As Crash Phillips says regarding how unbelievably fortunate a loser like me is to have a woman like Bethany for a wife, "Naughty, you really out-kicked your coverage on that one. If you ever do anything to blow that field position, I'll kick your ass."

Get in line, Crash. Get in line.

Like a Rock

I asked Dr. Naughton about making the transition from being a hard-core party boy to a responsible family man. "I don't know how responsible I am. I haven't held a steady job since Dubya was in office." He used a chapter from Reason for Leaving *titled* Like a Rock *about his inability to swim and his seemingly incompatible love of floating on a river to illustrate his metamorphosis:*

I can only recall taking three swim lessons as a kid. My mom enrolled me in a class for beginners at the old Hannibal YMCA when I was a very self-conscious third grader. When I arrived for the first session, I was mortified to see that all of the other students were pre-schoolers (half of them still in diapers). After one session, I refused to go back. My other two "lessons" consisted of Mom throwing me into the Pacific Ocean while we were on our great driving vacation out west and later into the La Plata City Lake. Her one and only instruction: "Hold your breath." Her methods did not prove effective. I was so traumatized by her sink or swim approach that I never accompanied her to another body of water again. But as long as Mom wasn't around to try to drown me, I loved being in a boat on one of my home state's many rivers. I guess there's a little bit of Huck Finn in every boy from Hannibal.

My dad and his wife moved to Steelville, Missouri, the float trip capital of the Missouri, just after I graduated from Hannibal High School. Dad was hired as the principal of the small town's high school, and as my freshman year of college drew to a close, he suggested I apply for a summer job at one of the canoe outfitters on the Upper Meramec River. The rustic cabin that he and Susan were renting was within walking distance of a campground and canoe rental place called The Canoe Company, so Dad arranged an interview with the owner of the business, a man named Will "Paulie" Paulson. The interview was a formality really, for I soon found out that a heartbeat and a valid driver's license were all the qualifications the job actually required.

I arrived for my first day of work excited about the prospect of working outdoors and reaping the fringe benefits of working in a natural setting rife with bikini-clad college girls floating by all day long in the slow-moving current of the river. The job was not all glamour though. On my first day, I was assigned to tear down an old wooden fence with another fellow named Earl. I was eager to prove my worth to the burly, labor-hardened Earl and hastily began to tear apart the rotted fence without paying the slightest attention to any potential hazards like, say an old board lying on the ground with two inches of a rusty nail protruding from it. I stepped directly onto the spike which sunk all the way into my foot, stopping only when the sole of my shoe met the wooden plank. I immediately fell to the ground and cried out in agony, which did nothing to impress Earl, but definitely got his attention. I was literally nailed to the six foot long board and could not stand or crawl to the truck to go to the doctor's office in town, so Earl was forced to help me extract the nail by slowly pulling on the board until my punctured foot was free. The pain from that maneuver almost caused me to black out and I could see that even Earl was queasy from witnessing the gruesome scene. He drove me straight to the doctor where I got a tetanus shot and an excuse to skip work for the next day or so.

When I returned to active duty a couple days later, I was told to take my first trailer load of canoes up the river to our put-in spot. New to the area, anyone would have understood if I would have gotten lost along the five mile drive to the riverside location we used to launch boats from. They were perplexed, however, when I took a wrong turn while trying to find my way out of the campground and wound up at a dead-end with two canoe trailers hooked up to my truck and no place to turn around. I struggled for about a half hour to get pointed in the right direction but I only succeeded in getting the truck hopelessly stuck in some mud with two jack-knifed trailers blocking the seldom used gravel road. I radioed headquarters for assistance and spent the next half-hour watching a frustrated Earl struggle to free the truck. He smashed the front bumper into a tree and a canoe fell off one of the trailers before he gave up and fetched the tractor to pull me out. First, he had to disconnect the trailers and turn them around by hand. Then he hooked a tow chain to the dented bumper of the truck and yanked it out of the deep mud. That evening, Paulie dubbed me "Wrong Way"- the name I still use to this day when I call him to book reservations for float trips and campouts with my friends. Come to think of it, I doubt he even knows my real name. Maybe it's better that way.

Weekdays at the campground were spent mowing and trimming weeds, collecting garbage, and preparing for the onslaught of the weekend visitors. Other than Earl, I was the oldest member of our crew of workers, so when it came time to divi-up the chores, I cherry-picked the ones that suited me. On a typical weekday, I could be found cutting the grass while on our company's only riding lawn mower. I made the high school kids trim weeds and use the push mowers while I rode in relative luxury on the 17 horsepower Allis-Chalmers lawn tractor. Each day at 8:00am, I would add a twelve-pack of Stag beer and a bag of ice to my employee tab, dump each into my Coleman cooler, and disappear to the far reaches of the campground until lunchtime. I came back to the general store only to grab a quick bite to eat and refill "Alice's" gas tank and then I was off again. No one would hear from me again until five o' clock.

By the time I had arrived in Steelville, my dad and Susan had already begun to move out after he accepted a job in another school district. This development left me the old cabin to myself for most of the summer. Living on my own, working at a place that catered to drunken college girls, and having the ability to deduct my beer tab from my weekly paycheck was a volatile combination to say the very least. At the first opportunity, I summoned my old high school buddies to join me for a weekend float trip. Rosie Crane, Dave Richards, Wes Douglass, and Chris Stevens all joined me for a weekend of mayhem.

At the last minute, my dad informed me that he would be

stopping by that weekend to gather a few of the things he had left behind in the move. I warned him that my obnoxious friends would be on hand, and he surprised me when he volunteered to entertain them while I worked all day Saturday before taking a day off to float the river with the guys on Sunday. I think he had more fun with them that weekend than I did. He drove them down to the river to drink beer in the hot summer sun while watching bikini-clad sorority girls float by in their canoes. By noon, Rosie had already puked in the river, but to his credit, (or by sheer dumb luck,) he at least had had the sense to face downstream. He was helped to the truck by Wes and Chris where he collapsed against the side of the little Mazda, putting a dent the size of his fat head in the driver's door. It took the additional help of Dave and Dad to hoist Rosie's 300+ pounds into the bed of the truck just to get him back to the house. By the time they returned to the cabin, a combative Rosie refused to get out of the truck and insisted that everyone just leave him there to "sleep it off." The rest of the crew proceeded indoors and waited for me to come home from work. By the time I got there, Rosie was as red as a boiled lobster after cooking in the sun all day. Undeterred, he woke up as the sun was setting and popped open a lukewarm Natural Light. "Hey Butch!" he slurred. "Sorry 'bout your truck."

"Tell it to my wife," my dad told him. "It's hers."

"I'm sure it'll all buff out in the morning," Rosie said. That's exactly the same thing he told his own father after he wrecked his Plymouth Horizon *[the car Rosie and Travis drove to Las Vegas and back]* while road-tripping on a dimly lit blacktop with Wes one night. (Mr. Crane gave Rosie only two rules to follow when he went off to college: "Keep the car shiny side up and between the fenceposts, and don't bring home any Asian women." Rosie broke both commandments before Christmas break.)

The next day, we floated the river in an inflatable raft that was big enough to accommodate the five of us plus two 48-quart coolers full of beer and jello-shots. What normally should have been a six hour float turned into nearly double that by the time our partially deflated, vomit-filled boat finally reached the take-out point. I apologized to my co-workers for the mess we left them, but they were used to such disasters. So was I. The natural beauty of the Ozark Scenic Waterways is often overshadowed by the carnage brought forth by marauding gangs of frat boys and sorority girls who use the river to blow off steam after a long school year. The Upper Meramec River is no place to take your children for a peaceful float on weekends in the summer. Weekdays are the best time to float (especially if you have kids) if you have a desire to experience the tranquility of one of the most visually appealing places in Missouri. Natural springs, limestone caves, crystal clear water, excellent fishing, and abundant wildlife are a few of the attractions of the river--when college students aren't defiling it for their own amusement.

When that summer in Steelville came to an end, I left The Canoe Company with a heavy heart. I loved working there. It was the first and only job I have ever had where I truly looked forward to going into work every day. The characters I met while living there were part of the attraction. We had old school buses that we used to ferry floaters up the river to the put-in and two of those drivers were among the most interesting people I've ever met. The first, named Lon, was a grizzled-old drunk who had lost a leg years earlier while straddling two moving cars driving down the middle Main Street in Steelville. He kept a cooler of Stag under the driver's seat of his bus and routinely emptied it before his shift ended at noon. At parties on the deck at the general store, he was known to remove his prosthetic leg, fill it from the keg, and pass it around for campers to drink from. One morning on his way to work, he purposely struck and killed a fawn that was crossing the road--destroying the grill and headlight of his brand new Ford truck. When asked to explain why he was late to work, he simply handed Paulie an aluminum pan of freshly shredded venison and said, "I stopped to grab us some lunch."

The other driver who worked for us had only three fingers on his left hand. Steelville is a major timber-producing region and he had grown up in a logging family. One day, when Jimmy and his sister were young, they were playing near their father's chopping block out behind their house. Jimmy had placed his hand on the old stump while his sister was trying to heft their dad's heavy axe. "You'd better move your hand or I'll chop it off," the little girl threatened.

No sooner than Jimmy said, "You wouldn't dare," did he lose his pinkie and ring fingers on his left hand. He retold the story with such glee that you'd swear he was glad his sister had done it.

When the time came to leave for Columbia, I told Paulie I'd be back next summer if he'd have me. He said he would and that he may even make me the manager. By the next spring I had convinced Paulie to let Dave Richard's work there, too, and together we arrived in time for the Memorial Day weekend crush of visitors. It was then that Paulie introduced me to a guy named Mick, who he had hired to manage the campground. I felt a little betrayed, but quickly got over it when I realized that I would have no additional responsibilities to hinder my good time.

Dave and I lived in a small pull-behind camper that Paulie had set up just for us that summer. We didn't have a TV, but we did have a kiddie pool and a make-shift deck made out of recycled shipping pallets. On our days off, we sat in the pool while drinking beers and laughing at the high school kids who had to trim weeds around our campsite. To keep me happy after giving the manager job to someone else, Paulie let me make a few extra bucks by working as the weekend, overnight security guard on the campground. This task entailed driving the company van from campsite to campsite, telling rowdy visitors to quiet down and ensuring that none of them tore anything up. Usually, campers could easily buy themselves more time before I shut down their parties by doing nothing more than plying me with shots of alcohol. After one particularly late and rowdy evening, I was awakened for work the next morning by a co-worker who after failing to find me in my trailer, discovered me passed out behind the wheel of the "security" van.

In the span of one week, the good times at The Canoe Company came grinding to a halt. While patrolling the campground with Dave one evening, floating around from party to party and getting hammered, we ran out of beer. Some campers suggested making a beer run to town, but I nixed the idea citing my marching orders to not allow anyone off the grounds after midnight (due to the high likelihood that anyone leaving at that hour would be drunk.) Dave implored me to look the other way, but I stood my ground and we eventually got into a full-out fistfight while driving the van back to our camper. Dave packed up his things and left in a cloud of dust to go back to his parents' house in Arkansas, swearing that our friendship was over. It was indeed a long time before we spoke again, but it wouldn't be until his mental breakdown years later that our friendship officially ended. The next day, I was forced to explain to Paulie why Dave quit. He took the news in stride and laughed it off by singing a line from Billy Ray Cyrus's "Achy-Breaky Heart" that said, "You can tell my ma, I moved to Arkansas, but I just don't think she'd understand."

Paulie and his wife were due to go on a short vacation later that week, leaving the inmates to run the asylum. One day, I had just returned from upriver after depositing a group of floaters by the riverside. While at the boat launch that morning, a woman actually asked me, "Which way do we go?" I was in an ornery mood and suggested she throw a leaf in the water and follow it. By the time I got back to the campground, I had had my fill of idiots for the day and was looking forward to lunch. Mick's voice came over the radio. "Hey Travis, I need you to take this busload of floaters upriver for me. You copy?"

"Negative, Boss. I see you're already behind the wheel and I'm on my lunch break. Why don't you just take 'em? Over."

"No, you're gonna do it. Now get off that radio and get your butt on this bus."

"Uh, I didn't copy that, Boss. Radio's breakin' up. I'll talk to you when you get back. I'm out."
"If you don't drive this bus you're fired!"

"Have a nice drive, Boss." The kid that was riding with me and I had a good chuckle over the exchange while we ate our lunch at the general store. We were just finishing our sandwiches when Mick walked in after his trip upriver.

"What the hell are you still doing here? I fired you, remember?"

"Yeah, sure you did."

"Do I need to call the sheriff? I said you're fired now pack up your shit and get out!" Mick was completely serious. To make matters worse, my firing was also an eviction since I lived on the campground in a company-owned trailer. Also, Paulie would not be back for days, giving Mick ample time to have me arrested for trespassing if I refused to vacate the premises. Just like that, the best job I ever had was over. I moved back to Columbia and started working at Westgate Foods, where I had almost as much fun, only without the constant presence of an endless line of bikinis floating by every day.

I've gone back to The Canoe Company as a paying customer a few times since that summer and am happy to have been welcomed back by Paulie with open arms. But some things have changed over the years--not necessarily at the campground, although the place has evolved a lot and become a top-notch RV park. The real changes took place within me.

I finally realized once and for all that being a drunken idiot was not a sustainable lifestyle choice when Bethany was seven months pregnant with Alex. Wes Douglass stopped by the house one day and suggested that we go for a little road trip on the gravel roads near my home along the banks of the Missouri River. Never one to turn down an opportunity to climb into an old truck and have a few beers with an old friend, I readily agreed. Eighteen beers later, Wes and I finally returned home, one hour late for the dinner I was supposed to cook for my pregnant wife and my mother. I parked the truck, opened the door, and fell flat on my face- too drunk to stand. I looked up and saw my mom manning the barbeque grill and Bethany holding a tray of pork steaks while simultaneously slicing me to shreds with the daggers that were her eyes. We ate our dinner in an uncomfortable silence and the next day I decided to announce my decision to quit drinking. Everyone supported the idea with the possible exception of Crash Phillips, who was at that time the "manager" of our slow-pitch softball team. It bothered him that I was the only one not drinking beer in the parking lot following our blowout losses, so he declined to invite me to return to the team the following season. His justification: "Quitters never win." (This coming from a guy who thinks drinking and driving should be taught in Driver's Ed classes, so we'd all be better at it.) Getting kicked off the high school baseball team was bad enough, but who gets booted off a slow-pitch softball team?

I never touched a single drop of alcohol for the next two and a half years. During that time I learned to be a functioning adult, a good husband, and a pretty damn-good father. I finally realized that I didn't need to drink a case of beer to impress my friends or to cope with life's disappointments. I figured out that life is actually pretty livable sober. After doing a great deal of reflecting over the course of my hiatus from drinking, I decided I would try what many other responsible adults had been doing successfully for years; drinking in moderation. This had been a foreign concept to me ever since that fateful afternoon at Dave's. Nevertheless, I thought I'd see if I could make it work. And it has worked--for me. My new motto is "Everything in Moderation," an improvement from "Everything to Excess." I realize it is not common for self-admitted alcoholics to find a middle way after so many years of out of control drinking. There will be those people who claim that either I was never an alcoholic to begin with, or that I am simply in denial now. Either may be true. But if I've learned anything in my thirty-eight years, it is that people don't always conform to nice, easy to label categories.

It pains me to admit it, and I shudder to use this word, but I think I've *matured*. Well, maybe not much, but just enough. When it comes to drinking beer these days, I go for quality over quantity. I like to drink thick, tasty microbrews (another motto is: "If I can't chew it, I won't drink it") and I usually limit myself to just two or three drinks in a given evening. I never, ever drink and drive and only on the occasional New Year's Eve or St. Patty's Day do I allow myself to become intoxicated. My liver and my family are very happy with this new and improved lifestyle. I have no regrets though. I am a better man for having experienced and survived the trials and tribulations of my youth and I can honestly say that I am perfectly pleased with the man I am today. Do I miss those carefree days of wanton self-destruction? Well, don't we all miss being young and stupid every now and then? Sure. But do I miss urinating all over myself while passed out drunk in my mother's recliner? ("Son, I love you, but I think you pissed in my chair.") No, I do not.

Several years ago, Wes and his wife Lynn, Rosie Crane, and Bethany and I went on a weekend float trip and campout at The Canoe Company. As it turns out, the years that I abstained from drinking and the period of personal growth that I underwent served to alter my idea of "fun on the river." Oh, I tried to act like my old obnoxious self, at times even hollering "show us your tits" to cute college girls who floated by our raft. But it felt forced and although several of them were kind enough to honor my request, I was left feeling strangely unsatisfied afterward. I haven't been back to Steelville since.

It is no small miracle that I survived to adulthood. In addition to spending much of my youth inebriated, I spent a lot of it around large bodies of water. Most of the credit for my survival should go to Crash Phillips, who once observed, "Naughty, you swim like a rock." Crash has actually saved my life three times: Once at a swimming area at Mark Twain Lake when I tried to swim out to the ropes with my buddies and failed miserably—almost tragically, and again during a float trip on the Salt River near his grandparents' farm when Chris Stevens flipped my canoe over immediately after I told him, "I can't swim so please don't flip my canoe over." The third time was when he helped me reconnect with Bethany.

I just don't have the desire to get hopped up and make bad choices like I used to. My priorities have changed since those reckless days. Having kids will do that to you I suppose. The next time I go to Steelville, I plan to take my family on a quiet, weekday float trip to enjoy the abundance of beauty that the Ozarks provide. I will be wearing my life vest, as will the kids. The cooler will be full of water and juice boxes instead of beer, and this time when I get out of the boat, it will be to show my boys a cave or some animal tracks--not to try to convince a raft full of drunken women to show me their boobs. (Of course I wouldn't try to stop them if they got the idea to do so all on their own. That would be just plain rude of me. I mean I have to set a good example for my kids.)

Dr. Cactus Fingers and the Prostate Exam

Travis and Bethany Naughton became parents for the first time on October 3, 2000 when they welcomed a ten pound baby boy named Alexander into the world. The infant was born healthy, but only after a scary incident during childbirth. From his memoir:

Bethany's labor had been progressing well, but after an extended period of pushing, there was still no baby. I was doing my best to comfort my wife, but her screams were drowning out my words of encouragement. Suddenly, I saw a look of total panic on a nurse's face. I knew something was terribly wrong. The doctor told us that the baby's heart rate had dropped dramatically and that they would have to get him out immediately. An emergency C-section was not an option since the baby had passed into the birth canal where he was stuck due to his large size. In typical Naughton fashion, my son decided to do things the hard way. He literally had to be torn away from his mother. It was not pretty. The doc told my beloved, "Bethany, I'm going to have to get this baby out right now. I'm sorry sweetie, but this is going to hurt." I'll be haunted by her screams for the rest of my life.

Mother and child survived and recovered quickly, and despite nearly passing out at the sight of so much blood, Papa did, too. When the newborn was cleaned up and handed to his exhausted mother for the first time, Travis told his wife that he never wanted her to endure such an ordeal again. "Next time, let's just adopt a little girl from China." For the next two years, life was good for the family of three. Travis got hired as the sales manager at a local automobile auction while Bethany resumed her career in health care. Happy, but feeling that there was something missing in their lives, the couple decided to have another baby.

They tried diligently for over two years to conceive a second child, but to no avail. On his blog, Travis explained how he was able to set aside his vow to never put his wife through the trauma of childbirth again and the consequences of breaking his promise:

Oh, but how quickly the thought of having sex almost daily under the guise of making a baby can make a man forsake such promises. I had more sex in those two years than I imagine I will for the rest of my life combined. Other than waking with a smile on my face pretty much every morning, our efforts were producing no results. So, Bethany and her "lady doctor" decided that we needed to submit to some fertility testing. Although I enjoyed the frequent sex, I must admit I was somewhat relieved to be told to abstain for a few days to build up my sperm count. After having sex a few hundred times with the only goal being to impregnate one's wife, the task becomes very goal-oriented and businesslike. Basically, the deed becomes more work than fun, which in and of itself probably contributed significantly to our lack of success. I for one am allergic to work, which is why I write.

I was told that I would need to submit a sperm sample to measure my little swimmers' population and motility. I wasn't thrilled with the idea of going to a clinic and performing on demand. Not to worry, said the doctor. As long as I could get a fresh sample to the lab within a half-hour, then I could make my submission from the comfort of home, and Bethany could take it to the lab on her way to work. That, I could live with. The next morning as my wife left for work, I gave her a kiss on the cheek, handed her a little brown paper bag that did NOT contain a sandwich and chips, and wished her a good day. The look she gave me was one of pity, disgust, and love. That afternoon, the lab called with the results. The few sperm that there were swam about as well as I did; which was not well at all. The doctor suggested that I submit a fresher sample, which meant that I needed to go to the lab to donate. But first, just to rule out any physical problems, he wanted to give my business-end a thorough inspection commonly known as a *prostate exam*.

My urologist called it a "physical examination" but by "physical examination" I could only assume that he really meant "torture session." Trust me, the prisoners at Abu Ghraib would gladly take electric shocks over what Dr. Prickly Pear Cactus Fingers did to me that day. In case aren't familiar with how to check a man's prostate health; a specially trained CIA operative with a passion for inflicting immeasurable amounts of pain and humiliation upon his fellow man slaps on a latex glove, dabs a whisper of "lubricant" on his finger, and... let's just say that he ignores the "EXIT ONLY" sign clearly posted on the hapless victim's posterior. Did I mention that Dr. Wire Brush Fingers was 6'6" tall with hands the size of catcher's mitts? To make matters much, much worse, I had to confess to Dr. Tree Trunk Fingers that the reason I was both shrieking and crying was because the ten tacos I had for dinner the previous night had spent the better part of the morning evacuating my body through the same EXIT ONLY that he had just driven his pine cone of an index finger into. Talk about "WRONG WAY- DO NOT ENTER!" To say that the affected area was tender would be a gross understatement. And I do mean gross. Here's a tip: hemorrhoids and hot sauce do not a good combination make, especially when a sadist with pineapples for fingers is elbow deep in your rectum.

Judging by the "Sorry about that," that he mumbled as I lay curled up in the fetal position upon the examination table while whimpering like a beaten puppy, I guessed the good doctor must have felt a little sympathy for me. After he was done, he handed me a tissue with which I dabbed the tears from my eyes, and I got dressed. He said that the Kleenex was actually for wiping the excess lubricant trickling from my sphincter. "Oops," was all I could say as I stared at the floor unwilling or perhaps unable to look him in the eye. I felt so violated that I wondered if asking if a rape kit was included in the price of the examination would be out of line. Dr. Footlong Frankenfurter Fingers told me that I was physically fine, (although I am certain that it will take years for my emotional scars to heal.) The final insult: he wanted me to submit another sperm sample. I couldn't imagine how I'd ever manage to get-it-up again.

You wouldn't think that I could have been more humbled and humiliated than I had been by Dr. Cheese Grater Fingers. You would be wrong. Bear in mind that by this time I had become a stay-at-home dad. We didn't have a babysitter to watch our son while I needed to be at the lab, so Bethany had to duck out of work and wait with Alex in the car while I went inside to do my duty. I wondered to myself, how many other dads make their children wait in the car while they go into a medical clinic to fill up a jar for a fertility test? *"Be back in a minute, son. Daddy has to run inside real quick to masturbate into a cup. You be a good boy."* Once inside, I rang the bell for service as if I were checking into a hotel (if only) and a friendly female lab technician came to the counter. "Can I help you?" she asked innocently. I pondered an appropriate response.

"Um, yes. I'm here for a semen analysis," I offered weakly.

"OH! Do you have it *with* you?" A loaded question if there ever was one.

"Uh, well…no. I need to do it here."

"Why? How far away do you live? Did you know you can do it at home and bring it with you?" she asked. *Please, no more questions.* I really wasn't planning on conversing this much with anyone associated with this unspeakable act.

"I live about a half hour away. My doctor says he wants… *a fresher sample.*" There were no secrets between us now. By the look on her face I could tell that the tech fully understood the situation. I couldn't bring a sample in with me because of the time it would take to get it to the lab. And as an added bonus, the lab wasn't a sperm clinic and therefore had no designated private area in which to complete the task at hand (pun intended) for maintaining some tiny portion of my dignity.

"Where do you want to do it?" she asked. *Again with the questions.* I was confused and concerned that she was asking *me* this. *I'm not the one that works here lady.*

"An exam room?" I timidly suggested.

"Oh, okay. Follow me." I trailed behind the tech through the labyrinth of the laboratory, convinced that I would never be able to find my way out without her help. "Wait here," she said. As I stood there in the hallway, I could hear whispers coming from around the corner. I imagined the conversation to sound something like this: "Betty, there is a gentleman here who needs to use a room to submit a sperm sample."

"Dear God! *Here?* Oh, he must be mortified."

"I'm sure he is. Although he seems remarkably calm. But I *am* deeply embarrassed for him. Do you think he can he use an exam room?"

"Sure, let's go find him one." Suddenly I was being led to a room by *two* women who knew exactly what I would be doing once the door was closed.

"Oh my. This room is freezing," Betty said. "I hope you are warm-natured." There was no escaping the fact that she was already picturing me in the frigid exam room, pants around my ankles with one cold, trembling hand trying to steady a specimen cup while the other hand...

"This will be fine," I assured her. She smiled unnaturally while the first woman offered me a sterile cup.

"Just come find me when you're finished and hand this back to me." *Great, I get to wander around this maze with THIS in my hand while looking for a woman to give it to.*

I'll spare you the details of what transpired next, but to paint a mental picture of the ambiance I was "enjoying," just imagine this ordeal taking place in an OB-GYN exam room with all of its wonderful pictures of fetuses, placentas, and what-not plastered all over the walls, and all the while I could hear the two ladies talking to each other outside my door. Not exactly a "get you in the mood" type of situation if you know what I mean. Then my male ego and insecurities kicked in. I thought, when I walk out this door, these women will know **exactly** how long this activity took to complete. How long *should* it last under these circumstances? If it lasts too long, they may think something is wrong and come knocking on the door at a most inopportune time. If it doesn't last long enough, they may think that I'm a little quick on the draw, or worse--that the little pervert actually *enjoyed* doing it in their office! "Maybe that's how he gets his kicks," Betty would say. Such thoughts did nothing to help ease the tension.

Eventually the ladies took their conversation down the hall and out of earshot and I was able to complete my mission. I located the first technician in a very loud room full of equipment at the far end of the corridor. She didn't see me come in so I blurted out, "All done!" She jumped like a cartoon cat being scared out of its skin by a dog.

"Oh my goodness! You surprised me." *With my speed? Duration? Delivery?*

"Sorry about that. Anyway, I guess I need to pay for the tests. Is there a receptionist?"

"Not today. You can pay me." I handed her the cup and she handed me a pen so I could write the check. We both knew what had been in that very hand just moments earlier. As I filled out the check, a spinning centrifuge filled with god-knows-what began to vibrate with such force that it rattled a collection of vials filled with more god-knows-what right off of a table which sent them crashing to the floor all around me. I was relieved that *my* sample was not among those lost in the disaster. "Don't touch it!" she warned. "It's glass." *Yeah, the glass is what I was afraid might come into contact with my skin.*

"Ok, you're all done," she said when I handed her the check. I explained that my wife would be coming by to pick up the results and I wished her a good day. I silently prayed that I would never have to see the woman again, although I was sure that one day we would bump into each other on the street and she would ask, "Hey, don't I know you from somewhere?"

The results of the second test were normal, eliminating my reproductive system as a suspect in the mystery of our inability to conceive again. According to Bethany's doctor, her plumbing was normal, too, with the help of an ovulation inducing lady-drug. Nevertheless, I have never been able to slip another one past the goalie, despite a glorious run lasting several years when no other married man on Earth had as many shots on goal as I did.

As Naughton continued to share stories about his experiences as a parent on his blog, he discovered that he was building up quite a loyal following. His writing voice began to shift from the edgy recollections of his youth to the more genial, yet equally hilarious "observations, confessions, and exasperations of being a stay-at-home dad." Readership of his blog grew swiftly and led to an offer to write a nationally syndicated newspaper column also called Stay-at-Home Writer. *Travis A. Naughton was well on his way to becoming a super-star.*

Finding Truman

Within a few months, hundreds of papers across the country picked up the column making Travis A. Naughton a household name. One particular story Naughton wrote for his column that appeared in a series of installments in the fall of 2008 solidified his celebrity and won the hearts of millions of readers across the country. This series documented the amazing journey that the Naughton's would embark upon in a quest to add another member to their family. This was the story of Finding Truman.

Four years of fertility testing and treatments plus a few thousand "hey, let's make a baby" sessions failed to add up to conceiving a second child. By October of 2006, Bethany and Travis began to accept that their dream to have another child may never be realized. Then one day, Travis reminded his wife what he had said after witnessing the ordeal that was Alex's birth. "Next time, let's adopt a little girl from China."

And so it was decided. They chose to use an adoption agency that a friend's wife worked at that specialized in international placements. They filled out dozens of forms, were fingerprinted, submitted themselves to criminal background checks, met with a social worker, and implored their friends and family to write letters of recommendation for them. By the time they completed all of these preliminary steps and were given a "log-in date" (LID) signifying that they had been officially approved to adopt a child, nearly nine months had passed. The couple was told then that the current wait time from LID to referral (being matched with a specific child) could be anywhere from twelve to eighteen months. It would be difficult to remain patient for that length of time, but what choice did they have?

As the pages of the calendar changed from month to month, so did China's estimate of wait time for adopting families. Twelve to eighteen months became eighteen to twenty-four months. Soon the Naughtons were hearing that they could expect to wait twenty-four to thirty-six months. When their agency asked the Chinese officials if families could expect the wait to continue increasing to forty-eight months or more, the answer was "Yes. It is conceivable." By that point, Travis and Bethany had already been trying to add to their family for almost six years. They decided that they could not wait an additional three or four more. *The following are several excerpts from* Finding Truman *that appeared in* Stay-at-Home Writer.

After working ourselves out of debt and saving up all the money we would need to pay for the adoption, the seemingly endless wait for a child started to wear me down and I was ready to ask the Enabler if I could spend the cash on an old hot rod instead. Having a classic car again would not make me as happy as having a beautiful baby girl, but it would be better than nothing. But The Voice of Reason had been checking the agency's website looking at the profiles of some special needs children who were available for immediate adoption. Many of these children were born with disfiguring birth defects such as cleft palates, hydrocephaly, or missing limbs. Others had congenital heart defects, cerebral palsy, or blindness. But one child, a beautiful eighteen-month-old boy, caught our attention. Born with two missing fingers and three missing toes on his left side, the toddler was otherwise in perfect health. Developmentally, he was right on track and his profile stated that he was lucky enough to be living in a foster home, instead of a miserable orphanage.

"He needs us to come save him," Bethany said. "What do you think?"

"I think we'd better snatch him up before someone else does."

We submitted our online application that evening and were informed a few days later that we were being given one week to decide for sure if we wished to adopt the little boy. We didn't need a week. We already knew in our hearts that he was our child. We told our adoption agency as much. I came home from work one day the following week and saw the light on our answering machine blinking. I pressed "PLAY" and listened as a woman's voice congratulated us on receiving our referral. Jiang Yi Zhan was ours. When we learned that he was born exactly two weeks before the day we decided to adopt a child, we knew beyond any doubt that we were meant to be his parents.

Our family had supported us throughout our struggle to have another child and they were as excited as we were when we told them about Yi Zhan. The news was especially well received by my mother, who had been diagnosed with terminal cancer just one month after we received our LID. As the wait time till referral for an infant increased, I feared that Mom would not live long enough to meet her granddaughter. Now, with the change in plans and decision to adopt a waiting child speeding up the process, there was a chance that Nonna (as she preferred to be called instead of "Grandma") would likely get to meet her new grandchild after all. At the end of October, we will fly to China to be united with our son.

Wednesday, October 29, 2008

China or Bust

Well, tomorrow is the big day. Unless you've been living under a rock, then you probably already know from reading my past few columns that Bethany and I are flying to China tomorrow to complete our adoption of the cutest little boy in the Eastern Hemisphere (Alex being the cutest in the West of course.) Tonight we will pack everything we need for the two week adventure. Bethany has made several lists to keep us organized. I don't deal with logistics very well, so she has taken that burden upon herself and done a wonderful job of keeping the process on track. Much credit also goes to our adoption agency. They have nailed down our itinerary, including our inside China travel and lodging arrangements, sightseeing tours, and official appointments to make the adoption finalized. So, what exactly have I contributed to this process you might ask? Well, does freaking out over every minor detail and writing about it count for anything? Probably not. But whenever Bethany gives me a list of things to do, somehow I manage to pull myself together long enough to complete my assigned tasks. And apparently, the only thing left on the to-do list is to pack.

When a woman is pregnant, she and her husband have nine months to wait in anticipation of the "big day." When that day comes, the mother does wonderfully and the father becomes a nervous wreck. Well, we began the adoption process over two years ago. That's two years worth of frustration, excitement, anticipation, and elation. And now the big day is finally close. (We'll meet our son on November 3rd.) And of course, the mother is handling things wonderfully while the father is a nervous wreck.

Be sure to read this column regularly while we're in China. Hopefully I can make you feel like you are right there with us, as you have demonstrated with your kind letters and show of support that you have been there with us all along. Thank you for the love you have given us throughout this process. We are blessed and humbled to have so many people who care so much about us.

The author included two or more daily updates in a single column when his entries were brief. Some newspapers even allowed him to include photos of the trip, largely as a result of overwhelming reader demand. Many publishers credit **Stay-at-Home Writer** *for helping bridge the gap between blogs and newspaper columns – creating a new hybrid "blog-in-print" format. Naughton gives all the credit to his subject matter. "People wanted to see Truman's picture. Once they saw his smiling face on my personal blog, they wrote letters to the editor demanding that photos be included in my column. I mean, have you seen that kid's picture? Who the hell could say no to that face?"*

Friday, October 31, 2008

Happy Halloween--from China!

Well, we made it. After leaving our house at 7:00 am, we checked into our hotel room in Beijing at 11:00 pm local time (10:00am Central Time Zone). Yes, that means we travelled for twenty-seven straight hours. We went from Hartsburg, Missouri to Kansas City to Minneapolis, to Tokyo, to Beijing. No problems whatsoever, although I was pulled out of the boarding line in Tokyo and was subjected to a thorough search of my person and possessions. (Thankfully the Japanese are a modest people--they stopped just shy of a strip search.) And Bethany will have to admit, that at least for the first day of our epic voyage, I have been a joy to travel with. No meltdowns or panic attacks whatsoever. I'm pretty proud of me right about now.

That's all I can manage to type for now. I haven't slept in about 30 hours or so. I think I may be hallucinating right now. I could swear I just flew half way around the world and landed in China. Can you believe such nonsense? Funny what sleep deprivation can do to the mind. Tomorrow, we will tour The Forbidden City, Tiananmen Square, and the Great Wall with about twenty other American families also adopting a child. If we manage to take any decent photographs, I'll try to include one or two in future columns. Stay tuned.

Saturday, November 01, 2008

TV doesn't do it Justice

Today, we toured the Forbidden City. What you can see of it on TV is only a fraction of the magnitude of this city. There are dozens of palaces, temples, and other buildings within the city's walls. It is so massive that there are actually over 8,000 rooms within the compound. We walked for hours and only got a fleeting glimpse of the amazing architecture. You have to see it in person to truly appreciate the intricate, hand carved adornments on every building in the city. It is simply amazing.

Speaking of amazing, on our way to the Great Wall of China we ventured past the Olympic venues known as "The Birds Nest" and "The Water Cube." Very impressive, but nothing compared to the wall of course. More than just the name of thousands of Chinese restaurants in America, the Great Wall is one of the most incredible creations in human history. We climbed a portion of the wall to the top of a mountain and got some great pictures along the way. We are pretty sure that we won't need any more exercise for the rest of the trip. Overcome with the magnitude of our surroundings I asked Bethany, "Did you ever think you would be climbing on the Great Wall of China?" Some of the other couples we are travelling with shared the same sentiment. It is important to remember that until 1978, China was not open to visits from Westerners. And until 15 years ago, China did not allow international adoptions. So while we are not the first Americans to visit China or adopt a child there, it still feels very special.

Tomorrow we will fly to Nanning, a city in Guangxi Province. Bordering Vietnam in the south, the weather is forecast to be in the 80s all week. (We think we packed too many cold-weather clothes, but who knows.) Then on Monday, November 3, we will meet our son. WOW!

Monday, November 03, 2008

Love at First Sight

Say "Ni hao" to the newest member of the Naughton family, Truman Jiang Naughton. Truman or TJ or Tru or Zhan-Zhan (his former nickname) is a feisty little guy who wasted no time at all in peeing all over his new ma-ma and ba-ba, which is Chinese for "daddy." (Incidentally, "da-da" is how one tells a Chinese child to go poo.) Call him whatever you want, I'll call him "son."

Truman is a brave little soldier. He cried quite a bit when his foster mommy left him. By the time we got back to our hotel he would just grab his handful of worn-out toys and head for the door. He just wanted to go home. After a while he calmed down and played a little. Then, he brought me his shoes. I put them on his feet, he grabbed his toys and he stood at the door again. He is fighting his new lot in life, but as time wears on, I hope he will begin to accept it. I managed to make him laugh a few times and he let Mama give him a bath. Apparently that stirred up some powerful memories. He cried a sad cry and right now is trying to get Bethany to put his shoes back on. He has his old toys in hand and looks ready to go. But he isn't screaming to leave this time. I think we're getting through to him. We tell him "hen hao" (very good) when he goes on the potty (which he has done 5 times in a row on demand with no accidents at all) and he claps and smiles when we praise him. And, he blew me a kiss a minute ago. That was freakin' awesome. It won't be easy, but we'll win him over pretty soon. We love him with all our hearts, that's for sure.

Tuesday, November 04, 2008

It's Legal

Today, after being interviewed by someone from civil affairs and a notary, our coordinator uttered the words, "Congratulations. You are now officially this child's parents." 'Nuff said. I have included some pictures in lieu of writing today. I'll bet you won't mind.

Thursday, November 06, 2008

A Day in the Park

We went to the People's Park today. We saw people doing Tai Chi, dancing, twirling swords, and playing traditional Chinese instruments. We fed the koi, rode amusement park rides, and took lots of pictures. Then we went to McDonald's and Wal-Mart. (Pretty exotic, huh?) When we went back to the hotel for naptime, Truman cried for nearly two straight hours while repeating his routine of putting on his shoes, gathering his things, heading for the door, and screaming "Mama, Mama!!!" He spent several hours yesterday and the evening before that doing the same thing. We *have* to get out of this hotel. When we're outside of this room, Truman is the happiest, most outgoing little guy you'll ever meet. Inside, he is miserable. We leave for Guangzhou on Saturday. Hopefully a change of scenery will make the difference. In the meantime, we will relish the moments spent outside of our room.

Saturday, November 08, 2008

A Change Will Do You Good

     This morning, we flew to Guangzhou. Truman didn't fuss a bit on the one hour flight. In fact, he has done pretty well all day. He even took a nap without starting World War III. He is still going thru his routine of gathering his things and standing by the door, but he's not screaming "Mama!" for hours on end. *Baby steps*. In about an hour, we are going to get his picture taken for his visa. On Monday he'll get a routine doctor's visit and then we'll have three days of free-time. Then, we'll go to the Consulate for final interviews and an oath of some sort. On Saturday we'll finally fly home. One week to go.

Sunday, November 09, 2008

A Good Day

     What a difference a day makes. The new hotel has a playroom for kids, which Truman enjoyed for quite a while. It also has a huge breakfast buffet, which Mom and Dad enjoyed. But for dinner, we went on an adventure. Six families walked in downtown Guangzhou to a local restaurant. For my brother Blake and anyone else afraid we would only eat at Western restaurants, you would be proud. As we were escorted to a dining room, we walked past cages of live snakes, tank of frogs, fish, and shellfish, and a pond with live gators/crocs in it. After we were seated, the waiter asked me (I sat closest to the "head" of the table) what we would like to order. I said I would like to see a menu and he said "No English on menu." I said that I would look at the pictures (which did not help at all.) By this time, everyone was concerned that we would wind up eating something undesirable/unidentifiable/unimaginable. One member of the group had some names of common Chinese foods written down on a cheat sheet and he and I were able to order dumplings, Peking duck, a nearly raw chicken (head included for no additional charge), noodles, rice, and some good ol' pijiu (beer). Twelve adults and five children ate cold chicken and drank warm beer and water for a grand total of just under $100. Truman had three full bowls of congee (rice porridge), which is about all he will eat. We all had a lot of fun getting to know one another and as we left the restaurant, a worker dropped a live frog on the floor that must have weighed over a pound. The "splat" sound it made was a perfect final note for the evening.

Monday, November 10, 2008

Another Good Day

      Today, we went to the medical clinic for Truman's required exam. The doctors were fascinated yet unconcerned about his unique left hand and foot. Clean bill of health. Afterwards, we went shopping and bought the little guy a traditional Chinese outfit and some souvenirs. Later, we went to dinner at a much tamer restaurant than the one we visited last night. Oh, and Truman slept the whole night through last night. Ten hours straight!

Tuesday, November 11, 2008

Chinese Democracy

      We went to a park in Guangzhou today. It was a good excuse to be outdoors on a beautiful day. I think the temperature is around 72 degrees or more. Truman fell asleep and as he lay in my arms a Chinese woman stopped to admire him. She felt the material of his shirt and gave me the international look of "shame on you for not having this child bundled in three layers of clothing plus a fur-lined parka." Some other parents have had strangers pull their child's pant legs down so that not an inch of skin would be exposed to the savagely cold temperatures. The well-meaning woman also pointed at Truman and then held up one finger to indicate "one year old?" I held up two fingers and she gave me a look that clearly said "You are crazy. You do not even know how old your child is." She held up one finger again. I held up two followed by the universal sign for "little." She nodded, but walked away in disbelief. She did smile and say bye-bye. Most Chinese are quite friendly. Take the gentleman I conversed with at the park for example. He walked right up to me and shook my hand. In rough English, he asked where I was from. I said the middle of America. He said what a great place that must be. I agreed. He then asked if I voted for Barack Obama. I said that I did. He said, "He only won 54% of the vote; that seems dangerous." I said that from where I'm from, you only need 51% to win. He said, "I don't understand your Congress. You have Senate. You have Representative. Only 100 Senate, but Representative I don't know." I explained the bi-cameral make-up of our legislative branch and he seemed to somewhat grasp the concept. (That's more than I can say for a lot of Americans.) He thanked me for visiting with him and wished me well. If China converts to democracy in the next few years, I will take full credit for it.

Wednesday, November 12, 2008

Wednesday in Guangzhou

Today, after breakfast, we went back to our room and just lounged around for a lazy morning. We didn't leave for lunch till about 2:30, when we walked across the street to McDonald's. Eventually, we decided to catch a cab and head back out into the city to do some shopping. We were back at our room by 5:30. And guess what. Truman has finally realized that being in a hotel room with his new ma-ma and ba-ba is not such a bad thing after all. He has gone to bed without fussing and slept through the night for three straight nights. He even let Mommy brush his teeth yesterday while I held him. He throws temper tantrums, gives kisses, and eats regular food (he is eating a panini from Starbucks as I type this). In less than two weeks, a scared little orphan has transformed into a typical two year old member of a family who loves him with all their hearts. Just two more days and a wake-up and we'll be headed home. We can't wait for you to meet Truman. If you've enjoyed his pictures, just wait till you see him in person.

Thursday, November 13, 2008

Thursday Sightseeing

     We just got back from a long walk at a local park. Paths lined with banyan trees, a huge former colonial mansion, a lake, ping pong tables and a tribute to former Chinese president Deng Xiao Ping were some of the highlights of the park. Thursday is drawing to an end, leaving us with one day left in China. Tomorrow, we plan on visiting the Six Banyan Temple, a famous Buddhist landmark. Then, we will take the oath at the American Consulate making the adoption and American citizenship of our son final. Later, Bethany has plans to do even more souvenir shopping while making time for one last Starbucks run. And I will have a final word on this blog about our experiences in China. Stay tuned...

Friday, November 14, 2008

Reflections of China

     On September 16, 2006 a boy was born in Guigang City, Guangxi Autonomous Region, People's Republic of China. A young couple's joy and anticipation likely turned to bitter disappointment when they saw that their child was born with physical defects including a malformed left hand and foot. To some Chinese, birth defects are a sign of bad luck and the mother is often blamed for them. She may be shunned or even kicked out by her family. Farming families, seeking healthy sons to help with the crops, often abandon daughters or deformed boys in hopes that they can try again for a normal son. No one knows exactly why five-day old Jiang Yi Zhan was left by the side of the road by his biological parents. What is known is that he became one of the thousands of orphans left to languish in dismal state run institutions with no one to love them.

"Zhan-Zhan's" luck began to change when he was slightly more than one year old. He was placed in a foster home and was well cared for there. He grew to love his "Ma-ma" and became settled in his new environment. Almost one full year later, he was torn away from the only mother he ever knew and placed in the arms of two red-eyed, pale-skinned strangers. For days, little Truman (as he has been re-named) cried endlessly for his foster mother. He was reserved and didn't eat much. His new parents worried that he was not handling the changes in his life well. But then, they flew to Guangzhou.

A change of scenery brought a change in attitude for little T. He didn't crawl out of his shell--he bounded out of it. He learned to eat pizza, throw temper tantrums, perform for crowds, and flirt with the ladies. He has, in a matter of days, become a full fledged member of the Naughton family with all the quirks that make us who we are. He is, at times, certifiably nuts--just like the rest of us. He will fit in just fine at the Hartsburg Homestead. Between him and Alex, we are no doubt the luckiest parents around.

Earlier today, Truman was blessed by a Buddhist monk at a beautiful temple. As I have recently been studying the ancient philosophy of the Buddha, the moment overwhelmed and humbled me. Later we shopped some more, which was of course a decidedly un-Buddhist pursuit, and then finalized the adoption at the American Consulate with a brief swearing in ceremony. When we land on U.S. soil, Little T will be a legal U.S. citizen. We will leave for the airport at 5:00 am tomorrow and be home in our own bed by about 10:00 pm Saturday night. Wow. Did we really just spend two weeks in China?

Sunday, November 16, 2008

Home Again!

This is a tidy little summary of our twenty-eight hour odyssey home yesterday. The trip was so long and crossed so many time zones that we saw the sun rise twice and saw darkness three times in the same day. (On a personal note of pride, I peed in three countries in one day. A new personal record!) We started in

Guangzhou China, waking up at 5:00 am to catch a ride to the airport. We flew for over four hours to Tokyo and another ten or so hours to Minneapolis. It was at that airport that Truman was processed as a new immigrant. When the officer stamped his paperwork and said "congratulations" I struggled to keep it together in front of the several hundred other immigrants and families in the room. My son had become an American. That's a pretty awesome distinction, and after spending two weeks in China, it's one that I'll never take for granted again.

    Finally, we flew to Kansas City where a large portion of our family was waiting for us. By "us" I mean Truman. Wow, can that boy work a crowd. He had everyone in stitches within minutes of landing. We even managed to snap a picture of Alex giving his little brother a kiss. At the exact moment when they first met! Then, Nonna landed in KC, returning from a visit with Blake and Meredith in Baltimore. And she got some Truman kisses, too, which we also got pictures of. I know I will treasure those for the rest of my days. After a lot of hugs, the travel-weary family drove home — together at last.

    What a great feeling it is to be back. Alex and Mommy helped Truman brush his teeth when we got home. At bedtime, I snapped a photo of the two brothers, cozy in their parents' bed, watching Winnie the Pooh and feeling happy and loved. I used to think the greatest sound in the world was that of a baby's laughter. However, during our drive home last night, I could hear my two sons playing and giggling in the back seat of the minivan. That sound filled my heart so full of joy that I could barely make out the lines on the road through my watery eyes. I reached over to Bethany and gave her hand a little squeeze and she returned the gesture. She looked into my eyes and at that moment, we both knew that our family was finally complete.

After some time had passed and little Truman had begun to understand English, Travis and Bethany acknowledged the child's missing fingers and toes one day when he was playing with a toy:

Bethany and I have been a little worried about how to answer the question, "What happened to my fingers?" whenever Truman got old enough to ask it. But as he was playing with some building blocks the other day, Truman looked at his left hand and said, "Missing." Trying our best to hold it together, we said that indeed he was missing two fingers, but quickly added, "That just makes you extra special." He accepted this as indisputable fact and continued playing with his toys. It wasn't long after that when we sat down together and watched the animated movie *Finding Nemo* in which the title character was was born with an irregular left fin following an attack on his nest by a hungry barracuda. Suddenly, Bethany and I both had a revelation. "Nemo has a lucky fin," (as it was called in the film), we pointed out to Truman, "just like you have a lucky hand."

"Lucky hand?" he asked excitedly.

"Yes. Do you know *why* your hand is lucky?"

"*Whyyyyy*?" he asked in his adorable, drawn-out toddler accent.

"Because thanks to your lucky hand, Mommy and Daddy were able to find you in China and bring you home with us. Instead of *Finding Nemo*, we were Finding Truman."

He laughed with approving delight and resumed his building project, perfectly happy for the time being to accept our explanation.

Travis continued to write about his experiences as a father and a husband for his column. His accounts of parenthood eventually made their way into book form with the publication of Stay-at-Home Rollercoaster *in 2011, which became his first best seller and established the author as the voice of a generation of men who had for one reason or another left the work force to become full-time dads.*

Stay-at-Home Rollercoaster

"I may not have a paying job, but rumors of my retirement have been greatly exaggerated." Naughton wrote in the preface to Stay-at-Home Rollercoaster. *"It may seem that my beautiful wife works two jobs while I just sit on the couch watching "my stories" and eating bon-bons all day, but nothing could be further from the truth. That's only half of my day."*

Naughton blogged about his time at home with his son Alex, well before he became famous as a columnist. Thankfully, he included several of his blog posts in **Rollercoaster**.

July 10, 2005:

I would venture to guess that the past week has been the stress equivalent of two years of pressure-packed work in the "real world." In just two days this past week, my four-year-old Spawn of Satan fed our fish a year's worth of food in one feeding, played with and talked to a dead bunny like it was his favorite toy, and urinated in not one but *both* of our dogs' water bowls. (I guess you could say he loves animals to death.)

Try dealing with a virtual clone of *yourself* sometime. Come on, you remember the hell you put your parents through. How will I survive this? What have I done?!

July 12, 2005:

Well, the Devil has stepped aside for a while and Alex, my little Angel, is back. After allowing me to sleep in past 9:00 this morning, he treated me to breakfast in bed. He actually made toast and slathered it with jelly all by himself. Then he brought it to me in bed and we ate it while he let me watch my morning news instead of his cartoons. What a difference a few days make. After a while, we got up and put on some music. Alex recognized the CD as the Blues Brothers soundtrack and proceeded to dance a jig that would have made Joliet Jake himself proud. And I was mighty proud, too. I suggested that for Halloween this year we should dress up as Jake and Elwood and he said, "You betcha!" I guess having a clone can be pretty cool after all.

August 19, 2005:

Just in case you are feeling down, I have the perfect pick-me-up. Take a kid fishing. Wednesday evening, Alex hooked and landed a nice bass completely on his own. (And yes, he kissed it good-bye before throwing it back.) We were both pretty proud. Later as our friend Wes was leaving, Alex said, "I'm sorry you didn't catch any fish, Wes." And then he gave him a hug. Alex didn't realize that he had just delivered some of the most powerful trash talk in the history of fishing. I couldn't begin to express how proud I am.

November 18, 2005:

How can a parent judge how well they are raising their child? Take him to a playground and see how he interacts with other kids. This test is especially helpful for those of us who don't get out much. Today, Alex was at Twin Lakes City Park when four kids showed up. The bigger kids left their little brother behind on the playground while they fed the geese. Alex stayed with the little one and kept him entertained. When the little boy couldn't crawl on top of a piece of equipment Alex explained how to do it and when that didn't work he actually picked him up. I was proud of how thoughtful he was. When the other kids came back they all started playing and talking. The following is a partial transcript of their conversation:

Little Girl: "How old are you?"

Alex: "I'm five."

Girl: "Well I'm six and he's seven, so we're older than you."

Alex: "Yeah because six is more than five. And seven is more than six."

Girl: "Well, you're not as old as we are."

(They played for a while and then Alex tried to show the kids a pretend dinosaur fossil on the plastic rock wall.)

Alex: "Hey guys come here. I want to show you something."

Older boy: "We know. It's a dinosaur bone."

Alex: "Do you know how the dinosaurs died?"

Girl: "No, do you?"

Alex: "A big meteor crashed to the earth and made lots of dirt go up in the air and all the plants died and then the dinosaurs died."

Girl: "Oh."

The kids' mom: "How did you know that, Alex?"

Alex: "I learned it in my history book."

Mom: "Wow, that's really good. What kind of dinosaur is that fossil from?"

Alex: "I think it's a brontosaurus."

Mom: "Is that written beside it?"

Alex: "No, I could just tell that's what it is."

Girl: "Well if you're so smart, what do cheetahs eat?"

Alex: "They eat other cheetahs."

Girl: "No they don't."

Older boy: "Well they might, but not usually."

Girl: "What eats lions?"

Alex: "Cheetahs."

Girl: "No they don't."

Older boy: "They could eat them if they're already dead."

Girl: "Vultures eat dead lions. You're not smart."

Alex: "Hyenas eat dead lions. You're not smart."

Girl: "No they don't. See, you're not smart."

Alex: "I am so smart I'm smarter than my dad even."

Oldest boy: "You're not smart. I'm smart."

Alex: "You're not smart, I'm smart."

Girl: "You can't be smart if you think cheetahs eat lions."

At that point I finally interjected and asked the little girl, "How do you know cheetahs don't eat lions? Have you ever been around cheetahs and lions?"

Girl: "No."

Alex: "See, you're not smart."

Me: "You're all smart, you just know different things. Alex, it's time to go."

Older boy: "I'm smarter than you."

Alex: "I'm smarter than you."

Me: "It's time to go son."

As we walked to the car, I whispered to my son, "If you are going to argue with someone about who is the smartest, you should know what you're talking about. Cheetahs probably don't eat lions. They eat gazelles and smaller animals. You shouldn't be arguing about who's smartest anyway."

We heard the kids following us to the parking lot, so we turned and walked back towards them. The boys were trying to apologize for arguing, but their tiny voices were drowned out by the little girl's as she was going on and on about something. I have no idea what she was saying and Alex had his hands over his ears to shut her out. I told him to just ignore her and listen to the boys' apologies. He did, and then he said sorry too. On the way to the car I said, "That was nice of them to say they were sorry."

"Man, I got tired of hearing her babbling on and on...blah, blah, blabitty, blah-blah!" he complained.

I wanted to say, "Get used to it son. It'll be that way for the rest of your life," but settled for, "Hurry, get in the car. Here she comes."

March 8, 2006:

Alex has seen animals mating on nature shows, but didn't understand the "ins and outs" so to speak. Today he heard something on the news about people being caught having sex in a parking lot and he said, "That's disgusting!" I asked him *what* he thought was disgusting and he said "sex." I asked him if he knew what sex was and he admitted that he did not.

Naturally I told him that I would explain it to him some other time. He wanted no part of that. "Tell me now, Daddy." I told him he wasn't old enough to understand it. He insisted that he was and wouldn't drop it, no matter how much I wished he would. I said that sex was the same as mating. He already knew that animals mate to make babies, so thinking that he had accepted my simple, vague explanation, I felt that I had dodged a bullet.

"*How* do people mate?" he asked. That one stopped me in my tracks. I was really hoping this wouldn't come up for a few more years. I was unprepared.

"You know that men and women have different private parts, right?"

"Yes."

"Those parts are made to fit together when people mate."

"Oh."

"People have sex to mate and because it makes them feel good."

"*Oh*."

"And since it is with their 'privates', you shouldn't talk about it with anybody but me and Mommy. 'Privates' means..."

"That it's *private*," Alex said knowingly. He flashed a sheepish grin and an embarrassed look of complete understanding. I felt awkward yet relieved as he went back to playing with his toys. Then I called Mommy and told her to bring home a six-pack.

June 10, 2008:

Earlier today Alex and I went to the new skatepark in Columbia. He rode his scooter and his board a little bit, but was ultimately too intimidated by the bigger kids to continue. One of the junior high school-aged boys said, "Outta my way, cowsucker" to him. Alex appeared to be more confused than insulted.

I told him that "cowsucker" just meant that he's young and

still drinks milk. (I hope that's all it meant.) I also suggested that he practice a lot and come back one day to show off his skills, but I could tell he was too discouraged to even think about returning. Frankly, I wouldn't mind if he never gets on a skateboard again. With a few exceptions, most of the skaters I've known had a tendency to gravitate toward anti-social behaviors. (Think: "Jackass The Movie.")

After we left the skatepark we played on the playground. We played "pirates" and "tag" and had a great time. I am happy that Alex is still young enough to prefer a swing-set to the trappings of the skater-set.

As the day grew closer when Alex would start kindergarten, his father worried if he had done enough to prepare his son for the anxiety some kids feel when they step onto the school bus for the first time, unsure of what lies ahead of them as they embark upon a new chapter in their young lives. Travis apparently had no reason to worry.

"How'd it go today, buddy?" I asked Alex when I picked him up at the babysitter's house after his first day of school. *[Naughton was working again at this point.]*

"Great. The kids already gave me a nickname."

"Really? What?" I hesitated to ask.

"Underwear Head," he said proudly.

"Why would they call you Underwear Head?" I asked, although I didn't know if I wanted to hear the answer.

"Because I took out the extra pair of underwear Mom put in my backpack and wore it on my head on the bus."

"Really?" *Dear God.*

"Yeah, and then I ran up and down the aisle of the bus until the driver yelled, 'Take that underwear off your head and go sit down!' All the kids thought it was funny. Then they started calling me Underwear Head. It was great."

I never wanted to run for school board anyway. Here's a parenting tip for you: Resist the temptation to pack an extra set of clothes "just in case" for your child on their first day of school.

(Younger): From some of the things I've read, it seems that there was never a dull moment in your house during those years when you stayed home with the kids.

(Elder): You're right about that. Those boys were too much like me for their own good—hell, for anybody's good. My friend Wes Douglass once told me when talking about Truman's antics, "I don't know how you did it. One and a half billion people live in China and you found the one that's exactly like you."

Naughton elaborated in Rollercoaster:

Truman is a wonderful test subject in the debate over "Nature vs. Nurture." Although he is not biologically related to me, there is no doubt that he, like Alex, is 100% mine. When Bethany comes home from work and sees a three-year-old Chinese boy being slid by his father across our hardwood floor into a set of plastic bowling pins, she can be forgiven for initially being a bit concerned. But when Truman the Human Bowling Ball laughs uncontrollably after my first roll and then runs back to me (like an automatic ball return) so we can pick up the spare, she understands that he enjoys the insanity at our house as much as the rest of us do.

(Younger): It seems that you really did enjoy your time at home with the boys. What are some other father-son activities that you shared with them besides "toddler bowling?"

(Elder): Fishing was a favorite of ours. Still is. I find that it's important for a dad to teach his boys how to fish, as well as bowl. *[laughs]* I still remember watching Alex reel in his first fish on his Spiderman pole when he was just three years old. I told him that before we throw fish back, we have to give them a kiss good-bye. I gave the small bass a little peck on its top lip and handed it over to Alex. He wrapped both arms around it the way a mother would cradle her newborn and planted a big, wet smack on the fish's flank. I say it was a "wet" smack because of the coating of slime that transferred from the fish's side to Alex's lips in the process.

(Younger): Did Truman take to fishing right away, too?

(Elder): About six years after I helped Alex with his first fish, it was Alex who helped Truman reel in his first, a bluegill hooked in our neighbor's pond. I think Alex felt as proud as I did when they hauled in their catch. I took some pictures and then I took a moment to reflect upon what a charmed life I was living. Of course, we've had our bad days as well as our good. The worst thing about adopting a two-year-old is adopting a two-year-old. For the first six months after we brought Truman home, we did not get through one single meal without an all-out battle while trying to get him to drink his milk, or juice, or water. Three meals a day, seven days a week, for at least six full months he refused to open his mouth to take a single sip of fluid. We tried everything we could think of to get him to drink, fearing he would become dehydrated otherwise. We tried leaving a cup of juice on the table to drink at his leisure throughout the day. We tried bribes. We tried punishments. We tried time-outs. We tried isolation and ignoring. Nothing worked. We tried frozen popsicles, but he wouldn't eat them. We did feed him some soup just to get some liquids into him. We even resorted to prying his little mouth open and pouring a few drops of liquid at a time down his throat. I practically waterboarded my kid to keep him from dying of thirst. A parent's love has no bounds.

(Younger): That sounds incredibly frustrating. How did you

handle the stress?

(Elder): Probably not as well as I could have. The more frustrated I got, the louder I got. He reacted either by trying to out-scream me or by shutting down into an almost catatonic state. Some days I would feel a little guilty after one of these battles, but within seconds after excusing him from the table he would be laughing and playing as if the past two hours of hell had never taken place. And it was hell. I liken the situation to that of a prisoner of war going on a hunger strike. In his little mind, I think he saw us as his captors at times, not his parents. We told him when to go to bed, we decided what he would wear, we sat him on the toilet and made him poop on command, and there was little he could do to resist. Apparently, you can lead a two-year-old orphan to water, but you can't make him drink.

(Younger): Didn't he ever pretend to drink just to get you off his back?

(Elder): Yes he did! He actually faked it in order to get us off his case. Giving him a sippy-cup or a cup with a straw made it easy for him to pretend that he was drinking. We could see his mouth move as if he were sucking on the straw, but his throat never made a swallowing motion and the level of the liquid in the cup would never go down. He did the same when drinking out of a regular glass, too. Nothing worked. And when we caught him faking, he would scream bloody murder and another battle would ensue. But when I gave him an ounce of milk in a shot glass one day, he drank the entire amount without fuss. After a while, I could get him to drink up to six "shots" per meal which soon began to turn the tide of the war. Gradually, as he accepted that Bethany and I were his parents and that we loved him, his resistance began to erode. I eventually found a two-ounce, plastic measuring cup made for holding a serving of salad dressing or something and switched him to using that instead of a shot glass. I thought that it would be a little safer for him to use and slightly less frowned-upon in public than the sight of a toddler drinking from a shot glass that had "Coyote Tequila" written on it.

I declared victory in the battle for hydration. But the cagey

P.O.W. still had a few tricks up his sleeve. One morning, I wasn't in the mood to prod him to get through his breakfast quickly, so I checked email and straightened up around the house while he fed himself. Truman didn't fuss. He didn't ask to get down from the table. He didn't whine about being full. He just sat in his high chair and drank his six ounces of milk and ate his one frozen waffle (which was a favorite meal of his) over the course of the next three and a half hours. I may have invented stubborn, but Truman perfected it.

It is abundantly clear from the way Naughton talks and writes about his children that he loved the time he spent raising them, despite the ups and downs of riding the "Stay-at-Home Rollercoaster." I asked him if he ever regretted his decision to stay home with them instead of working outside the home:

I honestly wouldn't have traded being able to stay-at-home with my kids for any other job in the world. My distain for performing physical labor is well known. I may even be allergic to work. Crash Phillips's grandfather thought I was.

In high school, Crash asked me if I'd like to make a few bucks walking his grandfather's soybean fields and pulling weeds. I said sure--I needed beer money. After an hour or so in the scorching Missouri sun surrounded by every type of weed known to mankind overwhelming me with their pollen, I started having difficulty breathing. I struggled along for a few more minutes until Crash, who was tired of hearing me whine said, "Let's head back to the house." I feigned protest, but was relieved to be put out of my misery. But the misery had only begun. Jack Phillips made me sit at his kitchen table while he wrote me a check for my hour and a half of "labor." I told him that it wasn't necessary to pay me, but despite my repeated protests, which only appeared to agitate him further, he insisted. He was making a point. I only lasted an hour and a half in his bean field. Yet he had been working that same field for over seventy years without complaint. I've never felt more pathetic.

But I felt greatly relieved and somewhat vindicated to be diagnosed with asthma several years later. I was almost happy that I suffered from a potentially fatal condition--at least I wasn't just being a slacker after all. It turned out that I really *am* allergic to work. Whenever Crash gives me a hard time about my work ethic (or lack thereof) that day at his family farm I say, "Hey, I could have died out there." Hell, now that I think about it, him taking me back to his grandparents' house before my breathing became any worse probably kept me from dying from a full-blown asthma attack. I guess that makes four times that Crash has saved my life. I probably ought to buy him a beer for that.

One story that Naughton wrote about in his column probably deserves most of the credit for landing the lucrative book deal that launched his career as a best-selling author:

Moments ago, I sat down to write a column about the ups and downs of pet ownership. I was feeling both a throbbing pain in my right index finger and inspired after having my hand bitten—again—by our pet bird Chi-Chi, a parakeet who apparently didn't get the memo about not biting the hand that feeds him. I had just typed the title to this future masterpiece when I was interrupted by the ear-splitting screams of righteous indignation coming from my three-year-old son Truman—a phenomenon more common than parakeet pecks and often much more painful. I set aside my laptop, meted out some swift justice to Tru and his older brother Alex, and settled back into my work station/easy chair to resume writing. But the moment was gone. The pain from the bird-bite had dissipated, as did my inspiration to write about my feathered and furry friends. I'll admit that I was tempted to pack it in and postpone writing until the boys' bedtime, but I decided instead to write this piece about a day in the life of a stay-at-home writer.

Just while I was typing the above paragraph, several distractions occurred that would derail most professional writers.

The phone rang while I was responding to yet another domestic dispute, causing me to threaten Truman with a life sentence in "time-out" without the possibility of parole if he refused to cease his screeching long enough for me to say, "Hello" to the person with bad timing on the other end of the phone. As I greeted the caller, Tru resumed his caterwauling, which forced me to repeat my initial cordial "Hello" with a more irritated one. The caller turned out to be a telemarketer, a fact that removed any guilt I may have had for sounding particularly rude. She wanted me to pass along a message to my wife Bethany that her prescription for her eyeglasses was now expired and that she should come in to get new glasses as soon as possible. First of all, I didn't know glasses had an expiration date. Do they get all brown and mushy like bananas or are they no longer legally valid after two years like, say, a driver's license? I was tempted to ask the caller these questions, but opted instead for the old stand-by, "I've got a screaming kid here. Have a nice day." Click. Minutes later, another sibling squabble ensued as did another phone call—this time from Bethany, who was "just checking in to see how everything was going." I kept my response short and not-so-sweet, which she correctly interpreted as "I'm a little busy right now, trying to write and not kill your children."

Although my kids can derail the creativity train that runs within me at the drop of a hat, or the taking of a toy, they do provide me with a wealth of material to write about—if ever I can find the time. Take this morning for example. I was drifting in and out of sleepyland at about eight o' clock, dreaming about peeing in the Pope's Jacuzzi--(I wish I were making this up, but it is unfathomably true)--when I heard the toilet lid go up in the master bathroom. I pried open an eye and peered through the doorway just in time to see Tru getting up on the potty like a big boy. I was surprised and pleased to notice him dabbing a stray droplet or two off the rim with a square of toilet paper. *What a conscientious little fella!* When he finished, I instructed him to dispose of his pull-up diaper and get a clean pair of underwear from his room, which he set out to do without argument. I was a proud papa.

Moments later, Tru returned to inform me that he couldn't

find any underwear in his dresser, and so I begrudgingly crawled out of my cozy bed—an unheard of act for a dad who is accustomed to burying himself under the covers and "watching TV" with his kids in the early morning hours (at least until *Sesame Street* is over.) I dug up a pair of skivvies that were as yet unpacked from a bag of clean laundry following a week's vacation and put them on my ominously smelly child. No sooner had I pulled up his Thomas the Train tighty-whities, than I spotted the source of the offending odor. An instantly recognizable brown streak had made its way from Truman's nether-region to his ankles. I sprang into action, fully awake now, putting aside all hope of waking to the dulcet tones of *"Elmo's World"* and how I would explain to the Pope why the water in his hot tub was extra foamy, and ran at a dead sprint--with filthy child in hand--back to the bathroom.

Upon re-entry, I flipped on the bathroom light. *The horror!* The first thought that came to mind was something along the lines of how relieved the Pope would be that I didn't do *that* in his Jacuzzi. Poo was everywhere, (and I don't mean the Winnie-the-Pooh sheets, jammies, and toys that were scattered about the house.) I'm talking real, non-Disney poo. I stood Truman on his feet in the middle of the room and like a CSI detective, began to piece together what had happened. Judging by the brown streak on the side of the tub, Tru must have leaned against it as he stripped off his diaper, which was now partially protruding from the trashcan like a brown and white bundle of shame. From there, the trail led to the toilet where it became apparent that the boy had not been dabbing a few drops of pee that errantly landed on the rim. *If only.* Instead, as he hoisted himself up to the seat, he very obviously smeared a British Petroleum sized brown slick all over the side of the commode.

I quickly peeled off his fresh underwear only to find that it was—not so fresh anymore. I began to clean up the bathroom fixtures while my patient but stinky child stood motionless and eerily emotionless in the middle of the floor. He seemed to be completely unaffected by the whole affair, unlike his father who was alternately holding his breath and gagging while depleting the disappointingly limited supply of wet wipes in a hopelessly vain effort to remove the now tacky substance from the boy's, well...boy parts. The only remaining course of action was a hasty shower, one that left no time for proper preparation or the securing of a washcloth. That unfortunate fact left me no choice but to use soap, water, and my bare hands to extricate the thoroughly stuck-on poo from the no man's land between Truman's bits & pieces and his little "peanut butt" as his mama calls it—a cute name for a portion of his personage that was anything but cute at that moment.

After some serious scrubbing, Tru was his old self again. I sent him back to watch his cartoons while I took a shower that I hoped was hot enough to sterilize my hands and burn away the nauseating memories from my mind. I guess I only succeeded on one of those fronts. And for that I'm somewhat glad. Without these types of experiences to draw upon, I would have very little interesting to write about. Oh, I could make stuff up and call myself a novelist, but in regards to my life I've found that the truth is much more entertaining than fiction.

Of course, Naughton did go on to write fiction later in life (his novel **Burning Couches** *became a runaway hit when it was finally published in 2035), but his strength was in his ability to relate stories from his real life to his readers. He would soon begin relating these tales to his fans face-to-face as he travelled the country during his first book tour following the release of* **Rollercoaster**. *He had no way of knowing what a rollercoaster ride he was about to embark upon.*

Dogma Day Care

Travis Naughton was a tireless self-promoter at the time his book hit store shelves. "Some folks would probably say that I was a shameless self-promoter--and they'd be right." Having promised his publisher to do whatever it took to publicize his new book, Naughton set out on a month-long book tour in the fall of 2011.

Beginning with the whirlwind day of appearances in New York City highlighted by an unforgettable appearance on The Late Show with David Letterman, Naughton's celebrity quickly caught fire. He flew to Los Angeles to tape the now famous segment with Jimmy Kimmel just one week after Rollercoaster's release, and was greeted with a standing ovation by the studio audience. "I was caught completely off-guard by the reception I was getting at places. I kept looking behind me to see who it was that everyone was so excited to see. After the Kimmel show, it began to sink it that they were actually excited to see me."

(Younger): With your new found celebrity and the demands of your book tour, how did you strike a balance at home?

(Elder): Well, I was on the road for a solid month after the book came out. I really started missing my kids after the first week or so. When I finally got back home, I didn't answer the phone or check email for a few days, just so I could unwind with my family without feeling the pull of the outside world.

(Younger): Were you still writing your column at this time?

(Elder): I had taken a month or so off while promoting my book, so when I got settled back in at home, I did resume writing for my column. It was kind of nice to get back to work.

One of the first columns Naughton wrote after getting back to work was a four-part piece called Dogma Day Care. *In it, Travis the Author explains the origins of Travis the Stay-at-Home Dad:*

When Bethany and I first discussed having children, I expressed my desire to be a stay-at-home dad, but because we still depended on both of our incomes by the time Alex was born, we decided to place him in day care. While Alex was an infant, an elderly African-American woman named Annie watched over him in her home and doted on him as if he were her own grandchild. She was wonderful, but after a while, we thought it would be beneficial to his development if he went to an actual day care center where he could have more structure in his day and an opportunity to interact with other kids. Although we weren't necessarily religious people, we found a nice center operated in a church in Columbia. It was convenient, affordable, and the folks working there seemed very nice. In the parent handbook outlining the center's official policies, a passage that read, "Corporal punishment will not be used under any circumstances" made us feel certain that we had chosen a safe and nurturing environment for our son. The clincher was that the day care was operated without a religious agenda, thus avoiding any risk of fundamentalist zealots indoctrinating our kid. *I'll do the brainwashing in this family, thank you very much.*

Over the next few weeks, Alex adjusted to his new "school" as we called it, and we became convinced that once again, when it came to finding good people to watch our child, we had chosen wisely. Then, one afternoon when I arrived at the church to take Alex home, the teacher handed me an "incident report." I dreaded what I might read; knowing that when it came to following the rules, the apple that was Alex didn't fall far from the Naughton family tree. Instead I was surprised and relieved to find that a two year old boy had bitten Alex during an argument over a toy. This was pretty typical behavior for kids this age, so I immediately forgave the offending child without giving it a second thought. As I continued to read toward the end of the report however, I was stunned to learn that as a punishment the biter was forced to ingest hot sauce. I had never heard of doing such a thing to a child. I know plenty of adults who find hot sauce to be intolerably painful themselves and would never consider pouring undiluted hot pepper sauce directly on a two year old's tongue. That's bordering on child abuse. I told the day care teacher exactly that.

"His mother gave us permission to do it," the teacher claimed.

"But it clearly states in your written policy that corporal punishment will not be used at any time," I reminded the woman.

"His mother had no problem with it. Why should you?" she countered.

"Because even if the boy's mother told you it was okay to do this, she does not have the right to give you permission to abuse her child."

"We don't abuse children here. Besides, why do you care anyway? Your son was the one who was bitten."

"I care because it sounds like this poor kid needs somebody to protect him since you and his own mother won't."

"Hey, if you've got a problem, then take it up with the director. She'll be here tomorrow. I can't talk to you while you're all worked up like this." At that, I nearly grabbed her by the hair, forced open her mouth, and poured the whole freaking bottle of hot sauce down her rotten throat.

"Don't worry. I'll do that." I took Alex home and explained to Bethany and later my mother what had happened. Both were as outraged as I was. Bethany and I agreed to pull him from the day care as soon as we could find an alternative. My mom was bent on revenge, as Alex was her only grandson, and she turned things up a notch. I received a phone call the next day from a newspaper reporter who wanted to get my version of the story before going to press. Apparently, Mom took it upon herself to notify the local newspaper to tip them off about allegations of child abuse going on at the church. Scores of people have learned the hard way not to mess with Donna Keller's kids or grandkid over the years. The members of the church were merely the latest in a long line of unfortunate folks who have felt her wrath. I was not pleased that Mom had forced my hand, but I couldn't contradict her to the reporter, so I confirmed the facts of the story. Soon thereafter I feared what the fallout might be for Alex if he was still at the center when the story went public, so I rushed there to pick him up before things escalated any further. As we were driving home, I received another phone call, this time from a local talk radio station. They had heard from the newspaper folks what had happened and wanted to know if they could interview me for an on-air discussion they were having about the incident. As it happened, I was only a block away from the station at that exact moment and when I said that I could be there in two minutes with my son if they wanted me to come in, they insisted that I walk straight into the studio and tell my story.

Not having any time to collect my thoughts or prepare a statement, I did my best to recount the incident to my interviewers while silently imploring my eighteen month old to "be a good boy and try not to break anything." Just an hour earlier, the incident was entirely a private matter and now I was in the center of a media storm that I was entirely unprepared for. In the back of my mind, a little voice kept saying, "You can't kill your mother. She was only doing what she thought was right." While doing my best to get the interview over with so that I could just be on my way, the radio personality asked the one question I was really hoping to avoid; "In your opinion, does forcing hot sauce down a child's throat constitute 'child abuse'?" I said that I thought it did. The lump in my throat sunk to the pit of my stomach upon hearing the next question; "Then will you be reporting this incident to the Department of Family Services?"

"Uh, I...well, yes. I suppose I will." There was no turning back now. *Thanks, Mom. Remember the pain I caused you during childbirth? Well, now we're even.* Later, I did call the agency that oversees day care centers in the state, and thankfully they were able to proceed without much further input from me. The investigator called me some time later and informed me that thanks to my report, the offending day care operation was being placed on probation and would no longer employ corporal punishment. I saw on a television news report not long after that the director of the day care center resigned and the pastor released a statement assuring the public that the church did not and will not condone such forms of punishment. My mother was immensely satisfied.

Of course this left us without child care, so I began asking around to find someone else to watch Alex. If you have ever tried to find a good pre-school for your child, you know that there is usually a long waiting list to gain admission for your little one. A friend informed me that his sister ran an in-home day care center that was licensed and located less than a mile from the automobile auction where I worked, and she currently had an opening for another kid. We were thrilled. We met Ellen, loved her right away, signed the papers, and deposited Alex within her home in the span of 24 hours. I know that if something seems too good to be true it usually is, but we were desperate. *To be continued next week…*

Dogma Day Care Part 2

Desperate to find childcare for our toddler Alex, Bethany and I put on our blinders and pretended not to notice that Ellen (the only employee licensed to care for children at her facility) was rarely ever at "Ellen's Day Care" when we picked up our son. We overlooked the fact that she worked a part-time job waiting tables while she was supposedly running her day care center.

One afternoon when I loaded Alex into my vehicle and waved good-bye to Ellen, I smelled feces. This was not the familiar stench of a poo-filled diaper. It was dog poo. I suspected that either Alex or I had inadvertently stepped in a fresh pile on our way to the truck, but after checking our shoes I found nothing. I buckled Alex's car seat and watched as he waved bye-bye to Ellen (it was one of the rare days when she was actually there.) It was then that I saw a brownish substance smeared between his fingers and across the palms of his hands. Ellen had a fenced in back yard and a German shepherd that was usually in a separate pen when the kids were there. Evidently, the separation of dog and kid was not always enforced. I unbuckled Alex and proceeded to wipe his hand on Ellen's front lawn as she watched through the window. Confused, she stepped outside.

"Is there something wrong?" she asked.

"You could say that, yes. Alex has dog crap all over his hands."

"Oh my God! I always watch the kids when they're out back and the dogs are never in the yard where the kids play. I don't even know when that could have happened." *Gee, I don't know. Could it have been while you were working at your other job maybe?*

"Well, he's got it all over him."

"I'm so sorry about that. I'll try to do a better job of cleaning up after the dogs when I let them in the yard." *So you **do** let the dogs run around and leave land mines in the yard where my baby plays. Wonderful.*

It wasn't much longer until Ellen informed us that she was going to start waiting tables full-time and that her assistant would be watching the kids from then on. Her *unlicensed* assistant. That was all we needed to hear. Burned-out at work, I decided to quit my job and stay home with Alex. Bethany agreed with the condition that I find a part-time job so that we could still pay our bills. I found a job at a boutique and bakery for dogs (yes, you read that right) where I would be working Tuesdays, Thursdays, and Saturdays, and we enrolled Alex in a pre-school close to home for those two days a week that I couldn't be home with him. We went with this arrangement until Alex turned three; at which time our son became the biter and not the bite-ee at day care. I had become bored with yet another job, and Bethany determined that we could survive on one income. *Hallelujah!* I announced to the world that I was "retiring" and for the next couple of years I lived a glorious existence raising my son and mooching off my wife. It was great--

while it lasted. With a few months to go before Alex was set to begin kindergarten, Bethany decided that he would benefit from trying pre-school again in order to get him used to the routine of being away from home. She also decided that there was absolutely no reason for me to continue my "retirement" if I didn't have a kid at home to take care of. She found Alex a day care center within a few miles of our house, and I found a full-time job managing the pet supply store. *To be continued next week...*

Dogma Day Care Part 3

Bethany had spoken with the director of a new pre-school who had us come in to fill out the requisite paperwork on a Friday. We arranged for Alex's first day to coincide with my first day of work the following week. The plan was for him to attend school for four hours per day until kindergarten started, at which time he would only need to be there after school until one of us could pick him up. This fit nicely with my schedule as I had arranged to work part-time until school started while I was training to become the manager of the doggie boutique I had worked at two years prior. When I dropped my son off at his new pre-school on the following Monday morning, I introduced him to the director by saying, "This is Alexander and this is his first day of school!"

    She said nothing. A blank expression was her only response. She just stared at me as if I were speaking a foreign language. After a long, awkward silence she finally said, "And what do *I* need to do?"

    Her assistant, recognizing that her boss had absolutely no idea who we were or why we were there told her, "I wrote it down on the list." I could only assume that by "it" she meant that a new student was starting on Monday.

    "My wife talked to you last week and said everything was fine for him to start today," I offered, hoping to jog her memory.

    "Okay?" she said, but it sounded more like she was asking a

question rather than confirming an established fact.

"We stopped in on Friday to pick up the paperwork and I have most of it filled out. But we didn't sign the "acknowledgement of fees" statement because we didn't see the amount written anywhere in our paperwork. We also didn't sign the form that says we received the policies and rules handbook because we didn't get that either."

"Well, we charge $120 a week."

"For part-time child care?" I was getting worried.

"Oh, wait. He'll only be here three days a week, right?"

"No, actually. He'll be here every day from 9 till 1."

"Oh, that's right," she said as if she were really remembering our previous conversation. "Well I don't know how much *that* will cost. We just changed our fees right before your wife called me. I'll fill out the form and have it for you when you come to pick him up. You can still sign the sheet that says you received a copy of the policies though."

"As I said, we didn't get that, so we can't sign it."

"Oh you didn't get that?"

Try to keep up, lady. "No."

"I'll get that to you, too then.""Thanks. Where do we put his backpack and coat?" We were conversing in the dimly lit basement of the converted ranch house that doubled as a pre-school. I could barely see my hand before my face, much less any sign of a coat rack.

"Oh, just go up the stairs, turn left, and walk down the hall until you see...Here, it'll probably be easier to just show you." It was.

"My wife said class starts at 9:00 am, so I should have him

here a little before 9. Is that right?"

"We actually start with morning prayers at 8:30 and then have activities and bible discussion at 9. Are you and your family Christians?" Morning prayers? Bible study? Never at any time did anyone tell us that this was a religious daycare center. *Those activities must have been mentioned in the handbook you never gave us.*

"Uh, well I...we don't...er, we're non-denominational." I mumbled while trying to regroup from her audacious question.

"We feel it is important to teach the children about God and Jesus in order to teach them how to be good Christians. That isn't going to be a problem is it?"

I wasn't ready or willing to debate religion or the existence of God with the woman in front of my young son.

"Well, we want him to be exposed to all sorts of new ideas and religions including Christianity." This was true, and diplomatic. But what I really wanted to say was, "Yes that's going to be a problem. A big problem. Do you think you could have mentioned at some point prior to Alex's first day here that you and your staff would be forcing him to participate in your religious practices. Yes, that's going to be a huge freaking problem."

I had to make a decision. I needed to be at my new job in 30 minutes. I concluded that even though the director of the facility had no idea that we were coming, had no idea what to do once we were there, never introduced herself to us, never welcomed Alex to his new school, and had planned to brainwash him without our permission, she probably couldn't ruin him in one day. I kissed my son good-bye, told him to call me if he needed me, and said, "I love you." I got in my car, drove to work, called Bethany to angrily voice my concerns (which she shared) and tried to concentrate on my new job. It was useless.

When I picked Alex up, he said he had a good time, and the director said that he did really well. I asked her if she had the forms we needed and she said she forgot. *Big surprise.* Alex said he spent the majority of his day in the windowless basement including during lunchtime, Bible lessons, and movie time. He said the cartoon movie they watched depicted two people in the jungle walking around naked with some sort of reptile. When they ate an apple, God made them wear clothes. Alex couldn't fathom why. Bethany called four other day care centers the next day and within a week had him placed in one. *To be continued next week...*

Dogma Day Care Part 4

Everything was going smoothly at Alex's new, in-home day care that was operated by a very nice lady named Darla--until Alex came home talking about all the guns he got to look at while he was there. He said that while Darla was busy changing a baby's diaper, her son led Alex into a back bedroom that is normally off-limits to the kids. There he was shown a glass display case filled with several high-powered hunting rifles, a shotgun, and some pistols. The case was locked, but the fact that my five year old son was able to sneak away with another boy to look at a collection of guns proudly displayed in an illuminated glass case in a licensed day care center while the only grown up in the house was completely oblivious bothered me greatly.

When I confronted Darla about this, she said that Alex was lying. She said there was no way he could have seen any guns in her house. I asked Alex to show us where the guns were and he led us straight to them. "Well, I don't know how he could have gotten in there. There's always a baby gate up in front of that hallway." This statement both amused and alarmed me. Did this woman actually think a couple of five year old boys couldn't get past a baby gate? And so what if the glass-front gun case was locked, I told her. Glass can be broken easily enough. I closed with, "If you went to any other licensed day care facility or school, would you ever expect to see guns on display? Of course not."

"Well, those kids aren't supposed to go in that bedroom. They know that. I promise it won't happen again." I made it easy for her to keep that promise. Alex never went back. I asked my employer if I could alter my schedule in order to be home in time to pick my son up from school and she graciously said yes.

Two years later, I convinced my wife the Enabler to let me "retire" again. We had decided to adopt a baby from China and as the date of the adoption drew near, all I had to say to convince Bethany was, "Hey, I'd love to keep working, but you know how hard it is to find good child care."

The Voice of Reason reluctantly conceded that I was right. I haven't punched a time clock since. Rumors of my retirement have been greatly exaggerated however. Being a stay-at-home parent is a lot of work. I'm not even sure how the title "stay-at-home" parent came about. We "stay-at-homes" don't stay at home for very long. We go out to do the grocery shopping, to take our kids to baseball, basketball, ballet, and band practice. We run to the post office, to the dry cleaner, to the DMV, to the vet, to the emergency room. When we are home, we cook, we clean, we change diapers, and we are expected to greet our spouses at the door with a smile, asking how their day was and not expecting them to return the courtesy, because it is they who suffer for having to have a "real job."

Of course Bethany understands that my job is not easy and the pay is lousy. She appreciates my efforts, even when she is positive that she could get the whites whiter. It's the excellent benefits package that goes along with my job that makes the slave wages worthwhile. All of my living expenses are covered. I have health, life, and auto insurance. I pay no social security or income taxes. I work from home. I get to spend a lot of time with my kids. On most days, I get to sleep in. I only rarely have to clean up a bathroom that's been "redecorated" by a kid with a woefully inadequate diaper. My life is pretty damn good. I never plan on having a "real job" again.

If that would be alright with you, Dear.

Bethany was more than happy to have her husband take care of the kids. The couple saved hundreds of dollars per month on child care expenses, to be sure. But more importantly, the boys enjoyed a close relationship with their father. "You just can't put a price tag on that," she admitted.

By the start of 2012, life for the Naughtons was very good. Travis's book royalties would make the family secure in their finances, allowing Bethany to decrease her hours at work to a less stressful part-time status. The couple adopted another child from China, this time a seven-year-old girl named Tian-Tian. (Travis confessed that ever since first deciding to start a family, he had always wanted a daughter.) Little Truman entered kindergarten in the fall, which freed-up Travis's days, allowing him distraction-free time to write a second book, **Reason for Leaving**, that was published in 2013. It immediately became a best seller, the author's second big hit in a row. Travis Naughton was hot, yet he was only getting warmed up.

Reason for Leaving

Travis Naughton couldn't have known that he had captured lightning in a bottle when he wrote Reason for Leaving. *The book was written in a completely original format — a rarity in the modern age. It amounted to a 284 page job application, the bulk of which consisting of the section "employment history." Naughton listed and described every job he had held up until his "retirement" in 2008. The hook, and the source of the book's title, was in the hilarious explanations and excuses that he gave for his "Reason for Leaving" each job. Naughton had long-since embraced his lack of a strong work ethic, (Chris Stevens once remarked, "You are the laziest sack of shit I know, but at least you own it.") and now, judging by the six million copies sold of his second book, so did his readers.*

(Younger): Did the response from your readers to *Reason for Leaving* surprise you?

(Elder): Definitely. I wrote the book mostly for my own amusement as a way to remember my days as a working stiff. I really didn't think anybody would be interested in reading it.

(Younger): Can you tell me more about one of your former jobs? Some details that were not in the book perhaps?

(Elder): Sure. After I convinced the Enabler that I didn't need to work full-time in order for us to pay our bills, I quit my job at an auto auction, (which was giving me an ulcer,) and applied to work at a store called "Goochie Poochie," which I mentioned in the book. I spoke briefly with the owner of the store, which was a pet boutique and gourmet dog treats bakery, a woman named Gayle Robinson, who said that she thought it might be nice to have a man working at the store for a change. She advised me to speak to the manager on the following Monday and ended our conversation by saying, "I think you might just be the perfect Christmas present for us." I wasn't sure exactly what that meant, but I took it as a compliment regardless.

I arrived for my interview with a resume in hand and a college education, which pretty much guaranteed me the job. The manager, a woman named Sally Myatt, asked only two questions: "What days can you work and when can you start?"

It didn't take me long to figure out how different Goochie Poochie [GP] was from all of the testosterone-driven jobs I had held in the past. The crudeness of the working environment and of my co-workers while I was a meat cutter, a groundskeeper, and used-car salesman was a stark contrast to the estrogen-infused serenity of the all female crew at the store. I took a liking to my new co-workers immediately, (although they later admitted that they were initially somewhat hesitant to allow a man into their inner circle,) largely because they were all young and beautiful college girls. But before long, they felt comfortable enough to tell me about their boyfriends and to ask me for advice about relationships and what-not. I was a good listener, and they appreciated me for it.

(Younger): I'll bet you had some pretty interesting conversations with those young gals.

(Elder): I did. One girl named Debbie felt compelled to confess things to me that were probably too much for her priest to handle. An old boyfriend had called her recently and wanted to get back together because she had given him the best head he'd ever had. She said that she was, in fact, quite gifted in that department. "Have you *seen* these lips?" she asked. She also confided in me that at a hot tub party with some of her sorority sisters, swimsuits were optional. She and a girlfriend were admiring each other's breasts when Debbie noticed that her friend had a pierced nipple. She asked her, "Would you mind if I licked your nipple ring?" Apparently her friend didn't mind and the rest of the story reminded me of some of the letters I've read in *Penthouse Forum*. She said, "You're such a good listener, Travis." Well of course I was.

(Younger): Of course you were.

(Elder): The store was rarely busy in those days, so we had plenty of time to talk> Sometimes the girls did homework. I'd take cat naps in the back room. The easy going pace and stress-free atmosphere was exactly what I needed. The store was founded on the principles of holistic pet care, and offered foods, treats, and supplements with only all-natural ingredients. We baked fresh treats with no added preservatives or fillers. We sold gentle shampoos and conditioners, and humane training collars and aids. Talk of hosting "yoga for dogs" and pet message sessions never came to fruition, but would not have seemed unusual in the slightest had they actually taken place. We even raised money for local animal rescue groups by selling pet photos with Santa and the Easter Bunny. (I look good in a bunny suit by the way. For years after I quit working there I continued to dress up for pet photos) It couldn't have been a more relaxing and fun environment. That is, until Gayle had a complete mental breakdown requiring an involuntary evaluation at the local psychiatric hospital. Gayle always seemed like a slightly quirky person, even before she paid a consultant to design a modification to her car that would allow it to be controlled remotely via a radio transmitter so that it would appear that her dogs were driving. And when she talked to customer's dogs and seemed to understand what they were communicating to her, we just thought she had a gift, not an illness. But after she started neglecting the store, was seen sitting in her car out in the parking lot for hours at a time, and then disappeared for a few weeks, we began to worry.

(Younger): That doesn't sound good. What happened to her?

(Elder): Her symptoms of paranoia and delusions forced both Sally and Gayle's cousin Grace to have her temporarily committed in a mental ward at the local hospital. But unfortunately, she held it together just long enough to get released without a proper diagnosis. One week later, a neighbor found Gayle Robinson's lifeless body lying on the floor of her garage behind the exhaust pipe of the car she planned to let her dogs "drive" one day. Apparently, as the engine was idling, Gayle drank two bottles of peach schnapps, laid down flat on her back, crossed her arms in the manner of an Egyptian mummy, and waited to die. As a huge fan of classic Hollywood, she always had a flair for the dramatic.

(Younger): So much for the stress-free part-time job, huh?

(Elder): Exactly. As the months wore on, rumors about the store's future began to circulate. Just as it seemed that the business would go under, a new owner came to the rescue. I doubted that the husband and wife who bought the store in order to fulfill a lifelong dream of owning their own business had any inkling of the nightmare that had made the store available to them. I also doubted that it was my place to tell them. I continued working at GP for another year or so until the Enabler determined that we could survive on one income if I was still interested in being a full-time stay-at-home dad. I jumped at the opportunity of course. But two years later, as kindergarten for my son Alex loomed on the horizon, the Voice of Reason told me to get a job. I called the new manager of the store and asked about getting rehired. Mary, (whom I worked with for a short time towards the end of my first stint on the job,) informed me that she would be leaving to pursue a job elsewhere soon and that I should apply for her job. So I did, and the store's owners were thrilled to have me back as the manager.

(Younger): Manager? That's pretty ambitious for someone who claims not to have a work ethic. How did that work out for you?

(Elder): Under my leadership, the store's profits increased exponentially. The natural pet food craze that was created following the massive recall of tainted, lower quality pet foods exploded just after I assumed control of the business. And because none of our products were involved in the recall, customers flocked to our store. As the business made money, so did I, and by the time Bethany and I were all set to adopt Truman, we had become debt-free. Once again, the Enabler gave me permission to "retire." "This time," I told her, "it's for good."

(Younger): It sounds like GP was a pretty interesting place to work. Even though it was "work," you did enjoy being employed there, didn't you?

(Elder): I did. I met a lot of interesting folks there. Some were quite bizarre in fact. We didn't sell animals, which was pretty obvious judging by the complete lack of animals in the store, but that didn't stop people from asking, "Do y'all sell pets in here?" on a daily basis.

"No, I'm sorry." I'd tell them. "We only sell pet supplies."

"Oh," a confused customer once said, "With a name like 'Goochie Poochie,' I figured you'd at least sell geckos."

Or the time I answered the phone, "Hello. Thank you for calling Goochie Poochie. This is Travis, how can I help you?"

"Um, yeah." The caller said. "I was wondering if you could tell me the best way to ship an alligator."

(Younger): Really? What did you tell the caller?

(Elder): I said, "Ma'am, we bake dog treats. I don't know anything about shipping alligators. Try calling the post office."

My all time favorite question was, "I'm building a rape stand for my pitbull. Do you sell muzzles here?"

(Younger): A rape stand? That doesn't sound good.

(Elder): Not good at all. I said, "No sir, we don't have any muzzles." I was lying.

"Damn," he said. "My bitch is meaner than hell and I'm afraid she'll kill my stud when I breed her."

"Gee, sorry I can't help," I said. "Maybe you should consider not breeding such an aggressive dog." I knew my suggestion would fall on deaf ears, but my conscience forced me to try anyway.

(Younger): What did the guy say?

(Elder): He said, "Naw, I want these pups to be the baddest motherfuckers on the planet so if anybody comes through my front door that I don't want coming through my front door, the only way to get back out will be in a body bag. You know what I mean?"

I thought, *No, I don't know what you mean, asshole. Don't you see that this store is a happy place where we spoil our puppies with handmade treats and expensive goodies? A place that sells sweaters for Chihuahuas? A place that sells toenail polish and hair bows for Yorkie-Poos?? Are you aware that our original owner commissioned an artist to paint wall-sized murals of each of her four dogs because she loved them like they were her own children? That she was building a car for her dogs to drive? That some people say she still haunts the store to this day and preys upon the souls of idiots like you? Can't you see that we'd be sorta opposed to building rape stands for dogs that are too dangerous to be handled, much less bred? I think you're fucking brain-dead. You know what I mean? No, you probably don't.*

(Younger): What did you really say to him?

(Elder): "Have a nice day, sir."

When Naughton set out to go on his second book tour, he called a friend of his named Paul Shields to see if he might be interested in joining him on the road. The two had met several years earlier while playing cards at the home of a mutual friend who Travis worked with at the car auction. They quickly realized that they each shared a similar, twisted sense of humor and hit it off immediately. Paul jumped at the chance to work with his old poker buddy.

Paul was a five foot five, half Chinese, half Irish, bespectacled employee of a company that rehabbed and/or demolished meth labs and crack houses. He was also a stand-up comedian and songwriter. Paul was the lone member of a comedy act called "Paul & the Violent Farmers." Paulie, as he was known by his friends, wrote absurdly funny songs and performed them while playing an acoustic guitar at comedy clubs and bars throughout the Kansas City area. When asked about the origins of the name "Paul & the Violent Farmers," Paulie was tight lipped. Travis took the opportunity to invent a back story on his friend's behalf. He repeated the lie everywhere they went:

Paul was drunk at the bar one night and noticed a group of rednecks playing pool in the back of the room. He stumbled over to them and put down a stack of quarters for the next game. All of a sudden this 6 or 7 foot tall corn-fed hoosier walks up and says, "This table's reserved for Ag students only." Paul slurred, "For your information, I was president of my high school's Future Farmers of America club."

Bubba got this wild look in his eye and says, "If you're a farmer, then I'm a 5 foot tall Chinaman lookin' to get his ass kicked." So Paulie punched him square in the neck and yelled, "We don't want your kind around here!" Then Bubba's overall-wearin' buddies proceeded beat to Paulie like an Oriental rug. Later when he woke up in the alley, a friend was standing over him telling the cops about what had happened in the bar between Paul and the violent farmers. Paul smiled, spit up some blood, and thanked her for inadvertently naming his act.

The pair would perform together, taking turns at the microphone, ignoring the traditional format of a featured performer followed by a headliner. They needed no opening act. Paul would sing a song or two, Travis would read from a chapter from Reason for Leaving, *and so on. Bored with the usual book signings and hour-long readings on the lecture circuit, Naughton (with Shields's help) blurred the lines of distinction between book tours and stand-up comedy. As word spread of this new and electric combination, venues sold out regularly, and the duo took their act on a nationwide tour.*

By the end of their first tour, Naughton had started including excerpts from some of his other original works in his routine. As a result, sales of his first book enjoyed a resurgence which caused it to appear on the New York Times bestseller list a second time. Travis Naughton and Paul Shields were bona fide celebrities now, and constantly on the alert for new ways to keep their act fresh and their pockets full. Travis had another wild idea in mind, but first he would need to track down his wild friend Dave Richards.

Going Overboard

Although their lives had gone in different directions after high school and they hadn't spoken to one another often since their falling out while working at The Canoe Company, it was only a matter of time before lifelong friends Travis Naughton and Dave Richards buried the hatchet. "We had a lot of history together," Travis said. "But like my father [who was a high school history teacher] always said, 'Those who fail to learn their history are doomed to repeat it.'" He elaborated in his memoir:

Coming out of high school, Dave Richards and I each received several offers to attend college on music scholarships. Dave accepted an offer from a small liberal arts college in northeast Missouri while I turned down an offer from the same school and another at a small college in Illinois--either of which would have paid for over half my tuition. Instead, I opted to go to the largest school in the state, which did not offer me a dime, but did offer me the opportunity to step out of the spotlight when I needed to. After being a very big fish in a very small pond back in Hannibal, I thought the anonymity of attending a university with over 20,000 students would be a welcome change of pace.

While I lost myself and my desire to play music in the sea of humanity that was the University of Missouri, Dave stood out as a talented trombone player at his school. He fell in love with college life and invited me to visit from time to time to share the experience with him. The first time I came to visit, Dave invited me to his fraternity house and introduced me to his new brothers. We played a little foosball and then answered the call to participate in a game called "The Circle of Death." About a dozen or so guys sat in chairs making a perimeter around a 55 gallon trash barrel, each with a six-pack of longnecks at the ready. Dave and I joined them in the circle and exchanged nervous glances. The rules were announced to the group: Rule #1: Players have 30 minutes to consume their ration of six beers. Rule #2: If a player must urinate, defecate, or regurgitate, he must do so in the barrel. Rule #3: The last player to finish his six-pack must clean out the barrel. Rule #4: Any player who leaves the Circle of Death for any reason must help the loser clean out the barrel at the conclusion of the game. After the rules were read, I wanted to make a break for it, but Dave was still just a powerless pledge in the fraternity and had no choice in the matter. I would not abandon my friend.

The game began. Guys cracked jokes to keep the mood light, but as the minutes ticked by and people started using the barrel as a toilet, the tension began to mount. Twenty minutes in, the first of the pukers started to buckle under the pressure. When the two minute warning sounded, I still had a full beer left to drink. I popped the top and started chugging as everyone in the circle made their sprint to the finish. Luckily for Dave and me, all of the time we spent at his parents' house cleaning out their liquor cabinet had prepared us for this moment. We each emptied the last of our beers just seconds before the buzzer sounded. I am both proud and embarrassed that neither of us had to use the barrel for anything other than tossing away our empties, and I still have nightmares about the poor schmuck who had to clean it out.

The next time I came to visit, Dave was living in an apartment off campus and was by then a full-fledged member of his fraternity. The first thing he said to me when I arrived was, "Tonight, we're gonna get you laid." Well, who was I to argue? I did seem to need Dave's help in that department. The truth is, without Dave by my side egging me on, I would probably still be a virgin today. While I was shy and self-conscious around women, Dave was bold and fearless. Once, he heard that a friend had some girls over at his apartment, so he went over to see if he could hook up with one of them. Without knocking, he threw open the front door, caught two couples going at it in the living room, and blurted out, "But who's gonna fuck *me*?"

During the party taking place at his fraternity house, Dave introduced me to a girl who I think was named Tracy. She and I started making out immediately, and for a moment I was worried that her instant attraction reflected the amount of money Dave must have been paying her to keep me company. In no time, she suggested that we excuse ourselves from the party and head over to Dave's place. For a puny, former second baseman who couldn't hit water if he fell out of a boat, I had just hit a home run. Moments after I finished rounding the bases, Dave came home and asked, "You kids have a good time?" A repeat performance the next night was answer enough. Whenever I'm asked if I've ever had a one night stand, I answer honestly, "Of course not. It was a two night stand. I'm no slut."

Each subsequent visit with Dave became more bizarre than the last over the next few years. I noticed a change in his demeanor that began to worry me. He eventually dropped out of school and landed a gig playing in a band aboard a cruise ship. It didn't last. Dave seemed to be stuck in a never-ending cycle of travelling to a friend's or family member's house, sleeping on their couch, wearing out his welcome, and moving on to the next stop to do it all over again. One day not long after I had gotten married, he called to ask if he could crash with me and Bethany for a while. I said no. We didn't see each other for another fifteen years.

Finally, Naughton found a way to reconnect with his old friend. His new brainchild was to form a blues band with Paulie, Dave, and a few other musician friends including fellow band camper and now famous Kansas City saxophonist/composer Joe Athon and world renowned drummer and former high school band mate Matt Kane. Dave, down on his luck and eager to get back into the music scene, agreed to let bygones be bygones and join the group. Paul reworked several of his songs into blues arrangements while Travis condensed some of his favorite stories into lyrics. Athon set the words to music and soon the band (which they decided to name "The Blues Farmers") had a formidable playlist. Travis talked about the thrill of playing in a band again with a reporter from Rolling Stone *magazine:*

"I had recently re-acquired an old trombone that I sold to a buddy over twenty years ago. It felt so good to be able to play again and I quickly realized how much I missed playing in a band. Even though Dave [Richards] does most of the playing while I sing, I still get to take a solo once in a while. I forgot just how much fun the whole experience is. I can see myself doing this for a long, long time."

The Blues Farmers appeared throughout the Midwest at bars and music festivals for the better part of the ensuing year. Naughton held book signings at local stores while the group was on the road, promoting both his books and the band. His agent knew the group's growing popularity would help sell books, so he suggested that the band cut an album. But there was a catch: they would need to change their name to "Travis & The Violent Farmers" in order to capitalize on their two most famous members.

The band unanimously rejected the idea of a name change. Despite being told by several record labels that their music was not strong enough to sell under the forgettable "Blues Farmers" name, they held firm to their conviction. After another brief tour in the summer of 2015, the band members decided to go their separate ways. When Travis told Dave "See you later" after their final performance, he had no idea how wrong he was. Richards' history of being a heavy drinker finally caught up with him. While working on another ocean liner later that year, he disappeared after going on an all-night bender and was presumed to have fallen overboard. His shipboard band mates testified that he was drunk most nights and was especially so on the evening of his disappearance. He was only forty-three years old.

Naughton was devastated by the loss. After Dave's disappearance, Travis retreated from the spotlight, back to his secluded home in the woods. He wrote in his journal some reflections of his life and what his old friend meant to him:

I still think about Dave all the time. Getting to play with him again after all these years was one of the highlights of my life. We had set aside all our past disagreements and really healed our friendship, although his drinking was still out of control. I even stopped blaming him for introducing me to alcohol at such an early age; someone else would have done the honors eventually. But I do wonder from time to time how things might have gone had I not strayed from the relatively straight and narrow path of my youth in favor of following my friend on the treacherous trail toward self-destruction that only one of us would eventually be able to walk away from. Would I have concentrated more on my musical pursuits? Would I have taken college more seriously? Would I have become a writer? Would I have met Bethany? Would I have had kids?

I would like to think that the contentedness I have finally found is owed to the choices, both good and bad, that I have made in my life. Mama always told me, "Everything happens for a reason." I simply would not be the man I am today were it not for the influences of Dave and the rest of the people I have met over the years. In that regard, I owe everything I have to Dave Richards. I just wish I could have told him that.

Are Those Goats?

Naughton's home in Hartsburg became his sanctuary. The stillness and isolation was conducive to his writing and helped inspire several of his most popular stories and essays. Travis had convinced Bethany to buy their "little house in the woods" in 1999, after growing weary of bouncing around from one cramped apartment to another during his college years. "Really, I just wanted to be able to walk around in the buff whenever I felt like it. Sure, one could make the arguments that in the country the air is cleaner, the stars are brighter, and the crime rate is lower, but for me, it was all about gittin' nekkid."

Their home is situated on ten heavily wooded acres, on the fringes of (appropriately enough,) the Mark Twain National Forest, near the Missouri River. The house itself is a modest 2,000 square foot, four-bedroom with a walk-out basement and a three-stall pole barn that serves as a garage. It is not visible from the road or their neighbors' houses, so it affords the residents a real sense of seclusion and privacy. "The rooms are cozy," Naughton wrote in his column, "which means 'tiny' in the language spoken by real estate agents, but we get by. I can clean the house from top-to-bottom in a single afternoon, often without the bother of getting dressed. I've done so several times, although whenever I turn-on the vacuum, I do get a little nervous."

(Younger): Do you still walk around the house in the nude, or is that a younger man's game?

(Elder): Oh, I still do it, but I try to avoid walking in front of any mirrors these days. *[laughs]* But before having kids, I took advantage of every opportunity I found to parade about in my birthday suit. I even enticed my wife to join me on occasion. People who live in the middle of nowhere shouldn't have tan lines. I think there might even be an ordinance that forbids them. I bet you didn't know that.

(Younger): No I did not.

(Elder): Nude sun bathing is a great way to spice things up for an old married couple. It also turns out that a tropical beach somewhere in Mexico is not the only place where two people can have sex outdoors. All you need is a reclining patio lounger, some mosquito repellant, and a secluded home in the country. Of course having children puts a damper on the whole nudity thing, but that just means you have to pick and choose your moments wisely. Whenever Bethany and the kids were out of the house for the day — or god help me--an entire weekend, I made the most of my opportunity. Sometimes I would take long baths while cranking some 80s hair metal on the hi-fi and drinking cheap red wine straight from the bottle. Just before the water in the tub got cold enough to induce hypothermia, I'd get out and dry off and wander around the house for a while before getting dressed. Sometimes I'd go outside and sunbathe, although it was not as much fun without my sexy, naked wife lying beside me. One time I laid-out too long and got a really bad sunburn on my ass, which was fun to show to friends but very uncomfortable when it came to sitting at the dinner table or typing on the computer.

(Younger): Besides the freedom to be nude, what are some other interesting aspects to living in the country?

(Elder): With clothes on, country living can be a little boring at times, but at others it can be quite an adventure. You may think that moving away from an urban environment full of gang warfare, drive-by shootings, and armed robberies would diminish the amount of gunfire to be heard on any given day, but you would be wrong. It's not unusual to hear shots ringing out from any given direction surrounding our property on any given day. As deer and turkey hunting seasons draw near, it becomes increasingly dangerous to walk through the hiking trails that I blazed throughout our woods. You would think ten acres should be enough of a buffer from our trigger-happy neighbors to keep us safe, but on one occasion, I found out that is not necessarily the case.

(Younger): Do tell.

(Elder): On a Sunday morning back in 2004 or so, I was working at the computer and sipping coffee while Bethany and Alex were downstairs watching TV. I heard several gunshots, which as I said was not unusual, except these sounded so loud that I became concerned that a trespasser might be hunting on our property. I was hardly dressed for a confrontation in my flannel pajama pants and paisley robe, but I stepped outside to investigate regardless. *Boom!* I could tell the shooter was close-by because I could feel the concussion of the blast in my chest. I walked out in front of the house and into a clearing near our sewage lagoon some 100 feet from our front door. (Yes, our front porch afforded us a breathtaking view of a fluorescent-green pool of excrement, but now that the trees have grown up around it, you can hardly notice.) As I stood in the clearing, quietly listening for the next shot in order to track down the trespasser, I heard what sounded like a cannon being fired followed by the sound of rain all around me. After a quick check of my underwear, I determined that surprisingly I had *not* shit my pants and that my neighbor was firing a shotgun directly toward my house. Sure, the distance the steel shot had to cover greatly reduced the chances that I would be injured by the blast, but nevertheless, I was under fire. Afraid to approach the gun-wielding maniac while unarmed, I decided to shout angrily in his general direction.

"Hey!" I yelled with every fiber of indignation I could muster. "You just shot at my house!"

I heard a gasp and some mumbling.

I shouted even louder, "That shot landed in my *front yard*!" I feared I wasn't making my outrage obvious enough.

"Sorry." That was all he said. I guess there wasn't much else he could say other than, *"Hey, I'm a real dumbass. I have ten acres of my own land that I could have been shooting over had I simply turned and faced the opposite direction, but for some reason I decided to stand on the property line and aim straight at your house instead. What can I say? I'm a mental midget, I guess. I would promise to never let it happen again, but I'd probably be lying."*

Well, it never did happen again. I made sure of that when I printed off an aerial photograph of our neighboring parcels of land with the property lines superimposed upon them. I took it and a carefully worded letter expressly discouraging anyone from taking aim at anything on my side of the boundary again to my neighbor, who mercifully was not home at the time. I taped the envelope to his door and prayed that I would never have to communicate with him in person. Unfortunately, after another neighbor reported spotting the same idiot trespassing at the bottom of our hill on other occasions, I had to make a face-to-face plea for him to please refrain from shooting at, camping on, or tracking live game through our ten-acre slice of heaven ever again. He of course denied any wrong-doing, but luckily he moved away a few months later--sparing me from having to confront him a third time and/or purchase my own weapon.

(Younger): Tell me more about your "ten-acre slice of heaven."

(Elder): The trails that I blazed in our woods rival the quality of those you would find in many state parks. I'm not kidding. The truth is that I've put more effort into creating and maintaining those paths than I ever did a paying job. But for me, it's been a labor of love. The rolling terrain features limestone rock formations, a small creek, a natural glade, and fields of various wildflower species. The network of trails takes the hiker past all of these natural attractions and over hills, through valleys, and around a huge stand of hundred-year-old oaks, sycamores, and cedars. I have seen white-tail deer, wild turkeys, possums, raccoons, coyotes, rabbits, rats, mice, moles, voles, squirrels, a flying squirrel, frogs, toads, salamanders, snakes, lizards, turtles, spiders, scorpions, and more insects than most city-dwelling folks could ever conceive of. Every now and then on a warm summer evening while all the windows in the house are open to let in the fresh country air, the unmistakable and unfortunate smell of a passing skunk will force us to close-up the house and enjoy some fresh country air-conditioning.

(Younger): Do you see a lot of birds around your house?

(Elder): We do. Before a cat showed up at our doorstep and proceeded to have kittens (which we had neutered and allowed to stick around) we had birdfeeders set up around the house. A person can only watch so many chickadees and blue jays become cat food before reluctantly taking down the feeders. To date, according to the check-list in my field guide to North American birds, I have spotted (or in the case of owls and whip-poor-wills *heard*) 52 species of birds on or around our property. Once, I even spotted a bald eagle perched in a tree on my neighbor's side of the property line. That was pretty neat.

Naughton wrote about some of his experiences on his homestead for Rural Living *magazine in 2014:*

There is one feature, albeit manmade, that sets our place apart from the typical country homestead. Our gravel driveway forms a big circle and in the middle of that circle, an "island" for lack of a better term sits. This island is elevated about four feet above the level of the driveway and the yard, and because our house is located on top of a hill, the view from that elevation is spectacular. A view too spectacular for say, a pair of pygmy goats.

In the weeks before Christmas when my son was two or three years old, my father-in-law Bill called to ask if Alex would like a pet goat for Christmas. Always up for a new adventure, I said, "I don't see why he wouldn't." A few days later, Bethany's father called again, this time to ask if we would be willing to take two goats, so the first one he picked out for us wouldn't be lonely. I said yes of course, and spent the better part of a weekend erecting a fence on our "island" to contain them. When Christmas came, we sat in the living room of my in-laws' farmhouse; apprehension in Bethany's eyes, anticipation in mine. A pair of baby pygmy goats was brought into the room, each kid wearing disposable diapers. In any other household, this might have seemed unusual, but not at the Lemon farm. Alex and I fell in love with them straight away and couldn't wait to bring them home. But homecoming would have to wait until after the chores were done on the farm.

Bill asked me if I would like to join him in constructing a whelping box for one of the Great Pyrenees bitches that was going into labor on that frosty night. I said, "No problem." Five hours later, after being driven in a 1973 Ford LTD sedan over every acre of the farm and to town and back twice, after building the dog bed, and after being shown Bill's "goldfinches" that he put in a 55-gallon barrel of water to keep the water from freezing, (to my great relief, after dreading what feathered horrors I might find floating belly-up in the barrel, "goldfinches" in Billspeak really meant "goldfish"), we finally returned to the house. I shot Bethany a look that said, "Never leave me alone with this madman again or so help me..."

Clearly, she understood. She returned my look with one of her own that said, "Oh my goodness! I'm so sorry. I'll never let that happen to you again." Her father was quite simply, a crazy person. To give you a sense of the insanity on his farm, I'll tell you that at one point Bill constructed some sort of a bomb (for reasons unknown to me) and after it was found and disarmed by the local authorities, with a devilish twinkle in his eye and an ornery chuckle he confided to a friend, "How do they know they got *all* the dynamite?" On another occasion he whispered to me, "I got these here vitamins from an outfit in China. The minerals come from outer space. You can't just buy this stuff at the store, you know? Don't tell Beth, or she'll think I'm crazy." *(Sorry Bill, but that spaceship has already taken off.)*

Bill was crazy, there was no denying it, but he wasn't all bad. He did give us goats for Christmas. We named them Ferdinand and Isabella.

Ferdie and Bella were a lot of fun to have around. Whenever I let them out of their pen, they stayed close by and often followed Alex, the dogs, the cats, and me on our walks in the woods. When I looked back over my shoulder on these hikes, I felt like the Pied Piper of Hartsburg, Missouri. It was quite a sight. Speaking of sights, a friend of mine *[Paul Shields]* held an online photo contest asking for submissions of snapshots of his friends doing something unusual while wearing an eye patch and a sombrero. My submission was a picture taken by then four-year-old Alex of me feeding Ferdie and Bella from an oversized beer mug full of goat chow while I was dressed in boxer shorts, cowboy boots, a sombrero, an eye patch, and nothing else. Paul emailed me and asked, "Dude, are those goats?" When I replied that indeed they were, I won the contest hands-down, although my friends did start to wonder just what the heck was happening at the Naughton Ranch while Mommy was at work. Hey, a stay-at-home dad has to entertain himself somehow. Not wanting to keep all the fun to myself, I dressed Alex in my odd-looking outfit and took his picture with the goats, too. I'm saving that photo for when he starts dating.

Those silly goats proved to be too smart for their own good. Aside from occasionally showing signs of being the dumbest animals on earth by eating a string of Christmas lights on the deck or a toy dinosaur, they were amazingly cunning escape artists. They tested their fence for weaknesses constantly and were able to break out all the time. I finally decided to relocate them to the pen that encircled our sewage lagoon because professional construction workers had built it, and after ten or so years it appeared to still be structurally sound. There was ample forage for them in the overgrown enclosure and so I moved them into their new digs one morning in early fall. Within days, I started seeing them in my front yard, casually grazing at my freshly seeded sprouts of grass. I herded them back into their pen, found the latest hole to open up, patched it as best I could, and repeated the daily. Finally, after several weeks of frustration, it seemed that the pen was at last escape proof.

One day after winter had arrived and a severe cold snap had settled in, I went down to the pen to give Ferdie and Bella their daily supplement of goat pellets. I noticed Bella was missing and was a little surprised by this discovery because Ferdie was usually the one who led the jail breaks. I went back to the house to fetch Alex and we set out to track her down. After nearly an hour of searching our woods and calling her name, Bella was nowhere to be found. I suggested to Alex that we go by the pen one last time to see if she had returned and as we came around the far side of the enclosure, I spotted something protruding from the iced-over lagoon. Too late to warn Alex to look away did I recognize that it was the bloated, drowned corpse of our beloved Bella. He spotted her immediately and let out a quiet gasp and whimper at the horror of what he saw. Ever the brave little soldier, he did not cry, but he was clearly upset, as was I. I felt responsible for her demise because had I not put her in that pen in the first place, she would have never walked out on the thin ice and plunged to her death. Try explaining that to a kindergartner.

Ferdie was acting pretty lonely without his sister in the dog pen I relocated him to after the accident. We decided as a family to send him to live with a small herd of goats that a friend owned. Life on the Naughton Ranch has never been the same without our light bulb-eating, fence-busting, four-legged friends. I really miss those little devils. Bethany's aunt Mary Lee said that she would give us some horses to help fill the void, but the Voice of Reason says until I develop the carpentry skills necessary to build an escape-proof corral, it ain't gonna happen.

(Younger): Did you ever build a corral, or did you stop trying to build things?

(Elder): No corral, but as bad as I was at building goat pens, it turns out that I do possess *some* carpentry skills. After years of promising that I would build a clubhouse for Alex, a gazebo for Bethany, and man-cave for myself, I had an epiphany. While I stared out the kitchen window at the empty island, I thought, "Why not combine all three?" Like a mad man bent on building a machine that would allow him to take over the world, I spent every waking moment of my free time for an entire month constructing a 12' by 16' deck located in the middle of the circle drive island. It was the first, last, and only wood-working project I have ever attempted by myself in my entire life. My good friend Wes Douglass did help me set the corner posts and floor joists (help I was immensely glad to have), but after that I built the remainder of the structure entirely by myself. Half of the deck is covered with a roof that shelters the hand-built wooden bar below, the other half is open-air. Furnished with a mini-fridge, a T.V., a stereo, and seating for a dozen of my best friends, the Party Porch, as I like to call it, serves its purpose well. I decorated it in the theme of a run-down bait shack complete with old fishing lures and poles, rusted metal signs advertising fishing tackle, a few real and fake fish mounts, photos of the boys and me with our best catches, some beer signs, and a large hand-painted sign that reads, "Naught's Landing, Live Bait & Cold Beer" hanging directly behind the bar. It is glorious.

(Younger): How does a bar double as a clubhouse for kids?

(Elder): Well, after an initial attempt to place the clubhouse on the rooftop of the porch (complete with railing and a secured ladder) failed due to the fact that flat roofs leak like — well, like flat roofs, I decided to build an annex on the back of the porch. The boys spent a lot of time playing in this fully enclosed and almost watertight "Discovery Club" (as Alex called it), while the grown-ups spent a lot more time in the main portion of the structure.

(Younger): What about the gazebo for your wife?

(Elder): She didn't get a gazebo per se, but she was pleased with the budget I worked within and was actually thrilled with the way the project turned out. We still spend quite a few evenings out there together. And when I needed a little "me" time while I was a stay-at-home dad, it provided a welcome refuge from the trappings of a life lived in absolute domestication.

(Younger): Naught's Landing sounds like a pretty neat place. But how do you entertain yourself during the winter months?

(Elder): In winter, it is sometimes a little too cold to spend much time on the Party Porch, but I still feel the need to get naked and be outdoors every now and then. One winter, we had about six inches of snow on the ground, and I had the house to myself for a few hours. The temperature hovered in the low 20s, but I didn't see why that should stop me from stripping off my clothes and stepping outside for a minute. As I tip-toed onto the front porch and into the frigid-air I spied a patch of pristine snow in the front yard. I knew what I had to do. I descended the stairs, stepped onto the walk, and lined-up my approach. Harkening back to my training in junior high gym class, I executed a perfect standing broad jump out into the fresh powder. (Okay, so it was really more like a belly-flop, but nevertheless.) I landed face-down in the snow, which of course meant that my penis instantly crawled-up inside of me seeking a warm place to hide. I imagined him saying, "Inside that house we have a perfectly good furnace and porn on the internet. What the hell are we doing out here?" Shocked by the cold, yet undeterred, I rolled onto my back and created what may have been the first naked snow angel in the history of mankind. My moment of glory was short-lived though as I was suddenly overcome by the sensation of a thousand icy needles tearing into my flesh. I sprinted into the house and took the longest, hottest shower of my life. Eventually, my penis re-emerged from his hiding place, tentatively at first, and I rewarded him with an unencumbered run of the house until my family returned home.

(Younger): What was Bethany's reaction when you told her that story?

(Elder): Let's just put it this way: Over the years, my wife has learned not to ask, "So what did you do with yourself while I was gone?" Some questions are better left unasked.

Returning home following the whirlwind that was two book tours and a concert tour helped Naughton recover from the loss of his old friend and the rigors of the road. It also allowed him to rediscover his love for living the simple life and writing about it. His willingness to share stories about his daily follies endeared him to his readers and lifted the popularity of his column to an all-time high.

Mr. Badwrench

During this period when Naughton returned to his writing roots, he penned a number of pieces that were later published in bound compilations of short stories and essays. The subject of one of these columns was Naughton's love/hate relationship with automobiles. It is a wonderful example of his "everyman" style of storytelling that is easily relatable to so many of his readers.

For reasons I can't begin to explain, I have an old truck fetish. This isn't to say that the sight of an old pick-up arouses me sexually. Rather, whenever I see an old Chevy or Ford that has suffered from neglect or abuse at the hands of its previous owners, I feel compelled to bring it home, tune it up, and slap a fresh rattle-can paint job on it. When I bring one of these jalopies home to show my wife, what she and most of my friends and family fail to recognize is the hidden potential in these buckets of rust. I am a visionary in this regard. I have discovered that dilapidated farm trucks make wonderful football tailgate party vehicles.

The first of these tailgaters was a 1966 Chevrolet C-30 that had served as a hog hauling truck over the course of its first 33 years of life. It had dual rear wheels, an 8'x10' flatbed, it ran, and most importantly, it only cost me six hundred bucks. I brought my friend Wes with me to go pick it up and when he first saw it he just shook his head as if to say, "Travis, I love you man, but you've lost your mind." He just couldn't see what I saw: *potential*. Bethany couldn't see it either at first. When I asked her what she thought of my new purchase after I drove it home, she said, "Well, as long as *you* like it dear."

My loving wife serves in two vital capacities within our

relationship: Voice of Reason and Enabler. It is a delicate balancing act that only she is qualified to attempt. More often than not, the Enabler eventually relents as I ignore the Voice of Reason. As I wear her down, "Do we really need a 34 year old truck?" is gradually replaced with, "I'll never have to drive it will I?", and I bring home another jalopy.

After Wes and I spent three hours removing the rusted and incredibly heavy steel stock panels from the bed of the old Chevy and I had applied a fresh black and gold paint job (the official school colors of our alma mater the University of Missouri,) Wes, and to a lesser extent Bethany, finally saw the light.

"I've got to admit," he said, "I just couldn't see it before. But man, that is one beautiful truck." And it was, too. The old truck served us well at countless tailgate parties including one when my son Alex was just a week old. Mizzou was playing against arch rival Kansas for the homecoming game the weekend after he was born, and there was no way I was staying home to look after a newborn while my glorious tailgatin' truck sat idle in my garage. Life is all about priorities you know.

But of course, my priorities changed a few years later. I bought a 1957 Chevy Bel Air that needed some mechanical work done on it and in exchange for the repairs a guy was doing for me, I bartered the old truck rather than part with the small amount of cash in my account. One morning I loaded the old steel stock panels and six old wheels and tires onto the flatbed and drove to work where the mechanic was going to drop off my repaired car and pick up the truck. Here's a word of advice for you: Never load one ton of material into the back of a 35 year old truck and then drive it at 75 miles per hour for 20 miles on your way to work. Bad things will happen. By the time I parked at my place of work, the truck could only manage a top speed of 15 miles per hour while a hideous knocking noise that sounded a lot like a jackhammer emanated from the engine. After I parked the old beast, I raised the hood and saw the vehicular equivalent to a blood-spattered crime scene: Oil coated every surface that was visible through the billowing smoke. I felt so ill I nearly vomited. "What have I done?" I cried out. I thought I should tell Ronnie about the blown motor, but he was the mechanic, not me, so I just handed him the keys. He hadn't planned on driving the truck back to his shop anyway; instead he would be hauling it on a flatbed trailer. As I drove my freshly tuned up and modified '57 Chevy hot rod home that evening, any feelings of guilt I had about giving Ronnie a truck with a bad motor were quickly replaced by a greater understanding of karma. The old car died less than two miles down the road; the victim of a horrendous wiring job at the hands of good old Ronnie.

Later I bought a 1976 Chevy dually, painted it black, tailgated with it until the transmission shot craps, and sold it at auction for beer money. Then I bought a 1975 Ford F-250, three-quarter-ton, four-wheel-drive, one-owner truck with only 80,000 actual miles. It was painted "Baby Poop Green" (I'm pretty sure that was Ford's official name for the color) and it was beautiful. It drove like a dream for the better part of a week after I brought it home. I hit it with a dozen cans of flat black spray paint, hand painted "Missouri Tigers" along both bedsides, and even applied a set of racing stripes that mimicked the pattern on Mizzou's football helmets. What a thing of beauty! But it still ran rough, so after spending all my money on paint supplies, I decided to make some repairs on my own. *Big mistake.*

The truck tended to stall periodically for no apparent reason even after it had warmed up and always at an inopportune time like when idling at a stop light in a busy intersection during rush hour. Frequently after driving it for a while and then shutting it off, it refused to start up again for at least a half-hour or so. This led me to theorize that dirt in the fuel filter canister was getting sucked into the filter when the sediment inside got stirred up while driving, thus blocking the flow of gas to the engine. (Does that sound like I know what I'm talking about or what?) So I decided to change the filter. I read in my repair manual how to remove the canister and filter. It said to remove them, discard the fuel in the canister, and replace. Nothing could be simpler.

Nowhere in the manual did it mention that because the filter is mounted at the lowest point in the fuel line (below the motor) a siphon would be created that would suck out every last drop of gasoline from the truck's 16 gallon tank when it was removed. As I lay under my truck, fuel splattered onto the ground, into my eyes, and all over my clothes. In a panic, I tried to put the canister back on, but since the 32 year old rubber gasket was warped, the unit would not seal and most of my upper torso became covered with petroleum distillates as a steady stream ran down my arms. Eventually I found a five-gallon bucket to contain the spill while I continued to struggle in vain to try to stop the flow of fuel. Have you ever wiped rubbing alcohol on your skin and felt its rapid-cooling qualities as it evaporated? Gasoline has the exact same effect. Oh, I should probably mention that I attempted to perform this "simple" maintenance project in 20 degree weather in an open-air pole barn. Within seconds, my hands were almost completely frozen. I could not move the fingers on my right hand at all and when I tried to manipulate them with my left hand, I noticed that the flesh on my digits was literally frozen solid. The tissue was so firm that I couldn't squeeze a depression into my skin. It felt like squeezing a piece of chicken straight out of the freezer. It was at that point that I started really freaking out. I think I may have even cried a little bit, although I am not sure if it was due to the pain, the fear losing my fingers to frostbite, or the frustration of knowing better than attempting mechanical work in the first place when I knew damn well from my past failures that no good could possible come from such an undertaking.

I ran inside the house, peeled off my gas soaked clothing, and took a long, hot shower. As I thawed, I realized that gas was still pouring out of my truck and that the five-gallon bucket would probably not have enough capacity to contain the relentless, toxic flood. I hollered for Alex to get dressed so we could go to town to find a fuel filter. A half-hour later we arrived at the parts store. I told them what I needed and they spent the next half-hour looking for it. None of their catalogs had any parts listed for vehicles older than 1985. Apparently, mine was the only 1975 Ford truck still running in the entire world. (I guess no one saw a need for replacement parts for trucks that should have been crushed decades ago.) Finally, after three different people got involved, I got the right part and headed home. I replaced the filter, gasket, and canister without many more tears being shed and poured the five gallons of gasoline collected in the bucket through a coffee filter (you should have seen the sludge in the bottom of that bucket) and funnel back into the truck's tank, and then went back inside to wash my hands a few hundred times. The fumes, a good cry, and three beers helped me sleep very well that night.

I realized that all of this effort was wasted however, when I discovered that the truck ran just as poorly after the fuel filter fiasco as it did before I risked frostbite and a permanent break from sanity to repair it. Eventually I paid a guy to replace the motor and transmission with freshly rebuilt versions, but even that brought no change in the way the vehicle ran. Disillusioned, I couldn't bear to look at what had become a very expensive lawn ornament any longer. Rather than asking the Enabler for more money to restore the old beast to its former glory, I sold it online for a substantial loss. Bethany said she didn't care about the money; she just wanted the eyesore gone. "Me, too," I said. "Now I can spend the $700 on my *next* project."

"Okay," said the Enabler. "But no more trucks," said the Voice of Reason.

Butterbean

One of Travis Naughton's favorite subjects to write about was his former college roommate and lifelong friend Rosie Crane. The two had made many outrageous if not blurry memories together over the years that found their way into Naughton's writing. It dawned on the author one day that he had accumulated enough material over the years to write a book about his unique friend. The Life and Lunacy of Roosevelt Crane *was published in 2017 and quickly became Naughton's third bestselling book.*

Prefaced with the disclaimer that the book, just like its star subject, was loosely based in reality, Crane *employed a literary device that allowed the author to mix several unbelievable but true stories about his friend with a few that were pure fiction. The result was a funny, disturbing, one-of-a-kind book that told the story of a friendship that spanned three decades. One chapter in particular, titled Butterbean, garnered the most attention from readers and from Hollywood. An adaptation based mainly on this chapter was made into a major motion picture called* The Wedding Guest, *released in 2019. The chapter, as written by the author, follows:*

"We didn't have a *real* wedding," my alleged wife has been known to tell people whenever the conversation turns to marriage and such.

"Does that mean I can start dating again?" I ask.

"If you can get someone to agree to go out with you, then more power to you Honey," she says. Frankly, Bethany was probably relieved that we didn't have a real wedding. What would she have told all those people when they saw who she was marrying? Instead, we got hitched in a tiny chapel that was tucked into an annex of a large church in Columbia. It cost only $50 to reserve the room and cover the minister's services. Our biggest expense was the $100 suit that I bought off the rack at Penney's (including a clip-on bow tie.) Bethany's sister Charla and her husband Doug were our only witnesses. Char was the Matron of Honor and donned the dress Bethany wore as Maid of Honor in her wedding. Bethany borrowed Char's wedding dress, which needed no alteration due to the fact that the girls are twins. Doug was the Best Man/photographer/videographer/director of music. A real multi-tasker, Doug took all of our wedding photos, set a video camera on a tripod in the read or the chapel, pressed "PLAY" on a portable CD player that blared "the Wedding March" through its singular speaker, and stood beside me during the ceremony. He put more effort into our wedding than I did.

"I think I could have the marriage annulled on a technicality if I wanted to," I tell Bethany. "You know the minister called me by the wrong name."

"That's true. But you corrected him, remember?" Damn. She was right again. When the minister said, "And do you, *Michael*, take this woman Bethany..." I had to interrupt him.

"Um, it's Travis."

"Excuse me?"

"My name is Travis, not Michael."

"Travis, Michael--what's the difference?" the minister laughed before pronouncing us husband and wife.

When our seventh wedding anniversary approached, I came up with a novel pick-up line for would be mistresses: "I've got a seven year itch--would you like to scratch it?"

Bethany responded, "If you can find any woman who will take you up on that, then more power to you." She knows that I like to flirt with the ladies, but she also knows that no other woman alive could put up with me and my obnoxious friends the way she has all these years. "Jealous?" she responds when people ask her how she feels when I make these kinds of remarks. "Jealous of what?"

Thanks, Dear.

Were she ever to feel jealous of anyone, it would probably of the women who were lucky enough to marry doctors or businessmen or anyone who didn't feel the need to tell his wife's friends, "I got a sunburn on my ass once."

Char and Doug had gotten married just six months before us and had a "real" wedding to which everyone was invited. Bethany and I didn't see the need to put people through that again so soon, so we decided that a small, private ceremony was enough. After attending the weddings of several of our friends in subsequent years, we stand by our decision. More than once, my bride has whispered into my ear at an expensive wedding reception or during an elaborate, lengthy ceremony, "I'm glad we didn't have a real wedding."

"Me, too, Babe. Me, too."

My brother, Blake, is the only person who expressed any displeasure with not being invited to our nuptials. None of my family was there, but he still took it personally. That didn't stop him from asking me to be his Best Man when he married Meredith though. I was honored, and his timing was good (for their sakes) because I was at that time in the middle of my two and a half year stretch of sobriety. But the prospect of delivering the toast at their reception, completely without the aid of alcohol to loosen my inhibitions, crippled me with fear. For weeks I struggled to come up with a speech that would make people laugh and cry, and not infuriate my new sister-in-law. Meredith is a former college athlete who could easily kick my ass on her worst day. But she's actually a real sweetheart, and I was glad Blake was marrying her.

Blake and Meredith decided to have a co-ed pre-wedding party, forgoing the traditional bachelor and bachelorette parties that have a tendency to get out of hand. I had no problem with their choice. Char and Doug had chosen this same route, as had Chris Stevens and his wife. Blake just isn't the type of guy who would enjoy having an exotic dancer gyrating on or around him. He and I are different that way. Nevertheless, the party was great fun. The highlight of the evening was when I challenged the Maid of Honor to a contest to see which of us could eat an entire sleeve of Thin Mint cookies the fastest. Kelly claims to have won, insisting that she had emptied her sleeve first. I, however, swallowed the last of my allotment while Kelly's cheeks were still packed like a chipmunk's. "What, are you saving some for winter?" I taunted.

    I don't remember any of the actual ceremony. This could be attributed to my Girl Scout cookie hangover or the fact that I was petrified because I still hadn't come up with a decent toast. After the wedding, everyone made their way to the reception hall and waited for the new bride and groom to make their appearance. I was hoping that they would get stuck in traffic, but unfortunately they arrived just a few minutes later. Meredith stopped by the table to wish me luck and to ask if I could work a reference to Blake's prior and questionable dating choices into the speech. I told her I would do my best. Then I broke into a cold sweat. There wasn't any way of getting around it: I would have to give this toast. Recognizing my distress, Bethany asked me if I was okay. "I could use a drink--or twelve."

    "You'll do just fine. Just be yourself."

    Just be myself? Are you sure that's such a good idea? Well, maybe you're right. I mean, why the hell not? Why was I stressing over choosing the right words and sounding perfectly polished and appropriate when everybody knows that quite frankly--that ain't me? Blake knew what he was getting himself into when he asked me to be his best man. Just wing it, I said to myself.

    I can't even remember who introduced me. I recall sweating profusely and grabbing a cloth napkin from my table to mop my brow with. My mouth was dry, so I took a sip from my champagne flute full of water and rose to my feet. I walked to the center of the room, dabbed at my forehead, took a deep breath, and paused. A few seconds passed. Every eye in the room was focused squarely on me. No one spoke. I dabbed again. Then, I began:

"Brothahs and sistahs!" I shouted in the style of a southern Baptist preacher. People in the audience were so startled that they jumped in their seats. "We are gathered here today to celebrate the Holy union of these two beautiful people--Blake and Meredith…" The audience started to giggle nervously, uncertain of how far I would take my routine. "…I said, Brothahs and sistahs! I want to tell you a story now. A story of a young man who had lost his way in life. This young man named Blake was a good man who had strayed off the path of righteousness and onto the road to eternal damnation. Brothahs and sistahs! Temptation and sin and serpents led this young man astray until a young woman, a woman pure of heart was Heaven-sent to save his soul! Can I get an Amen?!"

The crown yelled, "Amen!"

"This woman, this angel sent from Heaven came to bring this young man back from a life lived in darkness to a life lived in the sunshine of Pure Love! Hallelujah!"

The congregation yelled, "Hallelujah!"

"Brothahs and sistahs, I want to tell you that this woman, Meredith, saved my brother, Blake." I began toning down my theatrics. "She gave him the gift of her heart and made the finest man I know, the happiest man I know. For that, I am forever grateful. And I raise my glass and salute you, Mr. and Mrs. Naughton. Amen."

There was not a dry eye in the house. Several of Blake's college buddies who were familiar with his previous dating choices understood the inside joke and congratulated me on a job well done. During the dollar dance, my new sister-in-law thanked me and said it was a great speech. Blake later approached me, too, still red in the face from embarrassment, and thanked me for making his wedding day so memorable.

Of course Bethany and I didn't have a wedding reception

since we didn't have a real wedding. Instead, we used all of the money we would have spent on an elaborate ceremony and reception on our honeymoon. We flew to New Orleans and phoned our family and friends from the hotel in the French Quarter to tell them that we had gotten married. We loved the Big Easy, despite the fact that we were there in early August, when it's so hot that the garbage cooks on the curbs and the urine boils in the gutters.

Our honeymoon spot wasn't nearly as hot and humid as Wes and Lynn Douglass's was. They invited us to join them in Cancun for their destination wedding. They also invited Rosie Crane, a questionable decision at best, who wore blue jeans during the seaside ceremony and nearly passed-out several times from the heat in the gazebo. It didn't help matters that he had ignored Wes's plea earlier that morning to "Please don't get drunk before my wedding, Rosie." In Rosie's defense, it was an all-inclusive resort with swim-up bars in the pool. How could he *not* get drunk? Honestly, Wes knew it was a calculated risk inviting Rosie to Mexico for his wedding. I think he only invited him because he still felt guilty about shooting Rosie years earlier.

Back when Rosie and Wes had both been kicked out of college, they had a lot of free time on their hands. One of their favorite time-killers was to go shoot guns at a local firing range. One time as they went to retrieve their targets, Wes slipped in the mud and as he fell flat on his back, he accidentally squeezed the trigger of his .22 caliber handgun. The round hit Rosie in his left ass-cheek, dropping the 300 pounder like a bull elk.

"You shot me!" Rosie cried out.

"No I didn't," Wes said in disbelief, although he knew it was true.

"Yes you did. You shot me in the ass! You gotta drive me to the hospital."

The prospect of driving Rosie's Plymouth Horizon was almost scarier to Wes than that of watching his friend bleed to death. Wes couldn't drive a car with a manual transmission. He stalled the car several times and it bucked and heaved the entire way into town, causing Rosie immeasurable pain with each jostle. "Could you try driving a little more smoothly?" Rosie asked between clenched teeth.

At the hospital, Rosie calmly approached the registration desk and said, "I've been shot."

Without missing a beat, the nurse asked, "In the foot or the ass?"

"In the ass."

"Fill this out and take a seat."

"I think I'll stand, thank you."

"Shoot--I mean *suit* yourself."

In the years since the accident, many people have asked Wes, "Why did you shoot Rosie in the ass?"

"Because I didn't lead him enough."

The bullet entered and exited through Rosie's left butt-cheek. He asks anyone who will listen, "Do you know why I can't float?"

"Why's that, Rosie?"

"Because I have three holes in my ass."

After the denim-clad, drunken wedding guest nearly ruined the Douglass nuptials, Wes finally forgave himself for shooting Rosie. "Now we're even," he told his old friend.

Whenever one of my old high school buddies gets married and wants a good old-fashioned bachelor party, the Best Man invariably calls one particular escort service to provide the entertainment for the evening's festivities. Rosie has been to several of these parties over the years and has always managed to make a lasting impression. Even when two "entertainers" are present and are busy "entertaining" each other for the amusement of the guys leering at them, Rosie manages to overshadow the "talent."

"Find the butterbean!" he yells, referring to a certain part of the female anatomy that in his defense does appear that the girls are genuinely determined to "find." This usually causes the guys, and often the girls themselves, to break into hysterics. "It's right there!" he prods. "Get after it!"

The strippers always come with a male security guard/chauffer, whose job it is to make sure the guys behave themselves. At the bachelor party I threw for Wes, the security guy pulled me to the side and said, "Is that Butterbean over there?"

"What do you mean?" I asked.

"That bald guy. Isn't he the butterbean guy?"

Right on cue, Rosie hollered at the girls, "Find the butterbean!"

"Yep. That's him alright," I answered embarrassedly.

"I knew it! I love that guy!"

At Crash Phillips's bachelor party four years later, Rosie and I were sitting beside one another when the entertainment for the evening arrived. He leaned over to me and asked, "Hey, Trav. Is that the *same* security dude with those girls?"

"Hell, Rosie, I don't know. Who's looking at the *dude* anyway?"

Just then, the "dude" yelled from across the room, "I found the Butterbean!"

When I share these stories with my wife, I ask her, "Do you ever wish we had a *real* wedding?"

"No, *Michael*. I do not."

After the film's release, the real Roosevelt Crane became an overnight sensation. He reveled in the attention he received from fans of the movie and of the book loosely based on his life. But Travis Naughton had created a monster – and soon came to realize, much like Dr. Frankenstein, that perhaps it was not a question of whether he could *unleash his new creation on the world, but rather if he* should.

Rosie Crane Rides the Crazy Train

Rosie Crane was ill-equipped to handle the aftermath of his notoriety. For a while, he basked in the glow of his fame, landing dates with attractive women and sitting down for interviews with the local TV and radio stations in the Hannibal area. He even tried to parlay his sudden popularity into a political career. He ran for the office of mayor of his hometown and joked with potential voters, "Vote for me, or else I'll show up at your wedding." Rosie was on top of the world. At least for a little while.

After losing the election by a landslide, Rosie continued his hard-partying ways that dated back to his days as Travis's roommate in college. The constant drinking began taking its toll on his liver again and also his mind. As the book and the movie based on his life that had made him a minor celebrity became old news and faded into the shadows of the public's memory, Rosie tried desperately to cling to his fleeting fame. He crashed a couple weddings and made a pathetic,(rather than amusing,) spectacle of himself. Soon, he had alienated the few remaining friends he had left. His fifteen minutes of fame were up, and he found himself utterly alone and in severe psychological and physical distress.

Naughton recalls the day that Rosie's health issues became unavoidably clear. He wrote about this time in his memoir years later:

Rosie showed up at my house looking all disheveled and asked if he could sleep on my couch for awhile.

"How long are we talking about here?" I asked, wary of extending an open-ended invitation.

"Just long enough until my friends can come pick me up to

take me to California," he said.

"California, huh? Who do you know out there?"

"The girls from 'Baywatch,'" he said matter-of-factly.

"Really?"

"Yeah, really."

"You're serious? And who is it that's going to give you a ride out there?" I asked, not at all sure if I really wanted to hear the answer.

"Jennifer Anniston and Courtney Cox."

"Oh, I see. You're joking, right?"

"Not at all. So can I stay with you till they get here or not? I don't have anywhere else to go right now."

Hesitantly, I agreed. I had felt somewhat responsible for Rosie's current condition after the book and movie came out. I promised Bethany that I'd get rid of him as soon as possible. I later found out that he had been sleeping on the couch of a virtual stranger that he had met at a bar a few nights earlier. When he wore out his welcome there and was told that he needed to leave, Rosie convinced the hapless host to drive him to my house—a three hour round trip just to be rid of the house guest.

I knew right away something was terribly wrong with my old friend. He explained to me that everywhere he went, people were talking about him. Powerful world leaders like the Pope and President Obama were trying to tap into his mind to steal his ideas. He insisted watching TV news programs with the volume turned all the way up so that he could hear the commentators talk about him under their breath. And he was utterly convinced that the girls from "Friends" were on their way to take him to L.A.

As we sat and tried to carry out a conversation, Rosie gulped mouthfuls of air, which caused him to later rip the loudest belches

I've ever heard. "Why do you keep doing that?" I asked.

"I'm swallowing the psychic energies in the air," he said.

"I see." After coming to the conclusion that Rosie had suffered a complete psychotic breakdown, I tried to convince him to seek professional help. He just laughed and said that he was fine and would be out of my hair soon enough. A little more prodding got him to reveal that he had thought about harming himself after realizing that he was all alone in the world. Armed with this information, I formulated a plan to get him the help he so desperately needed.

The next day, I called our mutual friend Chris Stevens, who had also heard Rosie say some pretty strange things. He helped me put together an affidavit that we presented to a judge who ordered that Rosie be held in a mental hospital for a 72-hour involuntary evaluation. I explained this to my friend, who was insulted, but completely out of other options. A sheriff's deputy was dispatched to my house and as Rosie was taken away, I promised to visit him at the hospital. I felt like I had just turned over a Jew to the SS, but Bethany assured me that I did the right thing.

When I came to visit Rosie, he seemed perfectly normal. I knew that he was putting on an act so that the doctors would discharge him as soon as the involuntary evaluation period expired. Sure enough though, his plan worked. He was given a prescription for some sort of anti-depressant and after his release he convinced another friend to come pick him up. A few weeks later, he showed up at my house unannounced again. He asked for some money so he could get his life together and I reluctantly gave him a few bucks (admittedly just to get rid of him.)

A month or so later, Rosie called to say he was in town again and wondered if he could stop by. I said that would be fine and he arrived at my house a short time later. He came with everything he owned: a duffle bag containing his few remaining belongings, and the clothes on his back.

Once again he asked, "Can I crash here until my friends pick me up?"

"No you can't. Have you been taking your medicine?" I already knew the answer. He had only pretended to swallow his pills while in the hospital--he even showed me how he kept them under his tongue until the nurse left his room. I wanted to tell the doctors, but I knew that he had already fooled them and that he would be turned out into the world again regardless. I settled for cautioning him to take his meds for his own sake, but that obviously fell on deaf ears.

"Don't preach to me about medicine. If you won't let me stay here, then just drive me somewhere else."

"I'll drive you straight back to the hospital. That's it."

"Fine. Let's go." The ride to the mental hospital was a short one, but the silence between two old friends made it seem like it was an eternity. I helped Rosie get checked in and took a moment to study the expression on his face. The person I was looking at bore little resemblance to the Roosevelt Crane I had grown up with.

"Well, I guess this is goodbye," I said. "Have a nice life, my friend." I knew that he would be out again in no time, and would never accept the help offered to him that he so greatly needed. I had done all I could to help my old friend, and unless he was willing to meet me halfway, there was nothing more I could do for him. Rosie shot me a disconcerting look, and then forced an awkward smile as he unnaturally shook my hand almost as if he and I were merely business acquaintances and not the all-but-blood brothers we had been since the high school. I'll be haunted by the memories of that moment for the rest of my life.

After conning his way out of the hospital a second time, Rosie emailed me and tried calling a few times. I ignored his attempts to contact me, hoping that he would quietly go away. But he persisted until I was forced to spell things out in brutal, black and white. I sent him an email explaining my decision to end our relationship based on his refusal to seek help for his illness. I told him that I wouldn't subject my wife to this emotional turmoil. I ended by telling him I loved him but unless he was willing to take his medicine and get the help he needed, never to contact me again.

I received a reply to my email in which Rosie said that *I* was the crazy one (a point that is admittedly up for debate) and that he wished he had never met me. He said that all the years he wasted on being my friend were a huge mistake. I knew it was just his illness talking, but those final words from Rosie cut me to the bone.

Ask Bethany and she'll tell you that as recently as a few months ago I was still shedding tears over the fate of my old friend. I found out from Rosie's older brother that he is currently getting the help he needs as a permanent resident of a mental hospital after finally being correctly diagnosed as a schizophrenic. His doctors don't think he will ever be able to function on his own outside of the facility and anticipate that he will spend the rest of his life there. This fact is hard for me to come to terms with, considering the brother-like bond we shared for so long. He is also battling liver failure, which may buy him a one-way ticket out of there soon enough, sparing him many years of "living" in the hospital.

In sharp contrast to the light-hearted fare to which his readers were accustomed, the tragic tale of Rosie Crane's demise was not the only dark moment of Travis Naughton's adult life that later made its way into his memoir Rude, Crude, and Socially Unacceptable. *The book, which he finished in 2041, became the final resting place of the story of his mother's passing, which came only a few weeks after Travis and Bethany experienced the overwhelming joy of bringing home their adopted son Truman. Although the memoir was published many years after the fact, the passages about his mother were written when the wounds were still fresh back in 2009. The sentiments Naughton expressed in the chapter about his mom required no flowery metaphors, no shameless attempts at humor, and no exaggeration. The raw emotion of the passages, some of which were written on his personal blog as his mother's illness progressed, gives readers a poignant, stark view of the writer's soul laid bare for all to see. These are among the most powerful, yet tender examples of prose Naughton ever wrote in his distinguished career. An excerpt from his memoir follows in the next chapter.*

Rude, Crude, and Socially Unacceptable

If I am guilty of acting in accordance with any of the above adjectives, I blame my mother, Donna Keller. In fact, she used these very words to describe my behavior on many occasions, but it was really a case of the pot calling the kettle black if you ask me. I became aware at an early age that my mom was nothing like the mothers I saw on TV. I don't recall ever seeing her wear a dress. She never wore pearls or an apron around the house. She enjoyed forcing Blake and I to dust, vacuum, and wash the dishes while she sat in her recliner and watched football or professional bowling. She was a Marine, but she swore like a sailor. She told me and my brother that we could cuss all we wanted, too, even as young kids, as long as we didn't call anyone a bad name. Of course, neither of us had the balls to actually curse in front of her for fear that she was merely trying to trick us. Believe me; the threat of being bent over my mom's knee was more frightening than the prospect of burning in the eternal fires of Hell. Whenever the classic insult, "Your mother wears combat boots and drives a tank to church" was repeated within earshot, Mom deadpanned, "Yeah, so what's your point?"

Mom had to be tough to survive living and working in a man's world. Refusing to accept a traditional woman's role in society, she rebelled by joining the Marine Corps immediately after high school. When confronting sexist male co-workers at the car dealerships she worked at, her battle cry became "Eat shit and die!" More times than I can count, I watched her emasculate man after man who dared to call her "babe" or "honey" in front of her sons. It was a mistake that no one ever made twice. During my rebellious teenage years, whenever I foolishly spoke out against my perceived oppression by my tyrannical mother, she calmly warned, "You ain't ever gonna be big enough or bad enough to take me down,

Big Boy." Naturally, she was right.

In 2007, Mom began showing signs that she was human after all. In her previous 60 years, the only weaknesses that I could see in her were her addictions to Diet Pepsi and cigarettes. By July of that year, my mother had lost nearly fifty pounds without even trying and had become very lethargic. She had been out of work for quite a while so I assumed that she had become depressed while looking for a meaningful job. When she drove to my home to join Bethany, Alex, and I for dinner one evening after the three of us had returned from a week in Colorado, I was shocked by what I saw. The driver's side mirror of her car, (a vehicle she took meticulous care of) was hanging by a wire and scratching the paint on her door. As I greeted Mom in the driveway, she was barely able to extract herself from the car and when she stood up, she nearly collapsed. She could barely speak and looked like a walking skeleton. I had to help her into the house and after unsuccessfully trying to get her to eat dinner, we took her to the E.R. in Jefferson City. After drawing blood and getting a urine sample, the doctor said she was probably suffering from depression and that she needed to go to her doctor to get a prescription for anti-depressants. I thought it strange that they didn't give an obviously dehydrated person an I.V. or run some more tests just to rule out any other physical problems, but I'm a philosopher, not a doctor.

Bethany called a behavioral health clinic for a consultation the nest day and I took my mom to her appointment on a Tuesday afternoon. The woman who met with us there said that she could see some signs of depression, but also some physical problems that were troubling. Mom was weak on her left side, could barely speak, and was slightly disoriented at times. The therapist said Mom was showing signs of having had a small stroke and advised us to go to the emergency room at the University Hospital. She faxed Mom's info over to the ER. and we headed across town.

When we arrived at the hospital, we were led straight back to a room. "Well," I said, "That's lucky. We didn't have to wait at all to be seen. Maybe that's a good sign." The doctor had Mom undergo a CAT scan right away and after a while, she came back in the room and sat down beside Mom.

"I'm afraid I have bad news," the doctor began. "You have a large mass in your chest cavity and another in your brain." It was one of those moments when everything around you goes completely silent. She explained that they would do an MRI to see the mass in her brain and then she would talk to us again. Then she said "I'm sorry" and left the room. I walked over to Mom and hugged her and cried on her shoulder. Then I realized that she wasn't crying or feeling sorry for herself, so I stopped blubbering and got a hold of myself.

"See, I told you I wasn't crazy," Mom said. It had really bothered her when I had suggested that she may have been depressed. Only my mother would rather have a brain tumor than a treatable mental illness. At least her dark sense of humor was still intact. I decided right then that my job would be to keep her spirits up. So we spent the next few hours in the ER talking and laughing. In between tests and nurse visits, the reality of the situation tried to sneak up on me, but I held it together for Mom's sake. She would need all of the strength that I could muster. After ten hours in the ER, Mom was finally admitted to the hospital and given a room. She had been receiving I.V. fluids and a steroid that reduced the swelling on her brain. She became more coherent and was looking forward to getting some rest.

The next day, we got the news that we had been dreading; Mom had stage-four lung cancer. A tumor the size of a baseball was in her right lung and the disease had spread to her brain where she had not one but two tumors. The larger one was in her frontal lobe (which affects mood and personality- which explained why Mom had been so emotionally flat and confused in recent weeks). The steroids that were given to her in the hospital reduced the swelling enough that Mom's old personality began to re-emerge quickly. When Blake and his wife Meredith came to visit from Washington D.C., Mom's spirits soared and she was released from the hospital soon after. Within days, Mom was able to drive, eat, and cuss normally again. It would take a lot more than a few lousy tumors to keep this woman down.

Over the next few weeks, Mom started receiving radiation and chemotherapy treatments, and as is the case with many cancer patients, she began losing her hair. Now to most women, this side-effect is devastating. My mother wasn't "most women." She called me one day to ask a favor. "My hair is falling out," she began. "Get your butt over here and shave it all off for me." She was never satisfied with the appearance of her hair anyway, so having an excuse to cut it all off was fine by her. So I grabbed my clippers and drove the 20 miles to her house, which gave me time to put the impending haircut into perspective. I remembered that Mom used to cut my hair when I was a child and that she did a pretty good job of it. I wish she would have talked me out of the ridiculous mullet (business in the front, party in the back) haircut that I wanted back in the late '80s, but she always encouraged me to be myself, and she happily obliged. I thought for a moment that perhaps I could give her a Mohawk as payback, but I knew that cancer or not, she could still kick my ass. The truth was that this haircut that I was about to give my mother was a gift- an opportunity to repay her in part for all of the things she did for me. She used to cut my hair, now I was cutting hers. She used to take me to doctor's appointments, now it was my turn to take her. It was an honor for me to do so. Out of the dozens of appointments, treatment sessions, office visits, and lab tests she had to go to, she never once had to drive herself. I didn't want her to go through it alone for one thing. And, as time went on, she suffered a few seizures and I was forced to take away her car keys. In doing so, I took away her independence and to some extent, I took away a part of her soul. She loved driving. She had a Datsun 280 Z when Blake and I were young, and one day she took for a joyride at 130 mph. It is worth noting that a. This was a two-seater sports car with three occupants, b. None of us was wearing a seatbelt at this face-melting speed, and c. This happened a few short years after Mom and Blake flew through the windshield of a VW Bus in a roll-over accident. Mom was from California, where driving is a lifestyle. It helped define who she was. It made me physically ill to take that away from her. To assuage my guilt and to ensure my availability to help with anything that Mom may need, I quit my job. I was planning to do so eventually anyway to stay at home with the child we were hoping to adopt from China someday.

After her haircut was through, I pointed out to Mom that she still had some stubble wherever my electric clippers failed to cut as close as a shave. She said she didn't care and tied a do-rag over her head. I was helping her straighten the cloth when I noticed that the stubble actually helped anchor the bandana in place. "Kinda like Velcro," I teased her. She laughed and said that she agreed. I hugged her and before I got all bleary-eyed again I excused myself to the yard, which I proceeded to mow for her. I left her to her thoughts and to sweep up the pile of hair on the bathroom floor, and after I finished with the lawn she swept the grass clippings off of the patio, too. It blew me away how she just carried on with her life, never stopping to have herself a "pity-party" as she called it. Her favorite band of all time was the Eagles and their hit "Get Over It" became her mantra. If there was anything she couldn't tolerate, it was when people felt sorry for themselves. She never allowed me or my brother to do it, and I'm pretty sure that her lack of sympathy for my father's own depression contributed greatly to the demise of their marriage. At any rate, I was humbled by my mother's inner strength and it was my privilege to be there for her when she needed me.

Throughout the duration of my mom's illness, I posted updates on my blog and sent emails to friends and family in order to keep them up to date on her status. I have included some of them here in their original, mostly unedited form.

April 13, 2008

Subject: My Mom...

For those of you who didn't hear, my mom had brain surgery on Thursday. *Successful* brain surgery. After checking the follow-up MRI, the doctor said he was confident that he got the whole tumor out. Just hours after the operation, Mom was sitting up in her chair in ICU, eating a full dinner and cracking wise. On Friday, she was moved out of ICU to a regular room. Her condition changed hour by hour. At times, she was looking and sounding like her old self. At other times she leaned toward her left side, couldn't walk on her own, and suffered temporary paralysis on the left side of her face. All those symptoms have since gone away for the most part, so it appears that she is on the road to recovery. In fact, she got to go home yesterday. Blake is staying with her for a few days before he has to go back to Baltimore. If she still isn't back to 100% by then, she will come stay with us in our home until such time as she can manage safely on her own. Of course she is so stubborn that she is just sure that she can manage on her own right now and is growing increasingly tired of her sons "bossing her around." We told her this may be our only chance to torture her, so we better make the most of it while we can. It really is amazing that a person can have their skull sawed open, a chunk of their brain removed, and then be home watching NASCAR on TV two days later. (No, that is *not* a commentary on watching NASCAR.) Thanks to all of you who have sent along well-wishes, warm thoughts, and prayers. It means a lot to all of us.

Sunday, May 11, 2008

Subject: Happy Mother's Day

This year for Mother's Day I wanted to give my mom something really special. As you know, my mom is battling stage four lung cancer. She first heard the diagnosis on August 1, 2007. By the time her cancer was discovered, it had already spread to her brain. Since that time, she has undergone whole brain radiation, stereotactic radio surgery (direct radiation to the two tumors in her brain), months of chemotherapy, and brain surgery. Throughout these difficult months, Mom has done an incredible job of maintaining a positive attitude. Whenever I have felt sorry for myself, I quickly snap out of it when I recall how she has not allowed herself to have any pity-parties. How has Mom been able to remain so strong throughout this saga? Because she's a mom.

Moms work harder than most any man. Most moms put in an 8 hour day at work then come home and cook dinner, do laundry, clean house, and put the kids to bed. My mom was no exception. Mom worked harder than most women, too. Not one for being the June Cleaver type, Mom enlisted in the Marines. She rose to the rank of corporal before meeting my jarhead dad and getting married. She agreed to turn her back on her beloved California in order to raise a family in Missouri where Dad was from. Not satisfied with being a bank teller or doing other traditional women's jobs, Mom started working in the car business. Although most of her misogynist employers and co-workers tried to keep her in the business office, Mom insisted on trying her hand at selling cars. Eventually, she became the general sales manager at a Chevy dealership (an unheard of position for a woman to hold in one of the most sexist industries around.)

Mom isn't all work and no play though. I fondly recall listening to "The Eagles" and many other bands on our buffet-sized home stereo with Mom. On Sundays, we'd snuggle together in her recliner and watch westerns all day. Mom helped coach my little league teams. Mom also loves to volunteer. She gives blood regularly, donates her time to the "Show-Me State Games," and trained to become a volunteer with the Columbia Police Department.

Anybody who knows her will agree that she is the "toughest broad" they've ever met. She uses that term to describe herself, so I can use it without getting in trouble. (Just weeks after having brain surgery, Mom was outside trying to start her lawnmower. Oh yeah, she's a little stubborn, too.) Her strength has been tested throughout her battle with cancer and last week, it was tested again. The primary tumor (the one in her lung) is growing again. It is too large to remove, so she will undergo another round of chemo beginning next Thursday. While this is not good news, Mom has remained her usual positive self. She is a fighter. Fighters don't feel sorry for themselves. They fight.

So, on this Mother's Day, my gift to my mom is to tell her and all the world how much I love her. I want her to know that I am the man I am today because of her. I want her to know that she inspires me. I want her to know that her whole family loves her. I want her to know that I am proud of her. Mom, I love you.

Friday, August 08, 2008

Subject: Cancer Sucks

    Lance Armstrong beat cancer. It is difficult to comprehend his recovery. His testicular cancer spread to his lungs, his brain, and throughout his body and yet he not only survived, he went on to have such good health that he won seven straight Tour de France bike races. Winning one Tour is one of the singular most difficult things to do in all of sports. Seven? Seven. It shouldn't be possible. He should be dead. But he isn't. And that fact gives hope to everyone who wears one of his yellow bracelets.

    My mom is one of those people. Her diagnosis of stage four lung cancer which metastasized to her brain is every bit as grim as Lance Armstrong's was. She chose to fight, like he did, and has survived a full year since her diagnosis. She has endured hours of radiation, months of chemo, three hospitalizations, and brain surgery in that span of time. This week, Mom had to be admitted to University Hospital due to complications caused by the tumor in her lung. You see, it didn't get the memo from Lance that it was supposed to just shrivel up and go away. It decided to fight back and has managed to keep growing throughout the past year. I won't go into details, but suffice it to say that the tumor is winning the battle right now. But it hasn't won. The doctors have a procedure planned next week that may help relieve some of Mom's symptoms. In the meantime, Mom checked herself out of the hospital (against her doctor's wishes) in order to wait for her surgery in the comfort of her own home. Have *you* ever tried to talk my mom out of doing something?

    Cancer sucks. My mom's mom died from it. Her grandma died from it. Bethany's grandma died from it. A good friend of mine who was 29 years old died from it. (Jen was an only child and I'll never forget watching her parents kiss her goodbye at her funeral.) Cancer killed John "I'm the toughest sombitch there ever was" Wayne for God's sake. But Lance Armstrong- he beat it. He beat stage four cancer that spread throughout his body. He went on to greatness. He proved that nothing is impossible. And guess what: he isn't half as tough as my mom. But then, you already knew that, didn't you?

So please keep sending those positive vibes Mom's way. But don't feel sorry for her. Feel sorry for the cancer whose ass she's gonna kick. (And feel a little sorry for the doctors and nurses who tried in vain to convince her to stay at the hospital.)

Tuesday, December 30, 2008

Subject: I love you Mom

My mom was a Marine. She took shit off of absolutely no one. When she was diagnosed with terminal cancer a year and a half ago, she didn't waste time feeling sorry for herself. She fought the disease with all her might. She endured three courses of chemo. She endured whole brain radiation to shrink the two tumors in her head. She endured stereotactic radio surgery to her brain twice. She endured traditional brain surgery when the radiation didn't work. She was a Marine, and Marines don't surrender. They fight. Despite her disease-ravaged condition, she only moved into our home three weeks ago at my urging. Even after suffering a massive seizure that rendered her incapacitated, she fought for three more days before finally succumbing to her enemy. She went out on her own terms, having never stopped battling. Mom passed away this morning in our home, surrounded by her sons, her daughters-in-law, and her grandsons. We were glad to have been able to keep her comfortable at home, so that she wouldn't have to endure the indignity of having strangers care for her at a nursing home or hospital. Because she hated funerals, we are having her remains cremated and later Blake and I will scatter her ashes at sea off the coast of her beloved native land of California.

I would like to thank all of my family and friends who have supported us throughout the last 18 months. I have not always been the comedian my fans expect of me, but I think you will probably forgive me for that. I would like to especially thank my wife, my brother Blake, and his wife Meredith. Without them, I doubt I could have survived these last few months. They are the greatest trio of human beings I have ever or will ever know. Last, but not least, I want to thank my mom. Thank you Mom for raising Blake and me to know the difference between right and wrong. Thank you for teaching by example how to serve others through your volunteer work. Thank you for loving me, especially at times in my life when I didn't even love myself. Thank you for not letting me get away with being less than the man I was destined to be. Thank you for indulging my whims throughout my childhood. Thank you for snuggling with me when I was little. Thank you for helping coach my little league teams. Thank you for teaching me how to bowl. Thank you for going to all my band concerts. Thank you for providing for my health and happiness. Thank you for holding out long enough to meet your new grandson. Thank you for being my mom. I love you. I will always love you.

Wednesday, January 21, 2009

Subject: Moving Day

     Today, I had to clear out the remaining items from my mother's duplex. Upon loading the last item into the van, I buckled the kids into their car seats and went back inside the house for one last look. Then it hit me, as it had my brother just before he returned to his home in Baltimore two weeks ago: This was the last time that I would ever be in my mother's home. Never again will I be able to go to Mom's for a visit. Never again will I be able to drop off the boys to spend some time with "Nonna." Mom's house was always a place where the family could convene no matter where any of us lived. Even with Blake and Meredith living on the east or west coast, we could always count on meeting at Mom's house for Christmas or other occasions throughout the year. The loss of my mom and the loss of that comforting place called her home cannot be replaced. The emptiness of that house left me with a feeling of emptiness in my soul that hopefully time and the love of my friends and family will fill in.

Monday, January 26, 2009

Subject: Closure

    Our mom was originally from northern California, so Blake and I decided to scatter her ashes there after she passed away. The location was chosen by Blake who recalled Mom talking about going to the Santa Cruz boardwalk with her grandmother when she was very young. There, we chartered a 34' yacht to sail us off shore to a beautiful spot a few hundred yards off the coast. The captain and his first mate were very professional and surprisingly thoughtful as they guided us through the process. They circled the boat in the pattern of the infinity symbol to signify our perpetual love for our mother and to calm the waters just before Blake released the ashes. They gave us as long as we needed to sit and reflect and be in the moment. It was one of the most beautiful and intensely painful moments of my life. I know Blake felt the same way. After a while, the captain rang "eight bells," in the nautical tradition, to signify the changing of the watch, in a sense dismissing Mom from her duties as the leader of the family and handing over the business of carrying on to my brother and I. We let the wind guide us back to shore as we watched dolphins, seals, and sea lions swim by as if to say, "Life does go on." It was a perfect way to say goodbye to our Mom.

    Back on shore, Blake and I rode the rickety, 80-year-old wooden roller coaster that Mom rode with her grandmother so many years ago. It felt so good to laugh out loud again and to think about Mom doing the same in that very place. Finally, we went to the area of land closest to where we scattered Mom's remains and took a moment to breathe in the fresh salty air of the sea and to listen to the waves crashing on the rocks below. That's when I finally felt at peace. I knew at that exact moment that Mom had found peace, too. Our mom was watching us from above and giving us a big thumbs-up that said, as she often told us in life, "Ya done good, boys. Ya done good."

Big Fish

*As Travis regrouped at his Hartsburg home following the chaos that accompanied a third bestseller (*Roosevelt Crane*) and yet another draining book tour, he took some time to indulge in one of his favorite hobbies: fishing. He stopped writing his column and focused all of his spare time on developing the skills his father taught him as a boy in order to become a serious fisherman. In 2021, Naughton celebrated his fiftieth birthday by announcing that he would be joining the professional bass fishing tour known as the Bassmaster Elite Series. "My brother-in-law Doug joined the senior golf tour when he turned fifty," Naughton explained. "I've never shot below 120 on a golf course, but I could fish. So I bought a brand new boat and a restored 1966 Chevy four-wheel-drive to pull it, and started entering some tournaments."*

(Younger): Did you ever win any of those tournaments?

(Elder): Hell, I never even came close. But I had of a lot of fun. My family tagged along for a few events and laughed at the whole crazy scene. I even brought my dad along a couple times, although he was pretty frail by then. I think he was about as old then as I am now, *[seventy-six]* but he seemed to really enjoy himself.

(Younger): Your father was the one who taught you how to fish, isn't that right?

(Elder): He sure did. He was the best amateur bass fisherman I've ever been around. I remember when I was about seven or eight he used to take me to the La Plata Lake and catch the hell out of those largemouths in there. One evening he caught more big bass than I've ever seen any pro catch in any tournament. I was his net man that day. All I did was scoop lunker after lunker out of the water when Dad brought them up to the boat. He told me that he really appreciated my help landing those things. He said he probably would have lost half of them had I not been there to lend a hand. He wasn't just blowing smoke up my ass either. When we got back to the dock, Dad pulled the stringer of fish up out of the water to show to a bunch of kids who'd been swimming in the lake and they all let out this collective gasp at the sight of it. They sort of freaked out when they realized that they'd been swimming around with all of those monsters. We had an eight pounder, two seven pounders, and four five pounders on one stringer. In all my days of fishing I've never seen another haul like that. Ever.

Naughton's year spent on the Bassmasters tour sparked some powerful memories of his childhood that he knew he had to write about. He decided to begin working on a new book about fishing with his father, his friends, and of course his own sons. The end result was a book called One More Cast, *which was published in 2023. Naughton's fourth book was easily his best work from a literary standpoint. Critics praised his use of the vernacular of fishing and hailed the book as a throwback to the Americana of days gone by. In an age of ubiquitous computers, 3D television, and virtual reality,* One More Cast *was a dose of nostalgia the country sorely needed.*

One passage from the book revealed more than just a child's love of fishing. It painted a touching picture of a son's love for his father:

In those simpler days gone by, Dad would load up our old lime-green Chevy and we'd head out for a day of adventure together at our favorite fishing hole, a farm pond that a buddy of Dad's owned just south of town. There, the scents of wildflowers and red cedars wafted over us as Dad rowed us out to our favorite cove while the calls of red-wing blackbirds and the screech of the occasional red-tailed hawk replaced the noise of civilization. Often times, the chorus of locusts in the trees or the humming of dragonflies' wings were the only sounds to be heard--until a nice bass was on the line. The stillness of the day would then be shattered by whoops and hollers and words of encouragement from a father to a son or vice versa. "It's a big one, Dad! I think its Oscar!" Oscar was the nickname my dad gave to the mythical "big one" that we were always in search of. Every battle was played out as if Moby Dick himself were on the hook. When it got too dark to continue, Dad would row us back to shore, stopping countless times for "one last cast." During the drive home we would recount the day's events, bragging about our hits and lamenting our misses. Regardless of our successes or failures, we always had fun.

One such fishing trip took place when I was nine years old. It was a July afternoon as I recall, and I had one of the most memorable outings of my life. The water was calm, the air still, and the temperature reminiscent of a pleasant day in early spring rather than the typical oppressive heat and humidity of mid-summer in Missouri. It was a great day on the water. I caught a dozen or so nice largemouth bass and at least as many sunfish. Every one of them was a keeper, too. Usually we would release what we caught, but on this occasion the old farmer told us to keep as many as we cared to clean. "There's too many in there," he said. "Don't want 'em gettin' stunted." So we decided a fish fry sounded pretty good. I caught a fish on almost every cast. Dad put the fish on a stringer, doing his best to keep up as I landed them, leaving nary a moment for him to throw his own line in the water. He didn't mind. It made him swell with pride to convey stories of his son's fishing prowess to his buddies at work.

When finally it was determined that the mosquitoes were biting more often than the fish, we decided to call it an evening. As Dad rowed the old "V" bottom boat to shore, I leaned way back in my seat and gazed up at the canvass of stars just beginning to peek through the twilight. At that moment, I felt a level of contentment that was usually reserved for people far older than a kid my age-- people who have had a lifetime to gain enough perspective to be able to reflect upon and appreciate such sublime moments. I was just a boy fishing with his dad and I was as happy as a soul could be. As the boat reached the bank, I sat up and looked back toward my father. I could tell by looking at the gentle expression on his face that he too was pleased with way the day had turned out. "Pull up the stringer, Son. I'll grab the poles," he directed me.

I untied the line from the boat and tried to hoist it from the water. "It's too heavy. I can't lift it," I said as I struggled to pull up the haul of fish.

"You must have done even better than I thought," Dad said proudly as he carried our gear toward the truck. "Just hang on for a minute. I'll be right back to help."

As I stood there waiting for Dad to return, it was all I could do to just to keep a hold of the nylon line full of fish that seemed to be swimming in unison to escape their fate. "Hurry! I can't hold on much longer!" Just as the rope slipped through my fingers, Dad reached down, grabbed the end, and pulled it toward him. It pulled back. He could hear me whimpering behind him, my hands stinging from the rope burn that the fleeing stringer inflicted upon them.

"Dip your hands in the water to cool them off, Son. You'll be alright," Dad said. I did as I was told while he walked backwards from the water's edge with the line in tow, thus pulling it to shore. As what should have been a beautiful mess of fish breached the water's surface a few inches from my submerged hands, Dad shrieked with alarm when he saw a dozen or so disembodied fish heads dangling from the stringer and an enormous snapping turtle with its scissor-sharp jaws gnawing on the last relatively intact fish on the line. In an instant, both of us turned and ran toward the truck, stopping only when we realized it was highly unlikely that we would be chased down by a fifty-pound turtle. We were grateful to still have all of our fingers and maybe more grateful that no one was there to see us screaming and running for our lives. We realized that had there been anyone else present to witness our folly, we would have surely been laughed out of every bait shop and sporting goods store in the tri-state area.

"You shoulda seen the look on your face," I managed to say between gasps for air, my sunburned face stretched in a painful grin from ear to ear.

"I did," Dad laughed as he composed himself, "in the reflection of your wild-eyes when you saw that turtle coming out of the water instead of your of fish." We turned to look back at the snapper but saw that it and the stringer of fish heads were already long gone. "What do you say we head back home before Jaws makes a return appearance?"

"Good idea."

Even today, whenever I go fishing with my father, I become transformed once again into a boy out fishing with his dad. I remember the time when I invited Chris Stevens to come with us when my friend and I were about twelve years old. Dad said we could walk around the pond on our own while he went out in the boat, if it suited us. We said it would, since we could find more mischief on our own than under his direct supervision. He had but two rules for us to follow: "Don't fall in, and don't hook any frogs." If we hooked a frog, Dad knew from experience that it would bleed like, well, like a hooked frog. We said we understood and began to work our way around the pond, casting and retrieving as we went, pausing to examine snake holes and mostly just goofing off. Long about the time Dad had rowed almost exactly half-way across the pond, which was a good two or three hundred feet from where he started, Chris spotted a big ol' bullfrog sitting on the bank. As we approached, it just sat there staring blankly at the water, waiting glumly for a little excitement to come along. It was practically begging me to put a lure in front of its nose, if for no other reason than to just have something different to look at. So I obliged. And I'll be damned if that fat old lump didn't come flying up off his haunches and grab on to my rubber worm before I had a chance to pull it away. He held on tight, and straightaway sunk the hook right through his lower jaw. I knew Dad would be mad as hell if he saw what I did, so I tried to get the slimy little bugger off by myself. The more I struggled, the more the frog struggled and in no time he had hooked three of his four webbed feet while trying to pry himself free. Chris roared. He thought it was just about the greatest spectacle he'd ever witnessed. I was not as enthusiastic. Inevitably, I was forced to yell for Dad to come help. I could hear him cursing me in rhythm with every stroke of the oars he made.

By the time he ran the boat aground, he was huffing and puffing and cussing and spitting. Though I wasn't laughing at the time, Chris and I have had many a laugh about it in the years since.

Dad remembers the frog story quite vividly, too. "You remember that time when I told you boys not to catch any frogs?"

"Yep."

"And what did you do no more than five minutes later?"

"Caught a frog?"

"Caught a frog," he laughs.

One More Cast was a benchmark in the maturation of Travis the Author and Travis the Man. He refrained from embarking on a lengthy book tour following its release, opting instead to rededicate himself to his family and close friends. He took his family on several vacations, making occasional impromptu appearances at local book stores to meet his fans and autograph copies of his books, but always spending as much quality time as possible with his wife and kids. For the first time since Rosie Crane's illness and Dave Richard's death, Travis Naughton was truly happy again.

Great Scot

In 2025, the Naughton family went on a working vacation to Scotland, the motherland to both halves of Travis's family tree. While the author gave several book readings over the course of their two-week stay, he fell in love with the land of his ancestors and confided to Bethany that he wished the family could live there permanently. Not prepared to move so far away from her mother and sisters, she offered a compromise: One year would be her limit, with trips back home for Christmas and her birthday.

"Deal!" an excited Travis declared.

On July 25th, 2025, Travis A. Naughton announced to a large audience gathered at the Merchant City Festival in Glasgow that he had appointed himself to the unofficial post of United States Goodwill Ambassador to Scotland. Having previously made it known to his Scottish fans through the local media that his mother's side of his lineage (Clan Keller or Kellar) as well as his father's (Clan MacNaughton or MacNachten) could be traced back to their country, Travis was embraced as a native son. At a sold out reading in an historic theatre in the city's arts district, Naughton was asked to reveal how he came to be a writer. His speech was recorded by the local newspaper and transcribed for the morning edition:

"What do you want to be when you grow up?" That's what every adult asks you when you're a kid.

"I want to be a professional race car driver." It was my standard answer as a child, whenever I was asked this question.

"No, silly," adults say. "I mean what sort of a *real* job do you want to have?" And that is precisely how childhood dreams begin to start fading away. Grownups are just children who have given up on their dreams. I, for one, refuse to be a grownup.

The better question would be, "What do you want to do to earn money to keep yourself alive in a world full of disappointments after you have given up on pursuing your childhood dreams following countless years of hearing adults tell you that you need to grow up, face reality, and get your head out of the clouds?"

"I want to be an accountant?"

"Now you're thinking straight, sonny. You'd better run along. You don't want to be late for your first day of kindergarten."

I never bought into this way of thinking. The world would have no artists, musicians, or spoiled heiresses if everyone settled for a regular job. Who would want to live in a world without Paris Hilton for crying out loud? Not me.

When I was in high school, a career counselor came to talk to our class about our plans for the future. The woman asked each kid in the classroom to stand up and tell her what they wanted to be when they grew up. The standard answers were given. A doctor here. A lawyer there. An engineer. A teacher. "And what about you there in the back row?"

"I want to be a deejay." I had by that point already given up on my dream to race cars for a living, having heard so many adults tell me that it just wasn't practical. I thought spinning records on the radio would be fun, and since Wolfman Jack, Rick Dees, and Casey Kasem seemed to make a pretty decent living doing it, I figured why couldn't I?

"A disc jockey?" the woman scoffed. "Well, I guess if you want to be homeless and living on a beach somewhere looking for change with a metal detector, then go knock yourself out."

All of my classmates laughed their heads off. I was glad that I could at least provide an amusing memory for them to look back on while they sat at their boring desk jobs that would slowly sap the will to live from their crushed souls in the not-so-distant future. Was being a deejay really such an outrageous idea? I didn't think so, but just to be on the safe side, I decided to study political science when I went to college in the fall. After all, what could suck out your soul faster than going into politics?

It took only one semester in college to accumulate enough skeletons in my closet to rule out a career in politics, but just to play it safe I spent the next several years ensuring that any run for office would be completely out of the question. I dropped out of the university in 1994 and when I re-enrolled following a winter of discontent spent living in my father's basement on a hog farm in Iowa, I decided to pursue my dream to become a deejay. My friend Tony Lipper was hosting a three-hour blues show on our college radio station at that time and asked me if I would like to alternate shifts with him every other Sunday afternoon during his time slot. I said yes, and for the next year, I could be heard hosting "Blues 101" every Sunday afternoon on KCOU 88.1FM.

I didn't get paid to spin records, but it was a step in the right direction towards the goal of having a paying career in radio one day. Plus, I had full control over what went over the airwaves and absolutely no one to tell me what I could or couldn't play. The station had a large music library and I got a kick out of thumbing through the shelves full of old records and CDs as I prepared for each show. I especially enjoyed playing classic vinyl. By that time, virtually no other radio stations used the antiquated format any longer, so I picked from the stacks of old albums as often as I could. I loved my "job." But, being that it was a college radio station staffed entirely by students, when I finally graduated I was forced to resign.

Tony and I signed on to cover a weekly shift at a public radio station in town after we graduated, but I was turned-off by all the rules and formality, so I quit after one show. *Prima donnas.* It didn't help matters that the job was non-paying, which forced me to continue working full-time as a meat cutter in a grocery store. Once again, the practical world of having bills to pay won-out over childhood fantasies. Incidentally, Tony carried on without me and is still spinning tunes to this day at another public radio station in Colorado. Now *there* is a man who patently refuses to ever grow up. I commend him for that.

A few years after we got married, I nearly convinced my wife the Enabler to let me pursue my first childhood dream job: race car driver. While working at an auto auction, I made a few contacts with folks who raced cars on the local dirt track every Saturday night. I grew up at these types of tracks, accompanying my mom every weekend to watch the mayhem that was small town dirt track racing. She even took my brother Blake and I for a spin around the track one night when she was chosen by the car dealer she worked for to drive the pace car for the championship race. *That* was awesome.

I researched start-up costs and maintenance costs for owning a race car. I discovered that racing is not for people who are dedicated to getting themselves out of debt. The Voice of Reason wisely declined my request for funds. I begged a co-worker, whose father owned a beat up stock car, to convince her old man to give me a turn at the wheel one night if he ever wanted a relief driver. He said he'd think about it, but I never got the call. No, it was not practical to dream of becoming a race car driver, but I still wasn't ready to give up and work for the rest of my life. Surely there existed a way to be myself and get paid for doing it and nothing else.

While I was busy selling gourmet pet food part-time and used cars in my spare time, and staying at home with Alex the rest of the time, I stumbled upon a help-wanted ad for freelance reporters at a local business-oriented newspaper. Writing was a hobby that I enjoyed in my youth, but after seven years of scrambling to hand-in college term papers on time, I swore that I would never take on a writing assignment again. And although I had no interest whatsoever in the world of business, I was intrigued by the prospect of getting paid to write.

I was hired by the newspaper's editor and promptly assigned to write an article about the impact of state budget cuts on the local economy in the capital city. I had no training as a reporter, but I did my best to interview a few local officials and business owners before cobbling together the story. I submitted it to my editor and was surprised to hear that she loved my work. The article went to press without a single editorial revision. My mother was so proud that she framed a copy and gave it to me as a birthday gift a few weeks later. I had found my calling. My next assignment was to write a story about an indoor league football team, (that's American football by the way), based in the area called the Show-Me Believers. I was thrilled to be writing about sports instead of the economy and attacked the project with all the gusto of a linebacker.

When my second story went to press, I received my fifty dollars U.S. and a complimentary copy of the paper. I sat down to read it with great anticipation. The people that I had interviewed for the feature were looking forward to its publication as well. Theirs was a semi-professional sports franchise that was rooted in the core values of spirituality, family, and giving their fans a good show. I think I captured that essence in my writing and could hardly wait to see the finished product in print. To my horror, the story had been shredded by my editor, into little bits of random sentences and soul-less statistics. She had eviscerated the emotional aspects of the feature and turned it into a boring, mildly informative article barely worthy of the readers' attention. I was upset, and when my next story assignment was to write about the economy again, I declined and tendered my resignation, citing time constraints as my reason for quitting.

I *was* busy. That much was true. In addition to my duties at work and at home, I had also stumbled upon on new medium that occupied more and more of my time: blogging. With my blog, I was able to write about whatever I chose. I never had to worry about an article being edited to death. I never had to meet a deadline. My work wouldn't be graded by a philosophy professor with an unabridged dictionary and the Encyclopedia Britannica floating around in his head. I didn't worry about punctuation. I was able to simply sit at the computer and tell the world whatever was on my mind. And the world noticed (an admittedly tiny portion of the world, but at least there were a few people who were interested in what I had to say.) Finally, I had found my *true* calling.

The principal difference between bloggers and columnists is a paycheck. Therefore, the next logical step in the evolutionary chain of my writing was to try to get hired as a columnist for a local newspaper. I submitted a cover letter and writing samples to the publisher of a small weekly in the area along with a plea to be given a chance. I had met the publisher on a prior occasion, and hoped he would remember me. He responded promptly and said that in fact he did know who I was, but unfortunately, he did not need another columnist. When he purchased the newspaper a few years earlier, he found that there were more columnists on staff than reporters, so he cleaned house. "If you would be interested in working as a reporter," he added, "I would love to hire you." With respect, I declined, citing my desire to be in sole control over what I choose to write. *Prima donnas.* I would not have been so choosey were it not for the fact that the Enabler made a decent wage at her career. Thank you, dear.

Wanting to be a professional writer is a lot like wanting to be a professional race car driver. Both endeavors require a great deal of skill and luck. Both require a passion and a determination to succeed. But only one of these professions requires an investment of thousands of dollars to purchase and maintain equipment. And typically, only one of these occupations is potentially lethal. The Voice of Reason is glad I chose writing.

I eventually did get hired as a columnist. And eventually I wrote a book or two that found an audience. I'll admit that it's nice to make my own money nowadays, if for no other reason than if an old hot rod comes along with my name written all over it, I can buy it without having to ask the Bethany for money. Okay, that's not true. The Voice of Reason still controls all of our family's finances. And that's probably a good thing. Besides, were it not for The Enabler's willingness to work five or six different jobs to support my lazy ass while I pursued writing, I would probably still be frying chickens somewhere.

I guess that was the long answer to the question, "How did you become a writer?" The short version is simply this: I married extremely well.

Naughton didn't stop writing while he lived abroad. Over the course of his stay in Scotland he wrote yet another book. This one would be dedicated to his muse, his Enabler, his Voice of Reason, the love of his life — his wife Bethany. The book, called How I Love Your Mother, *was written for his children, who were by then grown, so that they would know their parents' love story and understand how much their father adored their mother. "I once read somewhere that the greatest way to show your kids how much you love them is to show them how much you love their mother," Naughton wrote in the book's introduction. By all accounts, he succeeded.*

The author's fifth book became a bestseller within three months of the family's return home.

Paging Doctor Naughton

Returning to the United States after a year abroad, Travis felt re-energized. Instead of going on yet another book tour in order to pad his more than adequate bank account, the author decided the time had come to build up his spiritual wealth. Not since declaring himself an atheist back in his college days in Columbia had Naughton given much thought to the meaning of life or the condition of his soul. "I was too busy living life to search for its meaning," he told me.

(Younger): You referred to yourself as an atheist, but you became a legally ordained minister years ago, isn't that right? Please explain.

(Elder): After attending the wedding of my dear friends Tony and Tina Lipper back in 2010, I had an epiphany. Their ceremony took place just a few miles down the road from here at a place called Beaver Meadows. It was a resort nestled high in the Rockies that had a special, almost spiritual vibe to it — it was just so beautiful. Tony and Tina were no more religious than I, so they asked a friend of theirs to officiate their wedding. Their friend became ordained by the Universal Life Church solely to perform the service. I thought this was a wonderful gift from her to her friends. The ceremony was very spiritual and moving, and afterward, I couldn't stop thinking about this priceless gift the Reverend Mandy Earlywine had given to the happy couple. I decided shortly thereafter to become ordained, too, on the outside chance that a friend would ask me for the same gift someday.

(Younger): Did anyone ever ask you to perform their wedding?

(Elder): Oh yes. I've joined seven couples in matrimony to date. It sure beats giving someone a toaster for their wedding!

(Younger): Has becoming a minister changed your spiritual views in any way?

(Elder): Yes and no. I still do not subscribe to any organized religion. Christians, Jews, and Muslims all worship the same God yet each group insists that their religion is superior to the others. How many millions of people have been killed in the name of God—all believing that they were the chosen children of the Heavenly Father? Organized religion divides us more than it unites us. However, spiritualism brings people together. Most people believe in a higher power of some sort. Be it God, or the Architect of the Universe, or Karma, or whatever you wish to call it, many feel that their existence fits into the plans of a Divine Design. I think most of us want to feel that our lives have meaning and that we each fulfill a purpose in a Great Plan. As a non-denominational spiritual leader, I have been fortunate to minister to people from all walks of life in their times of need.

(Younger): Early on, after you were ordained, detractors accused you of doing so as a publicity stunt. How did you respond to such criticisms?

(Elder): Those folks weren't entirely wrong. Everything I do is fueled by my ego to a certain extent. I admit that I enjoy the attention I get when I'm signing autographs or when I'm introduced as The Right Reverend Travis Naughton. Whether smashing a guitar on a stage in a high school auditorium, or pronouncing a happy couple "husband and wife," I relish being in the spotlight. But what my critics don't understand is that I can stroke my ego *and* make the world a better place at the same time. The two aren't mutually exclusive.

(Younger): What about the virtues of being humble and showing humility? How do you reconcile those with being a flamboyant minister?

(Elder): Martin Luther King, Jr. was a humble man. But

when he delivered a speech or a sermon, I'd say that he was pretty flamboyant, too. He was certainly the most dynamic public speaker — and minister — that the world has ever known. So, I don't think there's anything wrong with that approach. I would ask people to judge me simply by the amount of good I have done for others.

(Younger): What would you say is your greatest contribution to mankind?

(Elder): I have always said that mine is a Ministry of Laughter. When people are laughing at me, they become happy. Happy people are not preoccupied with negative thoughts. When a large number of people laugh with one another during one of my speeches or after reading something I've written, then their collective positivity will prevent them from doing harm to one another. Therefore, when I make people laugh, I am also making the world a better place.

(Younger): So what do you say to people who claim your ministry is a joke?

(Elder): I'd say they're absolutely right. But that doesn't mean that it's a meaningless mockery of religion. On the contrary, the Ministry of Laughter is the most meaningful thing I've ever done with my life. I have received thousands of letters from fans who wanted me to know that something I said or wrote made them laugh for the first time in weeks or even years following a personal tragedy or a long battle with the blues. I like to think that my sense of humor has saved more than a few souls over the years — including my own. And that, my friend, is no joke.

In 2029 Naughton's alma mater, the University of Missouri, conferred upon him an honorary doctorate in recognition of his lifetime achievements in the fields of literature and humanitarian work. He accepted his Doctor of Humane Letters degree and gave the commencement speech at the spring graduation ceremony for the School of Arts and Sciences. The following is a transcript of his address:

Members of the Board of Curators, Madam President, Dean Johnson, faculty and staff, friends and family, my fellow graduates; I stand before you today a humbled man. Receiving this degree on this most magnificent of days — a day that all of you who are wearing caps and gowns have worked so hard for so many years to finally enjoy — has lead me to ask two questions: What have I done to deserve such an honor, and have the decision makers at this institution completely lost their minds?

When Dean Johnson first called to tell me that I was to be bestowed with an honorary doctorate from my alma mater, I thought he was joking. After all, as an undergraduate here in the 1990s, I narrowly avoided expulsion on several occasions and escaped with a "something-point-five" grade point average (as my dear friend and fellow Tiger Rosie Crane so eloquently phrased it.) After assuring me that the offer was legitimate and that I was also invited to give the commencement address, my already bloated ego swelled to what my wife will tell you was an absolutely intolerable level. For days I bragged to anyone who would listen that I would be joining the likes of my literary hero Mark Twain in the elite circle of celebrities who have been awarded such an honor by the University of Missouri. I could not have been more full of myself. That is until the day that I came home after signing some autographs and discovered that my one hundred and forty pound Saint Bernard had had an explosive bout with diarrhea in my front hallway. She may have lost the battle to "hold it" until I got home to let her out, but I was the real loser. Nothing can take an egomaniac back down to earth faster than having to get down on his hands and knees and clean up after a canine nuclear explosion. All notions of my greatness instantly vanished as I expended the entire supply of paper towels in the house in a futile attempt to erase the carnage. As my desperation mounted, I used everything from napkins to toilet paper to the nice linen towels in the guest bathroom to wipe-down the floor, the dog's food and water bowls, and both walls in the hallway. For nearly an hour I scrubbed, gagged, and cried until finally the disaster was cleaned-up. And then my wife walked in. Any remaining trace of my ego was obliterated when Bethany looked down at the floor and saw a trash can overflowing with the ruined towels her mother had given us as a Christmas present the previous year, a scattering of empty paper towel and toilet paper rolls, and the red-faced, sweat soaked, broken shell of a human being that was her husband curled up in the fetal position praying for the sweet release of death. She didn't say a word. There were no words. She simply went back out the way she came in and called a few hours later to say that she was done towel shopping and to ask if it was safe to come back home yet.

So, as I said, I stand before you today a humbled man. I am truly humbled that you have chosen me to speak to you on one of the most important days of your lives. Little did you know that I would be talking about my dog having a case of the scoots, but nevertheless—I am proud to be here to share this day with you. I hope that you all take some time after graduation to enjoy your accomplishment. It is no easy task to earn a degree from a quality institution such as ours. *Earn* is the key word there. You have *earned* it. You sacrificed time with your friends to study for finals. You missed going home on a few weekends to see family when you knew you had papers to write. Many of you held jobs to help pay for your tuition while simultaneously attending classes--hopefully with greater regularity that I did. You deserve to feel good about yourselves.

But do be cautious to avoid the mistake I made by letting the ego run amok. It is easy to fall into that trap. You start to feel like maybe you're a little better than the guy next to you at the carwash who's scrubbing the mud off his rusty old Chevy while your Mercedes is getting hand-waxed by someone you think might have been in your freshman algebra class, but dropped the course after the first test. You should be proud of that diploma, but you need to understand that it doesn't entitle you to any degree of superiority over your fellow man. As you prepare to set out into the real world and embark upon your life's journey, remember to look out for the other guy along the way. When you go to a restaurant with your colleagues, be sure to give the waitress a generous tip—not to impress your co-workers, but because that server may just be walking a thin line between being able to afford college or having to drop out to support her family.

And always remember where you came from. I remember applying for financial aid during my senior year of high school and looking over the application my dad filled out. Under the heading of "total annual household income," Dad put down "$13,000." *Thirteen thousand for a family of four.* You see, my father was working toward earning his doctorate at Mizzou at the time, commuting 180 miles round-trip each day. That left him no time for a job. His wife supported us by working as—you guessed it—a waitress. On days when her customers were lousy tippers, we ate bologna sandwiches for dinner. The next day, we ate bologna for lunch *and* dinner, and when we couldn't afford to buy dog food—we had to share our bologna with our Labrador mix named Oreo. Now and then, despite all of the good fortune I have had since I graduated from the University of Missouri, I sometimes have to stop and remind myself what it was like—and what it is still like for many families—to struggle to survive.

You will experience incredible highs as you venture down the path of life. But earning a degree, landing a dream job with dream wages, and being able to afford a new Mercedes won't even come close to offering the satisfaction that getting married, watching the birth of your first child, or volunteering within your community will. And there will be unimaginable lows, too. The trick to surviving the rough times is to focus on the good times and create more of them. Be grateful for those good times and never take a day of your life for granted. Consider yourself blessed to be a graduate of the University of Missouri. Consider yourself blessed if you realize one day that you are so well-off that the worst thing that's happened to you in recent memory was when you had to clean up after a Saint Bernard with a wicked case of the squirts.

Again, congratulations Class of 2029 on your wonderful accomplishment. Enjoy this moment and every moment you are blessed to be alive. And good luck to you all. Thank you very much.

The Intercontinental Man of Letters

Throughout his adult life, Travis Naughton has been a letter writer. Beginning with notes sent home to his friends and family while he was away in boot camp and continuing to this day, Naughton has clung tightly to the antiquated tradition of hand writing/typing letters and sending them out via the U.S. mail. In 2011, he wrote the following letter to his friend, jazz drummer Matt Kane:

Dear Matt,
Feb 21, 2011

    Greetings from Mid-Mo. Since you indicated that you are a fellow writer, I thought it appropriate for you to be the first person I write to in my new snail mail campaign. It's funny you mentioned seeing the picture of me and Chris Stevens on facebook the other day because your name came up that night while we were reminiscing. It is a supreme testament to your musical abilities and your personal character that twenty-some years after you left Hannibal, your old friends and former band mates still speak very highly of you both as a friend and a musician.

    It was fun hangin' with Chris. I have only run into him a couple times since college but we were pretty tight back in the day if you remember. I've decided finally that facebook is good for re-connecting only to a certain extent and that face-to-face contact (or at the very least a personal letter once in a while) is the far superior way to communicate with friends. I don't know if you're a fan of Jack Kerouac (wrote *On the Road* and other Beat Generation classics) but I have really gotten into his writing and his life lately. In an age before affordable phone rates or the internet, Jack and his pals wrote numerous letters and visited each other in New York,

San Fran, Paris, Mexico City, Tangier, Denver, and all points between over the years. I just read a collection of letters written to and from Jack and his friend the famous poet Allen Ginsberg. It was fascinating to follow their friendship over the course of 20 years with all of their spats, professions of love for one another, and the creation of their now legendary writing styles. At one point, Kerouac wrote to his editor, "One day, America will read the letters of Allen Ginsberg and cry." What's really cool is that these cats *knew* they were changing the face of American prose and poetry. They knew they would be famous some day and actually kept all of their letters from one another! That blows me away.

Well Hoss, we may be famous one day, too. Your musical career is obviously taking off and hopefully my writing career will soon follow. Who knows, maybe our letters to each other will wind up in an anthology of famous Hannibalians someday. How about visiting the "The Matt Kane Dinette" or the "Travis Naughton Boyhood Home and Museum" instead of all that Twain crap?!

I want to share something with you that I wrote sometime in the mid 1990s that I just now found while looking for an envelope to put this letter in:

"And so the clock keeps ticking. Impatiently waiting for me to fill these blank pages with strokes of genius. I submit that the clock will not be satisfied soon. Inspiration escapes me as does the memory of my last contented moment. My mind, too, is a blank page thirsty for the ink of imagination to saturate its parched fibers. It has been countless empty lifetimes since music filled my soul. Countless blank pages in my book of life. Beethoven went mad trying to recall the intoxicating memories of the music he could no longer hear. He was forced to confront his loss by writing about it. His writing voice was in a language of key signatures and sonatas, mine is not yet discovered. My emotions are prisoners of my mind, unable to freely express themselves since I stopped playing music. Music was my confessional, my soapbox, my love letter, my white flag of surrender, my voter registration card, my mating call, my roadside billboard, my one phone call, my unanswered prayer, my letter to the editor, my best friend, and now..."

Pretty heavy, huh? Today is the first time I've read that in a long, long time. I wrote it when I was searching for a way to express myself, since music was no longer the immense part of my life that it once was. Writing has become my salvation. And it is serving me pretty well these days. I have written and re-written my book three times now. It is finally close to being done. I don't really know how to classify it, which sounds just about right for something coming from me.

Enough about me. Tell me about your life. I know you're married now and banging the skins, but what else floats your boat? What is your next big thing in life, what's coming down the pike? Kerouac and Ginsberg went to Columbia U, so you should stop by there sometime and sniff around for some real beat history. If I ever find myself in your neck of the woods, maybe we can check out their archives and catch some jazz in the city. That would be sweet.

Take care, man. And thanks for indulging my latest whims,
Travis

During the next decade, Naughton wrote both at his home in Missouri and at the dream home he and Bethany had built in the mountains of Colorado. He continued to churn out personal letters, occasional guest columns for newspapers, and essays for various other publications. He also completed his novel Burning Couches, *a semi-autobiographical story about a group of friends in high school, and his long anticipated memoir* Rude, Crude, and Socially Unacceptable *which was published in 2041 and became his seventh best-selling book in a row. I began interviewing Dr. Naughton in his mountain home in 2048, by which time he had reduced his writing output to occasional letters to his children and a few close friends.*

(Younger): Dr. Naughton, I find it hard to believe that a prolific writer such as yourself has ceased writing professionally entirely. Tell the truth, do you have another book in the works?

(Elder): Well, I'll never say never, but I just don't have the energy to work on such a lengthy and involved project these days. That isn't to say that I don't have something up my sleeve to keep me busy.

(Younger): Do tell.

(Elder): Well, my old friend Paulie asked me to collaborate with him to create a musical based on his comedy routine.

(Younger): You mean Paul Shields of *Paul & the Violent Farmers* fame?

(Elder): One and the same. We've been writing back and forth sorting out the dialogue and musical numbers for years now. I think we're getting pretty close to being done once and for all.

(Younger): What's the musical about?

(Elder): It's a story about a guy named Dwight who is a forklift operator and he and his best friend who happens to be a mime are out at a bar one night when Dwight spots this cute girl across the room. He talks to her and after some convincing he takes her to his lumberyard for a joyride on his forklift. One thing leads to another and she falls off the thing, cracks her head, and loses her memory. Her ex-boyfriend visits her at the hospital and convinces her they're still an item, leaving Dwight twisting in the wind. The rest of the musical is the saga of how Dwight and the mime try to jar her memory loose while she resumes her former life as a stripper.

(Younger): Wait, how do you write for a mime in a musical?

(Elder): Hey, you're talkin' to a pro here. If anyone can work a mute character into a musical, it's me.

(Younger): I won't dispute that. Will you actually use a forklift in the production?

(Elder): No, and this is the genius of Paul Shields. The entire production is staged in an actual bar. The scene with the forklift is recalled by Dwight to the mime after the accident. All of the other action takes place in a bar. The plan is for the actors to spontaneously break into character and begin the show while seated among the actual patrons of the bar. The only props we'll need are a guitar, a microphone, and a stripper pole. Paul is writing the music and I'm doing the dialogue. It should be a real gem.

(Younger): I can't wait to see it. Have you cleared a place among your many awards for a Tony?

(Elder): Not yet. This musical will be way off Broadway, that's for sure.

(Younger): What's the name of the show?

(Elder): *She Don't Know My Name is Dwight*. More of Paulie's genius.

(Younger): I love it. Speaking of things I love, during the course of my research for writing your biography, I have read and re-read all seven of your books. They are generally classified in most libraries and bookstores as creative non-fiction with the exception of your novel *Burning Couches*, which is largely autobiographical, but fiction nonetheless. How much of what you wrote in those other books actually happened in reality?

(Elder): How can we define "reality"? The philosopher in me describes it as a subjective observation by an imperfect individual of the world around him. Because no two people have the exact same eyes, ears, and other tools of perception, no two people are able to see the world in the exact same way. Therefore, who can definitively say what is real and what is not?

(Younger): Fair enough. Then let's be more specific: For example, did you really go outside in the dead of winter and make snow angels in the nude?

(Elder): I did indeed. And I even managed to convince my wife to join me a time or two over the years.

(Younger): Really? And I thought she was The Voice of

Reason.

(Elder): She is, but I'll let you in on a little secret that she taught me years ago. There are times in life when you need to laugh. Take for example the time I ruined our gravel driveway after attempting to smooth out some ruts with my neighbor's Bobcat tractor. It was the winter of 2010-11 and after we were trapped in our home by two feet of snow covering the road, my neighbor taught me to use his Bobcat in case he couldn't dig us out on the outside chance that he was either out of town or ill (he was hospitalized during that blizzard). After the snow melted, the neighbors went on a month-long vacation and the mud on our road made it almost impossible to drive on. So I hopped on the Bobcat and spent five hours scraping and sculpting our 500 yard long driveway into shape. I was fairly satisfied with the results, but knew we needed some fresh gravel soon to prevent the quagmire from recurring during the next storm. Sure enough, it poured that night—harder than it had in years—about four inches of rain. Bethany called me on her way home from her mother's house where she and the boys had been that evening and said, "We're stuck in the driveway." I couldn't reply. I was physically and emotionally spent. "Did you hear what I just said?"

All I could say was, "I'll be right there." When I drove down to the van, I saw it was buried to the frame and the storm was getting worse. I stood in the driving rain long enough to become thoroughly soaked and to realize the situation was hopeless. I couldn't sleep at all that night. Guilt and helplessness wouldn't allow it. After working so hard on that road all day, I felt like a total failure. I lay in bed and waited for the light of day hoping that it would change my perspective. It did not. In the morning, I went out early to try to pull the van out with my truck, but my old Dodge decided to sleep in. It wouldn't start. (The starter had been going bad for a while.) So I walked over to the neighbor's and hopped on the Bobcat again. I drove up to the van to try to pull it out, but it was sunk so deep that I couldn't even get under it to hook a tow rope to it. At that moment, the hours and hours of wasted effort, the fatigue, the ruination of our only way in or out of our house, the frustration of having previously been trapped in our home for several days following the blizzard, the realization that we couldn't get Alex to school or Bethany to work, and knowing beyond any doubt that it was all my fault caused me to have a total meltdown. I started convulsing. I doubled over like I was going to throw-up. I yelled. I cussed. I threw things. I paced. I screamed. I kicked at the mud. I cried. I absolutely lost my mind. And at that moment, I looked over at my wife, desperate for her to wave her magic wand and make it all better. Instead, she just stood there and smiled. (She's good about seeing the humor in these situations as they happen. Me, I don't find them funny until years later.) Right about then I am pretty sure I had a complete break from reality. I really don't remember much after that.

Well, Bethany did manage to save the day. She always does. First, she called-in to work to take a personal day, and then she called a tow truck. She called the school to tell them Alex would be late. Then she called a gravel outfit and had six loads of rock brought in. As she calmly handled everything, I sat in my truck and turned the key about a thousand times while punching the steering wheel and shouting obscenities. I eventually got it to start and took Alex to school an hour late. I apologized to my forgiving spouse and then I hopped back on that goddanged Bobcat and spread gravel between dumptruck loads for the next four hours. Then I shoveled rock by hand onto the dirt floor of the barn and around the edges of the driveway. By that evening, everything was back to normal and the driveway was in better shape than it had been since we bought the house.

I learned a couple valuable lessons that day. First, I should never attempt to perform any type of manual labor ever again. Everyone who knows me will tell you that I hate work and am lousy at it, so I swore it off once and for all. We're debt-free for godssakes. I will gladly pay experts to do the work for me from now on. I also learned that when the going gets tough, I should beg Bethany to fix the stuff I messed up. Why do men so loathe asking for help? Finally, I learned that I need to laugh at myself.

Life can really wear you down—especially if you take yourself too seriously. At one point or another, you will feel like I did that day in the mud—that the fire inside of you is being snuffed out. Whether you've been laid-off from work and can't find a new job, or you've just inadvertently stranded your family miles from civilization, you need to find a way to laugh—and fast. I have found that almost nothing else in the world can resuscitate your soul and cause you to laugh out loud quite like making naked snow angels. It's a lot like having sex. Your heart races, your body convulses, your flesh tingles, your breath quickens. It makes you feel so alive. And it is all the better when you can do it with someone you love.

From his humble beginnings as an Incontinent Letterman to his accomplishments as an Intercontinental Man of Letters, Dr. Travis A. Naughton has lived a remarkable life. With seven best-selling books, two feature films, dozens of essays and short stories, a goodwill ambassadorship, an honorary doctorate, and an off-Broadway musical to his credit, The Right Reverend Naughton takes the most pride in having raised three beautiful children who have grown-up to become generous and happy adults while maintaining a loving marriage with their mother for fifty-two years and counting. He's inspired countless writers of the next generation to put pen to paper, including myself. Perhaps more importantly, he's inspired me to look forward to the next snowfall.

Timeline of Major Events

- September 25, 1971: Born in Kirksville, Missouri.
- 1980: Moved to Hannibal, Missouri.
- 1990: Graduated from Hannibal High School. Joined United States Marine Corps. Entered University of Missouri.
- 1996: Married Bethany Lemon.
- 1997: Graduated from University of Missouri with degree in philosophy.
- 2000: Alexander Blake Naughton (first child) is born.
- 2002: Quits job to be a stay-at-home parent.
- 2004: Starts blog.
- 2008: Essay *Tits and Asphalt* published. Writes first *Stay-at-Home Writer* column. Adopts Truman Jiang Naughton (second child) in China.
- 2009: Essays *Tromboners, Too* and *Tromboners Two* published.
- 2010: Essay *Incontinent Letterman* published. Ordained as a minister.
- 2011: First book *Stay-at-Home Rollercoaster* published. Adopts Tian-Tian Naughton (third child) in China.
- 2013: Second book *Reason for Leaving* published.
- 2014: Film *Paper or Plastic* released. Tours with *The Blues*

Farmers. Essay *Are Those Goats?* published.

- 2015: Second tour with *The Blues Farmers*.
- 2017: Third book *The Life & Lunacy of Roosevelt Crane* published.
- 2019: Film *The Wedding Guest* released.
- 2021: Joins *Bassmasters Elite Series*.
- 2023: Fourth book *One More Cast* published.
- 2025: Moves to Scotland.
- 2026: Moves back to Missouri. Fifth book *How I love Your Mother* published.
- 2029: Receives honorary doctorate from University of Missouri.
- 2031: Builds dream house in mountains of Colorado.
- 2035: Sixth book, first novel, *Burning Couches* published.
- 2041: Seventh book *Rude, Crude, and Socially Unacceptable* published.
- 2046: Celebrated 50th wedding anniversary with Bethany.
- 2049: *Naked Snow Angels, The Authorized Biography of Travis A. Naughton* by Travis A. Naughton published.

Made in the USA
Charleston, SC
20 May 2011